Saints

May 27, 1993

Mary Clare
    This is to remind you
of our walks and talks
    May your life be
watched over by all the
Saints

        Thanks for being a
        friend

            Sophia

Other titles in
Chambers Compact Reference

Catastrophes and Disasters
Crimes and Criminals
50 Years of Rock Music
Great Inventions Through History
Great Modern Inventions
Great Scientific Discoveries
Masters of Jazz
Movie Classics
Musical Masterpieces
Mythology
The Occult
Religious Leaders
Sacred Writings of World Religions
Space Exploration

To be published in 1993

Great Cities of the World
Movie Stars
Operas
World Folklore

(handwritten annotations) '89 LX Power Pack / Moon Roof 69,000 866-6808 866-1881 7445-7692

Saints

Alison Jones

Chambers

EDINBURGH   NEW YORK

Published 1992 by W & R Chambers Ltd
43–45 Annandale Street, Edinburgh EH7 4AZ
95 Madison Avenue, New York N.Y. 10016

British Library Cataloguing in Publication Data

A catalogue record for this book is available from the British Library.

Library of Congress Cataloging-in-Publication Data applied for

ISBN 0 550 17014 6

Typeset by Alphaset Graphics Limited, Edinburgh
Printed in England by Clays Ltd, St Ives, plc

Acknowledgements

Chambers Compact Reference Series Editor   Min Lee

Illustration credits

Page

xii	courtesy Tate Gallery
21	courtesy Mansell Collection
24	courtesy National Gallery
34	courtesy Mansell Collection
37	courtesy Mansell Collection
47	courtesy Mansell Collection
67	courtesy National Gallery
69	courtesy National Gallery
73	courtesy Mansell Collection
80	courtesy Mansell Collection
82	courtesy Mansell Collection
96	courtesy National Gallery
118	courtesy Mansell Collection
129	courtesy Mansell Collection
132	courtesy Mansell Collection

Page

147	courtesy National Gallery
154	courtesy Mansell Collection
162	courtesy National Gallery
171	courtesy National Gallery
175	courtesy National Gallery
177	© Giraudon – Photeb
179	courtesy National Gallery
188	line drawing by John Marshall
192	courtesy Mansell Collection
204	courtesy National Gallery
210	courtesy Mansell Collection
216	courtesy Mansell Collection
218	courtesy Mansell Collection
223	courtesy Mansell Collection

Contents

Chronology of saints   ix

Introduction   1

Adalbert of Prague   3
Adelaide   4
Adomnan   5
Adrian of Canterbury   6
Afra   7
Agatha   8
Agnes   9
Aidan   10
Ailred   11
Alban   12
Albertus Magnus   13
Aldhelm   14
Alfonso Maria de Liguori   15
Aloysius Gonzaga   16
Alphege   17
Amand   18
Ambrose   19
Andrew   22
Anne   23
Anselm   25
Anskar   26
Anthelm   27
Antonius of Florence   28
Antony   29
Antony of Padua   30
Apollonia   31
Arsenius   32
Athanasius   33
Augustine   35
Augustine of Canterbury   38
Barbara   39
Barnabus   40
Bartholomew   41
Basil the Great   42
Bathild   43

Bede, the Venerable   44
Benedict   45
Benedict Biscop   48
Benedict of Aniane   49
Bernadette   50
Bernard of Clairvaux   51
Bernardino of Siena   52
Blaise   53
Bonaventure   54
Boniface   55
Brendan the Navigator   56
Brice   57
Bridget   58
Brigid   59
Bruno   60
Caedmon   61
Cajetan   62
Callistus I   63
Canute   64
Carlo Borromeo   65
Catherine of Alexandria   66
Catherine of Siena   68
Cecilia   70
Chad   71
Christopher   72
Clare   74
Clement I   75
Columba   76
Columban   77
Cornelius   78
Crispin and Crispinian   79
Cuthbert   81
Cyprian   83
Cyril and Methodius   84
Cyril of Alexandria   85
Cyril of Jerusalem   86
Daniel the Stylite   87
David of Scotland   88
David of Wales   89

Denis	90	Hugh of Lincoln	140
Dominic	91	Ignatius Loyola	141
Dubricius	92	Isidore of Seville	143
Dunstan	93	James the Great	144
Dympna	94	Jean-Baptiste Vianney	145
Edmund	95	Jerome	146
Edmund Arrowsmith	97	Joan of Arc	148
Edmund of Abingdon	98	John Chrystostum	149
Edward the Confessor	99	John Fisher	150
Egwin	100	John of the Cross	151
Elizabeth of Hungary	101	John the Baptist	152
Elizabeth of Portugal	102	John the Evangelist	153
Eloi	103	Joseph	155
Erasmus	104	Jude	156
Ethelbert	105	Julian the Hospitaller	157
Etheldreda	106	Kentigern	158
Ethelwold	107	Leo the Great	159
Eusebius of Vercelli	108	Louis IX	160
Fiacre	109	Luke	161
Fillan	110	Madeleine Sophie Barat	163
Finbar	111	Malachy	164
Finnian	112	Margaret Clitherow	165
Frances of Rome	113	Margaret Mary Alacoque	166
Frances Xavier Cabrini	114	Margaret of Antioch	167
Francis Borgia	115	Margaret of Cortona	168
Francis of Assisi	116	Margaret of Scotland	169
Francis of Paola	119	Mark	170
Francis of Sales	120	Martin of Tours	172
Francis Xavier	121	Mary Magdalene	173
Gall	122	Mary, Blessed Virgin	174
Geneviève	123	Matthew	176
George	124	Michael the Archangel	178
Gertrude of Helfta	125	Nicholas	180
Gertrude of Nivelles	126	Ninian	181
Giles	127	Odilia	182
Gregory of Nazianzus	128	Odilo	183
Gregory Thaumaturgus	130	Odo of Cluny	184
Gregory the Great	131	Olaf	185
Helena	133	Oswald of Northumbria	186
Hilarion	134	Oswald of Worcester	187
Hilary of Poitiers	135	Pancras	188
Hilda	136	Patrick	189
Hippolytus	137	Paul	190
Hubert	138	Paul of the Cross	193
Hugh of Cluny	139	Peter	194

Peter Claver	195	Thomas Aquinas	214
Peter of Alcantara	196	Thomas Becket	215
Philip	197	Thomas More	217
Richard of Chichester	198	Thomas of Hereford	219
Rita of Cascia	199	Timothy	220
Robert Bellarmine	200	Turibius of Mogroveio	221
Rose of Lima	201	Ursula	222
Samson	202	Valentine	224
Sebastian	203	Veronica	225
Simeon Stylites	205	Vincent de Paul	226
Stephen	206	Vitus	227
Stephen of Hungary	207	Wenceslas	228
Swithin	208	Wilfrid	229
Teresa of Ávila	209		
Theodore of Tarsus	211	Glossary	231
Thérèse of Lisieux	212		
Thomas	213	Index	233

Chronology of saints

Michael the Archangel no date
Anne 1st century BC
Joseph 1st century BC–1st century
  AD
Mary, Blessed Virgin 1st century BC–
  1st century AD
Barnabus 1st century
Bartholomew 1st century
Jude 1st century
Luke 1st century
Mary Magdalene 1st century
Matthew 1st century
Philip 1st century
Thomas 1st century
Veronica 1st century
John the Baptist d.c.30
Stephen d.c.35
James the Great d.c.44
Andrew d.c.60
Peter d.c.64
Mark d.c.74
Timothy d.97
Paul c.3–c.66
Cecilia 2nd or 3rd century
John the Evangelist d.c.100
Clement I d.c.101
Hippolytus c.170–235
Christopher 3rd century
Margaret of Antioch 3rd or 4th
  century
Barbara d.c.200
Callistus I d.c.222
Apollonia d.249
Denis d.c.250
Agatha d.c.251
Cornelius d.253
Valentine d.c.269
Sebastian d.c.288
Crispin and Crispinian d.c.287
Cyprian c.200–258

Gregory Thaumaturgus c.213–c.270
Antony 251–356
Helena c.255–c.330
Eusebius of Vercelli c.283–371
Catherine of Alexandria c.290–c.310
Hilarion c.291–371
Athanasius c.296–373
Nicholas 4th century
George d.c.303 or c.250
Vitus d.c.300
Erasmus d.c.303
Agnes d.c.304
Afra d.304
Pancras d.c.304
Alban d.c.305
Blaise d.c.316
Hilary of Poitiers c.315–c.368
Cyril of Jerusalem c.315–386
Martin of Tours c.316–c.400
Basil the Great c.329–379
Gregory of Nazianzus c.330–c.389
Ambrose c.339–397
Jerome c.341–420
John Chrystostum c.347–407
Augustine 354–430
Arsenius c.355–c.450
Ninian c.360–c.432
Cyril of Alexandria c.376–444
Simeon Stylites c.387–459
Patrick c.389–c.461
Leo the Great c.390–461
Brice d.444
Daniel the Stylite 409–93
Geneviève c.422–c.500
Brigid c.453–c.523
Benedict c.480–c.547
Samson c.485–c.565
Brendan the Navigator c.486–577
Finnian d.c.549
Kentigern c.518–c.603

David of Wales c.520–c.589
Columba c.521–597
Gregory the Great c.540–604
Columban c.543–615
Gall c.550–645
Finbar c.560–c.610 or 630
Isidore of Seville c.560–636
Ethelbert c.560–616
Amand c.584–c.679
Eloi c.588–c.658
Augustine of Canterbury d.c.604
Dubricius d.c.612
Aidan d.651
Fiacre d.c.670
Chad d.672
Bathild d.680
Caedmon d.c.680
Oswald of Northumbria c.605–642
Theodore of Tarsus c.609–690
Hilda 614–80
Adomnan c.625–704
Gertrude of Nivelles 626–59
Benedict Biscop 628–90
Etheldreda c.630–679
Cuthbert 634–87
Wilfrid c.634–709
Aldhelm c.640–709
Hubert c.656–727
Bede, the Venerable 673–735
Boniface c.680–754
Adrian of Canterbury d.710
Giles d.c.710
Egwin d.717
Odilia d.c.720
Fillan d.c.777
Benedict of Aniane c.750–821
Dympna d.9th century
Swithin c.800–862
Anskar c.801–865
Cyril and Methodius c.826–869 and
    c.815–885
Edmund 841–70
Odo of Cluny c.879–942
Wenceslas c.907–929
Dunstan 909–88

Ethelwold c.912–984
Oswald of Worcester c.925–992
Adelaide c.931–999
Alphege c.954–1012
Adalbert of Prague c.956–997
Odilo c.962–1041
Stephen of Hungary c.975–1038
Olaf 995–1030
Edward the Confessor 1003–66
Hugh of Cluny 1024–1109
Bruno c.1030–1101
Anselm c.1033–1109
Canute c.1043–1086
Margaret of Scotland c.1045–1093
David of Scotland c.1085–1153
Bernard of Clairvaux 1090–1153
Malachy c.1094–1148
Anthelm 1107–78
Ailred 1109–66
Thomas Becket 1118–70
Hugh of Lincoln c.1135–1200
Dominic 1170–1221
Edmund of Abingdon 1175–1240
Francis of Assisi 1181–1226
Clare 1194–1253
Antony of Padua 1195–1231
Richard of Chichester 1197–1253
Albertus Magnus c.1200–1280
Elizabeth of Hungary 1207–31
Louis IX 1215–70
Thomas of Hereford c.1218–1282
Bonaventure 1221–74
Thomas Aquinas 1225–74
Margaret of Cortona 1247–97
Gertrude of Helfta 1256–c.1302
Elizabeth of Portugal 1271–1336
Bridget 1303–73
Catherine of Siena 1347–80
Bernardino of Siena 1380–1444
Rita of Cascia c.1380–c.1457
Frances of Rome 1384–1440
Antonius of Florence 1389–1459
Joan of Arc 1412–31
Francis of Paola 1416–1507
John of the Cross 1452–1591

John Fisher 1469–1535
Thomas More 1478–1535
Cajetan 1480–1547
Ignatius Loyola 1491–1556
Peter of Alcantara 1499–1562
Francis Xavier 1506–52
Francis Borgia 1510–72
Teresa of Ávila 1515–82
Carlo Borromeo 1538–84
Turibius of Mogroveio 1538–1606
Robert Bellarmine 1542–1621
Margaret Clitherow 1556–86
Francis of Sales 1567–1622
Aloysius Gonzaga 1568–91

Peter Claver 1580–1654
Vincent de Paul c.1581–1660
Edmund Arrowsmith 1585–1628
Rose of Lima 1586–1617
Margaret Mary Alacoque 1647–90
Paul of the Cross 1694–1775
Alfonso Maria de Liguori 1696–1787
Madeleine Sophie Barat 1779–1865
Jean-Baptiste Vianney 1786–1859
Bernadette 1844–79
Frances Xavier Cabrini 1850–1917
Thérèse of Lisieux 1873–97
Julian the Hospitaller date unknown
Ursula date unknown

The Temptation of **St Antony** *(by the Queen of Sheba) after Gustave Flaubert, by Louis Corinth. Tate Gallery.*

Introduction

In its earliest usage in the New Testament, the term 'saint' referred to all those set apart for God, all the members of the early church who had received the gospel message and who as a result had rejected sin to live in a state of sanctity. Gradually the word began to be applied to those who had died as Christians, who were therefore in heaven and able to intercede with God on behalf of the living, and finally to individuals as a mark of particular honour and veneration among the local inhabitants or members of the same religious order. During the Roman persecutions of the Church in the early centuries AD many martyrs were canonized by popular acclaim as examples of fortitude and faith to the suffering faithful. The anniversary of their death was commemorated more in celebration than in mourning; they had assured their place in heaven by their death and could now help those who still lived. As the process of canonization (the inclusion in a list or 'canon') developed and grew, it became desirable to invoke the highest authority and so the approval of the Pope was more frequently sought. Under Pope Gregory IX in the 13th century papal approval became the only legitimate means of conferring sainthood. The initial impetus remained the development of a local cult, but the process of investigation gradually became more intensive.

To fulfil the conditions for sainthood within the Catholic church, an individual must now satisfy an extensive inquiry into their life and death which seeks to establish whether the subject has performed a heroic service of virtue or piety. Often this will be one outstanding deed, such as the foundation of a holy order or martyrdom, the sterling test of sanctity. In other cases it may be an unremarkable death but a life of exemplary conduct and humility. Claims of miracles will be thoroughly researched to determine whether they are in fact the confirmation of holiness. It is probable that many traditionally revered as saints, canonized in less demanding times, would have failed modern investigations into their suitability. In some cases such saints have had their feasts reduced recently, such as St Valentine, St Christopher and St Nicholas.

To compile an exhaustive list of all the men and women who have been venerated as saints by the Church throughout its history would be an aim well beyond the scope of a quick reference work; the most comprehensive work so far attempted on the subject fills 12 volumes. There are many surviving calendars which give a name, a classification (eg martyr, virgin or bishop) and feast-day for many thousands of saints, but for the majority we have no further information. Where a legend exists, the details are often so fanciful, and written so long after the event, that the facts remain at best shadowy. The selection of saints included here is an attempt to present the histories of some of the most influential, interesting and, wherever possible, best-documented saints. Often a saint's influence on succeeding generations is out of all proportion to the reliability of his or her legend, but for the purposes of this reference work these important figures have been included wherever possible.

Hagiography, or the study of saints' lives, is complicated by the fact that most civilizations before ours have seen history as primarily a didactic exercise: more important than bald facts was the presentation of an inspiring, exemplary construct. Many cults of widely-venerated saints have grown from purely or mostly fictive accounts, not historically but morally 'true' since they illustrate the profound spiritual principles by which the world of the pious operated. So although we may reject as unhistorical many of the details of saints' lives recorded in Jacobus de Voragine's famous *Golden Legend*, we can acknowledge the instruction and inspiration they seek to convey. Other accounts which are based more securely on fact appear to have undergone radical change as the devout oral tradition exaggerated the anecdotes, miracles and teachings associated with the saint. Many legends borrow freely from each other or from popular myth, and most reveal as much about the subsequent generations of devout worshippers as about the original subject, but this synthesis is part of the richness and interest of the hagiographic tradition. It should be noted too that the notion of writing saints' *Lives*, practised notably by that patriarch of historians the Venerable Bede, was the beginning of the tradition of biography which developed especially in the 17th century to become the major genre it remains today. The most interesting and personal accounts of saints reveal them as fully human individuals, with failings and foibles of their own, who were nevertheless heroically engaged in their fight for personal holiness.

Where appropriate, I have given a guide to the saint's attributes, patronage and a list of the particular situations in which he or she is invoked. It would be impractical and unhelpful to exhaustively cover all the attested variations; instead I have tried to include the most common or influential instances which might be of interest to the general reader. The field of ecclesiastical art is a vast and complex one, and the symbolism of the saints and their attributes an entire field of study in its own right. The most common attributes include the palm leaves and crowns of martyrdom, the episcopal robes, mitre and crozier of the bishop, the appropriate habit for any member of a religious order, and the hermit's staff. Many individuals have their own idiosyncratic attributes however, such as the otters associated with St Cuthbert or the lion which usually accompanies St Jerome, and a few, such as the Blessed Virgin Mary and St Paul, are unmistakeable by their face alone. Although the patronage claimed for a saint is often logical, or at least deductible, from the legend, in many cases the cult develops in unexpected directions to give startling results, such as St Agatha's well-attested patronage of bell-founders. These developments are traced in the text wherever possible, but often the exact reasons for the changes can only be guessed at.

The biographical sketches of the saints contained within this book demonstrate the democratic nature of sanctity, for they are drawn from all levels of society and backgrounds, from convicts to kings, murderers to child martyrs. The saints even embraced widely different doctrines and ideologies within the Catholic faith. The one characteristic common to virtually all of them is their single-minded devotion to the God they served and whose interest they placed above the demands of self, family and often even the established Church. In many cases this fierce devotion manifests itself in ways which now seem extreme, such as the ascetic life of the Desert Fathers, the uncompromising and belligerent stance of many theologians, and the self-mortification of the 'pillar-saints' who spent most of their lives alone aloft their tall pillars, stretching to heaven. Nevertheless, a sensitive study of the saints and their cults will reward the reader with more than simply an interesting historical insight: their stories are alive with human interest and through them we can glimpse something more, an inspirational spark of the divine touching history.

Adalbert of Prague

c. 956 Bohemia — Pomerania 997

The apostle of the Prussians

Despite continual misunderstanding and opposition, he never abandoned his difficult work.

Born of a noble Bohemian family, he was baptized Voytech but at his confirmation took the name of his teacher in Magdeburg, St Adalbert. When Adalbert the elder died in 981 his protégé returned to Prague and was consecrated there the next year, the first native bishop of the city. He brought back with him an impressive collection of books, high ideals and a zeal for reform along the lines of the Cluniac model.

Difficulties in Prague

The opposition with which he met in Prague, however, both from unconverted pagans and from unreformed believers and clergy, discouraged Adalbert and in 990 he withdrew to Rome. He joined the Benedictine abbey of Saints Boniface and Alexis in Rome, but was not permitted to quit his episcopal duties so lightly. Duke Boleslaus of Poland campaigned for his return to Prague, Pope John XV concurred, and Adalbert was sent back under papal order, with the assurance of support from the secular authorities.

For a time the situation appeared to have improved, and he founded the famous Benedictine abbey at Brevnov. But hostility broke out anew when he attempted to give sanctuary in church to a woman convicted of adultery. The outraged populace dragged the woman out of the church and executed her, whereupon Adalbert promptly excommunicated everyone involved in the killing.

Once again he was obliged to flee to Rome, and once again he was ordered back to Prague by the Pope, Gregory V. But several of Adalbert's relations had been murdered by his enemies in Prague; it was finally agreed that to return him against his own will and that of the people would be inflammatory and might lead to further tragedy.

Mission to Prussia

Duke Boleslaus suggested an alternative mission, to the pagan Prussians in Pomerania. Adalbert went on to evangelize Hungary and possibly Poland and Prussia as well, but he and his fellow missionaries achieved only limited success. Eventually Adalbert was murdered, along with his two companions Benedict and Gaudentius, by Prussians who suspected them of being Polish spies.

Death and cult

Adalbert's body was flung into the water near Königsberg, traditionally believed to be the place of his death, and it was later discovered washed ashore in Poland. He finally received enshrinement at Griezno, and his relics were forcibly translated to Prague in 1039. Although his life's work seems characterized by failure, the influence of Adalbert was enormous. His example inspired many of the famous missionaries in central Europe, and he helped propagate Cluniac ideals throughout his apostolate. He is usually represented in art with the club and lances thought to have been the instruments of his martyrdom, and often with a two-headed cross.

Feast-day 23 April
Patron saint of Prussia and Poland

Adelaide

c.931 Burgundy — Seltz 999

The beloved empress

After an almost fairy-tale life of true love, rejection and restoration, Adelaide was venerated for her unfailing charity and holiness.

The daughter of Rudolf II, King of Upper Burgundy, Adelaide was wedded to Prince Lothair of Italy at the age of 16 as a result of a political agreement between Rudolf and Hugh of Provence, Lothair's father, which had been arranged when she was only two. In 950 however the newly-married Lothair died; he may have been murdered by Berengarius, who succeeded him and who tried to force Adelaide to marry his son. She refused and was imprisoned, but when Otto the Great of Germany invaded Berengarius's territory he freed this royal prisoner and took her back to Pavia with him, where they married in 951. This was a second marriage for Otto too; his first wife had been Edith, sister of the Anglo-Saxon king Athelstan. Shortly afterwards he was crowned emperor by Pope John XII in Rome, and he died in 973.

Outcast and regent

For the next 20 years Adelaide faced enmity and opposition from her husband's family. Otto II, son of Otto and Adelaide, succeeded his father, but his Greek wife Theophano disliked her mother-in-law intensely and managed to turn Otto against her. She found ammunition for her attack in Adelaide's habits of unstinting giving to the poor, and this became the basis of heated quarrels between mother and son. Adelaide was obliged to retire from the court and live for some time with a brother in Burgundy until Abbot Majolus of Cluny stepped in to heal the breach, when she returned to court. The reconciliation lasted only until Otto's death in 983; he was succeeded by his infant son Otto III and Theophano, acting as regent, once again forced Adelaide from the court.

When Theophano herself died in 991 the venerable Adelaide returned once more, to be invested with the power of regent. She used her new authority to found and restore monasteries in the area, and was much concerned with evangelizing the Slavs. She was a generous and likeable woman, who sought the advice of holy men throughout her difficult life, and she won the admiration and respect of her people.

Death and cult

She died at Seltz in Alsace, in the convent which she had founded there, and the centre of veneration of this remarkable woman was established at Cluny. St Odilo, the Cluniac abbot, wrote a *Life* in which he praised her exceptional goodness and we have no reason to doubt the popularity he claims for her. In art she is represented as an empress giving alms or food to the poor, often next to a ship.

Feast-day 16 December

Adomnan

c.625 Donegal — Iona 704

Supporter of the Roman tradition

Biographer of St Columba and ninth abbot of Iona, Adomnan's influence reshaped Celtic Christianity.

Also known as Adamnan, he was an Irishman traditionally descended from the grandfather of Columba. He enrolled as a novice at Iona under abbot Seghine at the age of about 28, whom he went on to succeed as ninth abbot in 679. At Iona Adomnan received and taught Aldfrith, son of King Oswiu of Northumberland, who was seeking sanctuary after his father's death had embroiled him in a violent dispute over succession.

After he had ascended the throne, Aldfrith granted the request of Adomnan when he visited on a mission to secure the release of 60 Irish prisoners held in England. On this journey and more especially on a later visit to Ceolfrid at Wearmouth monastery, Adomnan was converted to the Roman method of calculating Easter, which differed from the Celtic tradition practised at Iona. He returned to his own monastery and campaigned strenuously for the adoption of the Roman calendar and the introduction of the Roman rather than the Celtic style of tonsure, but although he achieved much success on his visits to Ireland, the monks at Iona resisted the changes until after his death. It is sometimes said that he died of despair

and disappointment at the stubbornness of his monastery.

Works

During his third and last visit to Ireland, Adomnan spoke at the Synod of Tara and convinced the assembly that women should be exempt from warfare, and that churchmen and children should not be killed in warfare or taken as prisoners. The resolution subsequently passed became known as Adomnan's law *Cain Adomnain.*

Adomnan's most famous work is his *Life of St Columba* (*Vitae sancti Columbae*) about the founder of Iona, which, although it contains some fanciful material, is an important and scholarly biography. He also wrote a treatise *De locis sanctis,* one of the earliest descriptions of the Holy Lands based on the account of a French bishop, Arculf. Sailing around the west coast of Britain on his journey home from Jerusalem, Arculf was shipwrecked near Iona and stayed for some time with the monks there. It is interesting that Bede refers to this work rather than to the *Life* of Columba. The mystical work *Adomnan's vision,* which purports to give an account of the saint's revelation of heaven and hell, was written in the 10th century at the earliest.

Death and cult

Adomnan died on 23 September at Iona, 12 years before the monastery finally accepted the Roman Easter for which he had fought so hard. His cult was soon well-established throughout Ireland and Scotland. He is usually depicted praying with the moon and seven stars about him, and occasionally writing his *Life of St Columba.* The identification with St Eunan, especially common in Ireland, is doubtful.

Feast-day 23 September

Adrian of Canterbury

Africa — Canterbury 710

The schoolmaster of Canterbury

In his positions as advisor to the archbishop and master of the cathedral school, Adrian contributed greatly to the status of Canterbury as ecclesiastical centre of England.

Nothing is known of Adrian's early life in Africa, until he became a monk and then abbot at Nerida, near Naples. At this time the archbishopric of Canterbury was unexpectedly vacant, following the death of the archbishop-elect, Wighard, in Rome in 665. Pope Vitalian was keen to appoint Adrian to the post, knowing of his reputation for learning, orthodoxy and holiness. He offered the post to Adrian twice; on both occasions the monk refused the honour, but he nominated the Greek monk Theodore of Tarsus as a suitable replacement. Vitalian acted on his suggestion, on the condition that Adrian accompany him as advisor, and so Adrian sailed for England with Theodore and worked as his helper.

The school at Canterbury

When Benedict Biscop left to found Wearmouth and Jarrow, Adrian became abbot of the monastery school there, St Peter and St Paul (later known as St Augustine), a post he held for nearly 40 years. Under Adrian's learned influence and skilful administration the school developed into a highly-renowned training ground for many future bishops and abbots, much praised by Aldhelm, and attracted pupils from every area of England, and even Ireland. Pupils were taught Latin and, unusually for the time, Greek, as well as theology, Roman law, poetry, astronomy and calendar calculation. Equally instructive as his academic teaching was his example of personal goodness and humility. It was this combination of learning and virtue which won him such deep respect and inspired generations of students in their religious lives.

Death and cult

Adrian carried on with his work at the school long after the death of Theodore. He died on 9 January and was buried in the church of the monastery in which he had taught. When excavations were made for alterations to the church in 1091 his body was discovered to be incorrupt, and this led to a revival of his cult with many miracles reported at his shrine. He was especially renowned for his miraculous intervention on behalf of the boys of the monastery school who were in trouble with their masters.

Feast-day 9 January

Afra

d. 304 Augsburg

The saintly prostitute

Although the facts of her life and death are disputed, her example of humble integrity has an unfailing appeal.

It seems clear that a martyr named Afra did exist at Augsburg, and she has been venerated for centuries in Cologne, but the historical details recounted in her *Acts* are extremely unreliable.

She is traditionally believed to have been a prostitute in Augsburg during the persecutions of Diocletian who was arrested as a Christian. When commanded to offer sacrifice to pagan gods at her trial she refused, saying that her body had sinned and might be punished but that she refused to defile her soul. Accordingly she was burned to death on a small island in the river Leech; her body was recovered and given an honourable burial by her mother Hilaria and her three servants, and they too were imprisoned by the Roman authorities. Like Afra they refused to offer sacrifice, and were burnt to death in their turn.

Cult

In some ancient calendars of Augsberg Afra is listed as a virgin: some scholars have suggested that her irregular legend came about through confusion with another martyr, Venerea of Antioch, whose name became confused in the popular mind with that of Venus, the pagan goddess of love, which in turn gave rise to the prostitution legend. Venerea shared a feast-day with Afra in Jerome's martyrology.

One further elaboration of the legend claims that Afra was a convert of the Spanish bishop of Gerona, Narcissus; whatever the facts, her cult in Cologne is ancient and popular. She is shown in art crowned and enthroned holding a dead tree, or being burnt to death.

Feast-day 5 August
Patron saint of penitent women

Agatha

d. c.251

Chaste and immovable

Agatha is said to have been subjected to the most horrific tortures for her faith and her virginity.

Although her cult at Catania in Sicily is ancient and well-attested in several early martyrologies, including that of Jerome, little is known of the historical figure of Agatha. The late, unreliable *Acts* associated with her name claim that she was a young noble Sicilian, born in either Palermo or Catania, who had dedicated herself and her virginity to God as a child. When she was pursued by an amorous consul named Quintian, therefore, she rejected his advances out of hand despite his threats to implicate her as a Christian in a climate of imperial persecution. Furious, Quintian condemned her; she was sent to Aphrodisia, keeper of a house of prostitution, in an attempt to corrupt her inflexible purity but she miraculously succeeded in preserving her virginity. She was tortured and

humiliated but refused to renounce her faith: one of her most famous ordeals was the cutting off of both her breasts, but she was healed and encouraged by a vision of St Peter coming to her aid as she lay in prison, mutilated and in agony. She eventually died after being rolled over red-hot coals, inviolate to the last.

Cult and iconography

Her cult became hugely popular in Sicily, Italy and beyond; she was invoked against fire, by extension particularly against the unpredictable eruptions of Mount Etna, and against the associated dangers of earthquakes and lightning. Her iconography is especially interesting. As she is usually shown as a virgin martyr, who carries on a tray before her her two shorn breasts, the resulting image has understandably given rise to much confusion and the breasts have frequently been wrongly identified as bells or loaves of bread. As a result Agatha is venerated as the patroness of bell-founders, and many churches celebrate her feast with a tradition of blessing bread. An alternative explanation for her patronage of bell-founders is the association of the warning bell rung to alert folk of fire or imminent eruptions with a cry to Agatha for help, or perhaps from the appearance of molten metal as it was poured into the bell-moulds, like a stream of lava. Other representations show her with pincers or shears, the instruments of her torture, and she sometimes wears the veil that is her most famous relic.

Agnes

d. Rome c.304

The victorious virgin

Little is known of this most famous of virgin martyrs, but she has become a powerful symbol of Christian chastity and innocence.

The various legends of St Agnes offer conflicting evidence, but most are agreed that she was born of a wealthy Roman family and, although exceptionally beautiful, consecrated herself to chastity as a child. When she was betrayed to the Roman authorities as a Christian by a rejected suitor, at the age of 12 or 13, she endured martyrdom rather than compromise her faith or her virginity.

To this basic story many traditions add elaborations, such as the story of the soldier who looked on her in her imprisonment with impure thoughts and immediately lost his eyesight; it was only restored by the prayers of Agnes. During her arrest she is said to have been unmoved by the govenor's range of torture implements, until in desperation and enraged by her radiant purity he sent her to a house of prostitution in Rome, where she might be supposed to lose her innocence. But Agnes, by her holiness of bearing and by divine intervention, was impervious to the corruption around her. She returned to the governor as virginal

and as intractable as ever, and finally he ordered her execution.

Martyrdom

Agnes is variously supposed to have been beheaded, pierced through the throat, and burned to death. These conflicting accounts of her martyrdom suggest that the details of her story were lost in myth by the time of her *Acts.* Together with the noticeable similarity to the legend of St Agatha, this suggests that it might be unwise to place too much confidence in the historical reliability of the legend. She was buried in a catacomb on the Via Salaria that was later named after her, and by 349 a basilica had been built over her tomb by Constantina, daughter of the emperor Constantine. A head was removed from the shrine to the Lateran Palace around the ninth century, and on examination in the early 20th century was pronounced to be that of a girl aged about 12.

The cult of the lamb

From the sixth century at least Agnes's emblem has been that of a lamb, from the similarity of her name to the Latin *agnus* ('lamb'). At St Agnes in Rome, where the nuns weave the pallia for archbishops, the lambs which provide the wool are specially blessed on her feast-day. Her cult gained immediate popularity, with influential figures such as Ambrose, Prudentius and Jerome singling her out for praise, and several early English churches were dedicated to her. In art she is usually depicted with long hair and a lamb, sometimes with the sword of her martyrdom at her throat.

Feast-day 21 January
Patron saint of betrothed couples, gardeners and virgins, invoked for chastity

Aidan

d. Bamburgh 651

The apostle of Northumbria

Founder of 'The English Iona' at Lindisfarne, which played such an important role in Christianity in the north of England and beyond.

Beyond his Irish origin, little is known of Aidan's early life until we hear of him as a monk at Iona. When Oswald, who had been converted while in exile in Iona, returned to recapture his Northumbrian throne from the Mercian invaders, he naturally turned to Iona for help in evangelizing the area. The first monk sent by the monastery soon returned declaring the Saxons to be unteachable. The monks apparently concluded that he had been too harsh in his teaching and practices; the milder and more diplomatic Aidan was sent to replace him.

Aidan was consecrated bishop and settled on Lindisfarne, well-positioned for evangelizing Oswald's land in the north of Northumbria but set apart from the world's bustle. His see lay between the Forth and the Humber, but the influence of his foundation was to extend much further. From Lindisfarne, Aidan made countless missionary journeys on foot into the surrounding area, founding monasteries and churches, while at the monastery he engaged wholeheartedly in caring for the needy and educating Saxons, often slaves whose freedom was secured by the monastery, as clergymen.

The prayerful bishop

According to Bede, whose affectionate *Life* is our main source of information, Aidan's many miracles increased his effectiveness and fame. Bede could not bring himself to condone Aidan's Celtic observance of Easter, being an adherent of the Roman system himself, but he speaks warmly of Aidan's personal qualities of humility, peacefulness and prayerfulness. Aidan was in the habit of spending each Lent secluded on Inner Farne, the island Cuthbert later made his own, in penitential meditation, and it is likely that Bede used such examples of holiness as spurs to the conscience of the more worldly bishops of his day. Along with many other saints, he is also famed for his love of animals; in art he is frequently depicted with a stag, after a legend that he once rendered a stag invisible by prayer to protect it from its hunters. Oswald was succeeded in 642 by King Oswin of Deira, who was on equally cordial terms with Aidan and is said to have given him a horse, which Aidan promptly gave away to someone in need.

Death and cult

Oswin died in 651, at the hand of Oswiu, and Aidan died soon afterwards at the church he had founded at Bamburgh. Cuthbert is reported to have watched his soul being transported to heaven as he stood tending sheep in the Lammermuir Hills. Aidan was buried in Lindisfarne's cemetery, from where his relics were later translated into the church. It is said that Colman, a later abbot of Lindisfarne who strongly opposed the introduction of Roman practices, took some of the bones with him on retiring into the Celtic stronghold of Ireland after defeat at the Synod of Whitby. The only ancient church dedicated to Aidan was that at Bamburgh, but his most enduring monuments are the record of his exemplary life and the influence of the monastery he founded on Holy Island.

Feast-day 31 August

Ailred (Aelred, Æthelred, Ethelred)

1109 Hexham — Rievaulx 1166

The Bernard of the North

The centre of his life was friendship, with Christ and with his fellow humans.

Born into a noble family, son of Eilaf the last hereditary priest of Hexham, Ailred was educated in Hexham and Durham and in c.1130 became steward in the court of King David, the half-English king of Scotland. He was popular at court, being a gentle and pious character, but despite his strong attachments to his friends he felt uncomfortable there and four years later left to begin a more austere and simple life with the Cistercians at Rievaulx in Yorkshire.

Cistercian leader

In about a year he was promoted from novice to advisor to abbot, and in 1142 he was entrusted with a mission to Rome to oppose the election of William of York on behalf of Bernard. The next year he took on the abbacy of a new daughter house of Rievaulx at Revesby in Lincolnshire. In 1147 he returned to Rievaulx as abbot, and remained in the position until his death on 12 January. He governed the monastery with holiness and gentleness (Walter Daniel records that Ailred did not dismiss any monk in all the time that he knew him) and it flourished under his rule, becoming the largest monastic house of the time in England with over 600 monks and producing five new foundations. His health had always been poor, and towards the end of his life

he was confined to his monastery in agony, suffering from gout and stone. Ailred was buried in the Chapter House at Rievaulx, and his relics were later raised to the church.

Works and cult

Ailred was considered a saint even in his own lifetime; he was popular for his warm personality, respected for his intellect and counselling, and venerated for his personal holiness and his gift of preaching (he was chosen to preach at the translation of Edward the Confessor in 1163). He was often compared with the great saint of the Cistercians and known as 'The Bernard of the North'. His *Life* was written by Walter Daniel, a monk under him for 17 years and a personal friend.

Some of Ailred's own writings also survive, giving an indication of the breadth of concern and the warm humanism that characterized the man. The most famous is *De spiritali amicitia* based primarily on Cicero but drawing on the Christian tradition of Augustine, John and Bernard, it seeks to illustrate the centrality of Christ in true friendship. The influence of Augustine is seen further in *De anima*, an exploration of the nature of the soul which incorporates psychology, philosophy and theology. He also wrote several *Lives* of saints, most notably those of St Edward and St Ninian, and many beautiful prayers and sermons. Surprisingly, Ailred has never been formally canonized, but in 1746 the General Chapter of Cistercians at Cîteaux formally approved the local cult in England.

Feast-day 12 January

Alban

d. c.305

The first martyr of Britain

A pagan converted by the priest he sheltered, whose cult produced one of the greatest English abbeys.

Alban was a soldier and a leading citizen in the large Roman town of Verulamium (modern-day St Albans) in Hertfordshire, during a period of persecution. Bede claims this was in the time of Diocletian, but some modern scholars have suggested it may well have been earlier, perhaps in the reign of Decius or even Septimus Severus at the beginning of the third century. He gave hiding and shelter to a priest fleeing persecution, and was so impressed by his faith that he was converted and baptized. When the emperor's men came searching for the priest, Alban exchanged clothes with him; the priest escaped but Alban was arrested in his place and commanded to sacrifice to pagan gods. This was the acid test for Christian believers; Alban of course refused and was tortured and condemned to death.

Death

Alban apparently performed several miracles on the way to his execution, traditionally believed to have been on Holmhurst Hill, which are recorded in detail by Bede. The most famous is the dividing of the river to afford a crossing for himself and the vast crowd that accompanied him to witness the execution. One of his executioners was converted, while the eyes of the other, the one who actually beheaded Alban, later fell out of his head. This grisly episode has been a particular favourite of artists ever since.

Cult

He was buried near the city, and his shrine became renowned for the miracles of healing performed there. By Bede's time there was a commemorative church over his shrine on the hill. King Offa later founded the Benedictine Abbey of St Alban's on the site, and the town became known by that name. Alban's cult flourished along with the fortunes of the Abbey, soon one of Britain's wealthiest, with nine ancient churches in England being dedicated to him. It has been contested that Alban's remains were translated to Ely in the 11th century, and a feast of translation is celebrated there on 15 May, but St Alban's itself has always denied the claim.

A later version of the legend, recorded by Geoffrey of Monmouth, names the fugitive priest as Amphibalus, and the discovery of his supposed relics in c.1178 gave great impetus to Alban's cult. The name Amphibalus is now recognized as a mistranslation of the word denoting the cloak in which Alban wrapped himself, posing as the priest.

Feast-day 22 June

Albertus Magnus (Albert the Great)

c.1200 Lauingen — Cologne 1280

The universal doctor

The central achievement of his vast œuvre was the application of Aristotelian philosophy to Christian theology.

Albertus's titles of 'great' and 'universal' both refer to the phenomenal extent of his learning; he spoke so authoritatively on so many subjects that he was sometimes accused of magic by his bewildered contemporaries.

He was born in Swabia, the eldest son of the Count of Bollstädt, but while studying at the University of Padua in 1223 he overthrew his family's objections, rejected his inheritance and joined the recently-founded Dominican order. The next few years were spent teaching theology, mainly in Cologne where he tutored Thomas Aquinas, and he quickly became known and respected for his erudition and understanding. Albertus early recognized and loudly proclaimed the genius of his pupil Aquinas; the two men were close friends and intellectual soulmates until Aquinas's death in 1274. Both were pioneers of the scholastic method of learning, applying the principles of Aristotle to theology and insisting on the separateness and individual value of faith and reason.

Private and public careers

In 1254 Albertus was appointed prior provincial of the Dominican order and for a time was personal theologian to the Pope in Rome. But administration was not his true métier, and in 1257 he resigned and returned to studying. In 1259, along with Aquinas and Peter of Tarentasia, he proposed a systematic curriculum for Dominicans. His private studies were rudely interrupted when he was appointed bishop of Ratisbon in 1260, against his wishes. Having held the see for two years and proved to himself once again his unsuitability for administrative work, Albertus resigned the post and went back to teaching and writing at his monastery in Cologne.

Later life and death

He was not silent or ineffective, however. At the Council of Lyons in 1274 he called for reconciliation between the Greek Church and Rome, and when Aquinas's teaching was attacked by theologians from the University of Paris in 1277 Albertus spoke brilliantly in his defence. But in the next year he suffered a memory lapse: it was the beginning of a degenerative illness that was to lead two years later to his death in Cologne on 15 November 1280. He left an immense legacy: 38 quarto volumes filled with his thoughts and learning on a vast variety of subjects, and an enduring tradition of philosophical analysis.

Cult

Albertus was beatified in 1622 but only canonized in 1931 when he was pronounced Doctor of the Church by Pius XI, who also named him patron of students and of the natural sciences. In paying tribute to Albertus's 'scientific instinct' and his appetite for learning, Pius was echoing the verdict of Dante, who counts Albertus among his 'lovers of wisdom'. In art he is usually represented lecturing from a pulpit, usually dressed in the robes of a Dominican bishop, or in discussion with Thomas Aquinas.

Feast-day 15 November
Patron saint of students, scientists and all the natural sciences

Aldhelm

c.640 Wessex — Somerset 709

The first great English scholar

Equally renowned as a scholar and a popular bishop, his work edified the ecclesiast and the peasant alike.

Related to the King of the West Saxons, Aldhelm's early education was under the Irish monk Maeldubh at Malmesbury until he moved on to the famous school at Canterbury to complete his education as a Benedictine under St Adrian, the advisor of Archbishop Theodore of Canterbury. On returning to Malmesbury he was appointed director of the school there and later, in c.675, its abbot. His learning and personal holiness were famed, and in addition to his own extensive study and writing his special concern was to improve the quality of education throughout Wessex. He founded several monasteries to further this concern, including those at Frome and Bradford-on-Avon. It is believed that the Anglo-Saxon church which survives at Bradford incorporates elements built by Aldhelm himself. He also tried to educate those who followed the Celtic observance of Easter to follow the Roman tradition. King Ine of Wessex recognized the value of this earnest, wise abbot and appointed him his counsellor.

The Wessex bishop

On the division of the Wessex diocese in 705 he was appointed first bishop of the western half, with the privilege of retaining his authority at Malmesbury. He established his see at Sherborne and during his four-year episcopate built several churches in the area. His imaginative evangelistic techniques were unorthodox for the day but no doubt effective: he would mix in clowning and song along with his preaching to attract his listeners' attention when sharing the gospel with them. He died in 709 on a visit to Doulting, near Westbury, and there is evidence of an ancient cult.

Works

Aldhelm is perhaps most famous for his love of language and books. He wrote many vernacular songs and hymns (unfortunately none of these survive today) in an attempt to communicate the gospel more effectively to the poor and illiterate of his diocese. These received the approbation of King Alfred himself, and appear to have been immensely popular. Among the surviving Latin letters is one addressed to King Geraint of Dumnonia (modern-day Cornwall and Devon) which persuaded many to accept the Roman tradition of Easter observance in preference to the Celtic. He also wrote several Latin poems and a famous treatise on virginity in honour of nuns, specially dedicated to the nuns of Barking.

Aldhelm's love of language sometimes led him to an over-intricate, even incomprehensible style, and he delighted in metrical riddles and language games, but he impressed many with the importance of learning and is respected today especially by those who share his love for books. The Dorset promontory commonly known as St Alban's Head is more properly St Aldhelm's Head, presumably since it was on his estates.

Feast-day 25 May

Alfonso Maria de Liguori
(Alphonsus Mary Liguori)
1696 Marianelli — Nocera 1787

Founder of the Redemptorists

Excluded from his own order by deception, he bore this and everything with quiet humility.

The young Alfonso, whose father was a nobleman of Naples, distinguished himself at University there, gaining a doctorate in both civil and canon law at the age of only 16. From this promising beginning he went on to practise successfully at the bar in Naples for eight years, renowned for his eloquence, until one day a mistake cost him a very important case. It was a pivotal point for Alfonso; he turned to the priesthood and after much private theological study he was ordained with the Oratorians in 1726. Over the next few years he travelled the rural areas around Naples, preaching to the peasant folk and teaching in the towns.

Redemptines and Redemptorists

In 1731 Alfonso reorganized the convent of Sister Mary Celeste of Scala in line with her visions, which he acknowledged as genuine, thus founding the Redemptines. His more famous foundation however was the Congregation of the Most Holy Redeemer (the Liguorians or Redemptorists), which from its inception was fraught with difficulties. Alfonso's vision of an effective centre for mission was crippled by internal dissension. Mary Celeste left to found another convent, and in 1733 Alfonso found himself with only one lay brother left after the rest of his monks abandoned Scala to form their own congregation. Undaunted, he recruited anew and established a second community at Villa degli Schiavi, but this too collapsed after a few years. Somehow the community survived and even thrived despite all the setbacks; in 1743 Alfonso officially became superior and the male and female orders were formally approved by Pope Benedict XIV in 1749 and 1750 respectively.

Difficult last years

Although he had refused the see of Palermo, Alfonso was forced by papal order in 1762 to take on the bishopric of Sant' Agata de' Goti, where he endeavoured to reform the clergy and improve the condition of the poor. But in 1775, deformed by rheumatism, he was forced to resign the see because of ill health and returned to the community at Nocera.

Disaster followed in 1780 when Alfonso, by now ailing severely, was tricked into signing a forged rule for the Redemptorists that went contrary to his papally-authorized rule of 1750 and was rejected by Pope Pius VI. Deposed and effectively excluded from his own foundation, the next few years were filled with physical and mental anguish. He overcame his depression however and before his death was reported to have experienced visions, performed miracles and prophesied. He died peacefully on 1 August, was canonized in 1839 and named a Doctor of the Church in 1871 by Pope Pius IX.

Works

Alfonso wrote several influential works of devotion, history and theology, of which the most famous is his *Moral theology*. Although his written language is often rather ornate, he claimed that his preaching was such that the simplest person in his congregation could follow it without difficulty.

Feast-day 2 August
Patron saint of confessors and moral theologians

Aloysius Gonzaga

1568 Lombardy — Rome 1591

Patron of Catholic youth

Although some find his extraordinary piety unattractive, his unquestionable courage and devotion have won him the respect of generations.

Born on 9 March in the family castle in Lombardy, Aloysius was the eldest son of Ferrante, marquis of Castiglione and courtier to Philip II, and Marta Tana Santena, chief lady-in-waiting to the queen. Ferrante had military aspirations for his young son, and encouraged him to participate in army parades proudly bearing a real pike on his shoulder. But the child developed a precocious piety, displaying unusual devotion and self-discipline. Robert Bellarmine and others later doubted whether he had ever committed a mortal sin.

In 1577 he was sent by his father to Florence, to further his secular education, along with his brother Ridolfo. Here he was obliged to appear frequently in the court of Francesco de' Medici, and developed an extraordinarily disciplined regime to protect himself from the corruption and hedonism around him. He was similarly repulsed by the licentious court of the Duke of Mantua two years later, and immersed himself instead in the *Lives* of the saints, excused from court because of a painful kidney disease which was to haunt him for the rest of his life. Fired with dreams of sanctity himself, he now began to teach the Catechism to the young boys of Castiglione.

The road to monasticism

Visiting Spain in 1581 fresh from his recent reading, Aloysius determined to become a Jesuit missionary. His disappointed father was furious and refused his permission, threatening to flog him. The death of the Spanish infante released the family from their courtly duties, and they returned to Italy in 1584. Aloysius continued to plead for his father's consent and finally Don Ferrante capitulated; the succession was handed over to Ridolfo and Aloysius enrolled as a novice in the Jesuit house of San Andrea in Rome. Here he was forced to modify his excessively austere lifestyle under obedience, but secured for himself the most menial tasks of the monastery. He was sent to study at Milan, where he was warned in a vision of his approaching death, and because of ill health was soon transferred back to Rome.

Death and cult

In 1587 he took his vows, and that year when plague swept Rome he nursed the victims, disregarding his own safety. He caught the disease and died on 21 June, despite a partial recovery, aged only 23, after receiving the last rites from his friend and director Robert Bellarmine.

The surviving letters to his mother and others display a somewhat unattractive formality, but in his brief time as a monk, and under Bellarmine's influence, Aloysius developed a more humane attitude to friendship with others and less rigorous self-mortification, although his devotion and piety never slackened. He was canonized in 1726 and in 1926 was declared patron of Catholic youth by Pope Pius XI, because of his untimely death and the work he carried out among the poor of Castiglione.

Feast-day 21 June
Patron saint of Catholic youth and Jesuit students

Alphege (Ælfheah)

c.954 — Greenwich 1012

'The first martyr of Canterbury'

This kindly and courageous man has long been recognized as a martyr in principle if not in particulars.

The young Alphege enrolled as a monk at Deerhurst monastery in Gloucester, but retired after several years there to enjoy a solitary life in Somerset. His isolation ended when St Dunstan appointed him abbot of Bath, where the community included many of Alphege's own disciples, and in 984 he succeeded Ethelwold as bishop of Winchester.

Bishop

During his episcopate of 20 years Alphege became renowned for his generosity in giving to the needy and for the harshness of his personal austerities. His reputation grew, and in 994 he was sent by King Æthelred the Unready as mediator to the invading Danish forces under Anlaf and Swein. The Danes were so impressed with this godly man that, while still exacting tribute from the Anglo-Saxons, Anlaf was converted to Christianity and vowed that he personally would never lead his troops against Britain again. He kept his promise.

Capture and death

In 1005 Alphege was named successor to Aelfric, archbishop of Canterbury, and received the pallium in Rome from Pope John XVIII, but further trouble arose with the Danes, whom Æthelred had been unable to control. Much of the southern half of England had been overrun by invaders in 1011, and the tribute (or Danegold) paid by the fearful Anglo-Saxons did not prevent the Danes from looting and pillaging their villages. In September of that year the invaders laid siege to Canterbury. The city was betrayed by Ælfmar, an Anglo-Saxon archdeacon, and Alphege along with other leaders was held captive for seven months. He was released only once, and that briefly, to care for the victims of an epidemic. The other prisoners were ransomed and duly freed, but the price set upon the archbishop, £3 000, was exceptionally high.

Alphege refused either to pay the ransom himself or to allow others to do so, and his intransigence so infuriated the Danes that one night, when his captors were carousing, they set about him with ox bones in a drunken rage. One gave the death-blow with an axe. His body was removed to St Paul's in London for burial. Although not strictly a martyr for the faith, he became known as a national hero for his stand against the Danes and in the late 11th century St Anselm confirmed that he was a legitimate object of veneration as a martyr for justice.

Cult

In 1016 Cnut ascended the throne, preaching reconciliation between Danes and Anglo-Saxons, and Alphege's body was translated to Canterbury in 1023. It was discovered in 1105 to be incorrupt, which stimulated the cult's popularity. Before his death Thomas Becket is said to have commended his soul to God and St Alphege, whom he considered to be the first martyr of Canterbury, although Becket's own cult was later to outstrip that of his predecessor. In art, Alphege's emblem is an axe, and he is shown symbolically protecting his sheep from wolves.

Feast-day 19 April

Amand

c.584 Poitou — Elnone c.679

The itinerant bishop

One of the great missionary bishops, who brought thousands to Christ during his purposeful wanderings.

At the age of about 20, and without the permission of his family, Amand enrolled as a monk at a monastery on the island of Yeu. His father discovered him there after several months of searching and attempted to bring him home by force but Amand, unmoved by his threats of disinheritance, went on to be ordained at Tours and later moved to a cell near Bourges where he spent 15 years as a hermit under the direction of Bishop Austregisilus of Bourges.

He was consecrated as a bishop in 628 after a pilgrimage to Rome but was assigned no specific see, receiving instead a general commission to preach Christ to the heathen. In his efforts to carry out this somewhat vague brief, Amand travelled throughout Flanders and northern France, probably journeying also to Carinthia, Gascony and Germany. Some traditions claim that he was appointed bishop of Maastricht in 646,

a post which he would have held for only three years before handing it over to St Remaclus and returning to his missionary work. During his travels he founded several monasteries and convents, including those at Ghent, Elnone (later Saint-Amand) and Nivelles.

Overcoming opposition

Although Amand commanded the respect and support of most Frankish kings, he faced much opposition in his work of conversion. When he denounced the crimes of King Dagobert I he was banished for a time, but was later recalled and so far reconciled with the king that he baptized his son Siegebert (the future king and saint). He also suffered at the hands of the hostile inhabitants of Ghent, and for a time his labours there appeared unsuccessful, but his perseverance finally won many of the pagans to faith.

Death and cult

For the last four years of his life Amand was abbot of his monastery at Elnone, and it was at this time that he wrote the *Testament* which still survives. He died quietly at Elnone, and his cult spread quickly throughout France to Britain. He was especially venerated in the regions which now form northern France and Belgium, and the geographical association of his cult with these great centres of wine-growing and beer-drinking has led to his patronage of brewers and all those associated with the production and retail of alcohol.

Feast-day 6 February
Patron saint of brewers, wine-makers, hotel keepers and bar staff

---

Ambrose

c.339 Trier — Milan 397

Bishop and statesman

His fearless stance against heresy and imperial authority strengthened the Roman church in the midst of the Empire's decline.

Ambrose senior was praetorian prefect of Gaul, and on his death his young son was taken back to Rome to be educated. After distinguishing himself at his studies in rhetoric and poetry, he became a lawyer renowned for his oratory skills, and his success paved the way in c.369 to a commission from the emperor governorship of Liguria and Aemilia. Based at the capital of his province, Milan, he proved an industrious and popular ruler.

Bishop

When the Arian bishop of Milan Auxentius died in 374, turmoil broke out in the city as Arians and Catholics vied to have their candidates elected his successor. The confusion at the assembly in the cathedral was so great that eventually Ambrose was obliged to step forward and try to pacify the people. A voice from the crowd, traditionally that of a child, cried out 'Ambrose for bishop!', and the crowd unanimously took up the call. Ambrose was horrified and protested vigorously; although a Christian believer he had not even been officially baptized. But the people were insistent, and Ambrose was forced to capitulate when the emperor confirmed his appointment. He had actually fled to the house of the senator Leantius in an attempt to conceal himself, but on hearing the imperial edict his host handed him over to take up the episcopal seat. A week

later he had been baptized and consecrated, and feeling strongly the lack of a formal, in-depth religious education he launched into an intensive programme of studying the Bible and ancient Christian writers.

Confrontation

Ambrose lived simply, having given away most of his possessions, and he quickly became known as a great preacher and defender of orthodox Catholicism against Arianism, the doctrine which questioned the divinity of Christ. As advisor to the young emperor Gratian, whose uncle Valens was a notorious Arian, he successfully urged him to ban the heresy in the west of the empire. He also intervened to persuade Maximus, the assassin of and successor to Gratian, not to annex the Italian domain of the young emperor Valentinian II. When ordered to hand over a church for Arian worship Ambrose staunchly refused, reminding Valentinian that the emperor himself is within, not above, the Church. This was the principle on which he based his political activities throughout his life. He also successfully prevented a revival of the cult of Rome's goddess of victory by intervening to persuade Valentinian to reject a senatorial motion to return her altar to the senate-house.

The victory of orthodoxy

The politics and religion of the Roman Empire were both fundamentally affected when Maximus ignored Ambrose's advice and invaded Italy. Valentinian II fled for protection and aid to Theodosius I, emperor in the east, who took the opportunity to defeat Maximus in battle, thereby restoring the young emperor but becoming effective ruler in the west himself. It was Theodosius who finally convinced Valerian to renounce Arianism and to recognize the

19

authority of Ambrose, but he himself was later to bow under Ambrose's reproof by doing public penance after his troops led a horrific and indiscriminate massacre at Thessalonica in revenge for the killing of a governor there in 390.

Ambrose and Theodosius came into conflict on numerous occasions, but both were noble enough to recognize the greatness of the other. Theodosius complimented the integrity and courage of his sparring partner by saying that Ambrose was the only bishop known to him who was worthy of the name. When Valentinian was murdered by Arbogastes in 393, Ambrose refused to countenance this adventurer who was bent on overthrowing Christianity in the empire; Theodosius's victory over Arbogastes at Aquileia was effectively the death blow for paganism. The victory came only a few months before his own death, in the arms of Ambrose, and it was Ambrose who preached the funeral oration over the emperor who, despite his faults, had rendered such service to the Christian faith.

Death and cult

Ambrose himself died only two years later, aged about 57, and his relics were translated in 835 into his basilica in Milan where popular acclamation soon had him venerated as a saint. Ambrose is usually represented in art in his bishop's robes, and his emblem is a beehive (it was believed that in his infancy a swarm of bees landed on him, signalling his future eloquence). Occasionally his attribute is a scourge, recalling the penance which he so famously imposed on Theodosius. He is frequently shown together with Gregory, Jerome and Augustine as the fourth Father of the Latin church.

Works and Influence

One of the best-loved bishops of the church, Ambrose has also had an enormous influence on the history of western Christianity, not least for his part in the conversion of Augustine whom he baptized in 387. His emphasis on the use of hymns for worship and doctrine has become a central precept of the western Church: some of his hymns survive, along with some treatises and letters (the most famous written to Gratian in 377 to warn him of the dangers of Arianism, *On the Faith*). The present forms of the Ambrosian rite and the Ambrosian chant, although traditionally ascribed to him, cannot be proved with certainty to be his.

On the prompting of his sister St Marcellina he collected together his sermons in praise of virginity to produce an immensely popular treatise. Since the Roman Empire depended so heavily on a constant supply of new, loyal subjects to hold its frontiers he was accused of attempting to undermine the State with this teaching: he countered reasonably that the population was more at risk from war than from a number of consecrated virgins. It is certain however that his emphasis on the desirability of chastity had the effect of increasing the popularity of monasticism over the future centuries. Another well-known work is his treatise on Christian ethics written for the benefit of clergy, *De officiis ministrarum*. The Athanasian creed too is probably his.

Feast-day 7 December
Patron saint of Milan, bee keepers, wax refiners, domestic animals and the French Commissariat

St Ambrose by Pinturicchio. S. Maria del Popolo, Rome.

Andrew

Bethsaida — Patras c.60

First disciple and first missionary of Christ

One of Jesus's closest friends, his personality is often obscured by his more outspoken brother but his cult has always inspired devotion.

A native of Bethsaida, by Lake Genesareth in Galilee, Andrew was born into a family of fishermen. His father Jona and brother Simon worked on the lake with him, but it appears that by the time of Jesus's ministry the brothers were living in Capernaum, since Jesus stayed in their house while visiting the town. Andrew was an early follower of John the Baptist; he and another disciple heard their leader acclaim Jesus as 'the Lamb of God' and left John to follow him. Hence he is known in Greek as *protoclete*, the first-called. Andrew also proved the first missionary; he brought his brother Simon to Jesus, who then renamed him Peter. After baptizing both Andrew and Simon Peter in the Jordan, Jesus called them from their nets to full-time discipleship with the famous words 'Come, follow me, and I will make you fishers of men.' Andrew is also mentioned at the feeding of the five thousand, and in the Upper Room at Pentecost.

Legends and cult

Little is known for certain of Andrew's subsequent career. Various authorities attribute to him various preaching destinations, but most agree that he was crucified at Patras in Achaia. One famous tradition claims that he founded a church at Byzantium, appointing Stachys as its first bishop, but this is based on a late medieval forgery, later supported by the translation of his supposed relics from Patras. It was an attempt to give the influential church at Constantinople the same weight of apostolic authority as that of Rome, with its more sturdy claim to enjoy the relics and patronage of both Peter and Paul. Andrew's status as patron saint of Russia, then, is almost certainly based on a fiction.

The claim of Scotland is also dubious; it rests on the legend that St Rule carried his relics from Patras in the fourth century and was divinely directed to modern St Andrews in Fife, where he built a church and evangelized the neighbouring Scots for the next 30 years. It is more likely that the relics were indeed taken to Constantinople, stolen at its overthrow in the Crusades in 1204 and removed to Amalfi, Italy.

Representation in art

The distinctive saltire (X-shaped) cross associated with Andrew and used in the Scottish flag was an innovation of the 10th century, not common until the 14th; ancient art depicts him bound to a regular cross from which he is said to have preached for two days before dying. He is also frequently depicted with a fishing net, obvious symbol of his occupation as both fisherman and evangelist.

> **Feast-day** 30 November
> Patron saint of Scotland, Russia, Achaia, fishermen and old maids, invoked against gout and sore throats

Anne

First century BC

The mother of Mary

An immensely popular figure, she must certainly have existed but her legend is unreliable.

Absolutely no historical details are known about the grandmother of Christ, not even a name, but this popular cult is based on the apocryphal *Protoevangelium* of James. According to this unreliable second century document, Anne was the childless wife of Joachim, but she was visited by an angel as she prayed and was promised that she would have a child. Anne vowed to dedicate the child to God, and so the Virgin Mary was born. There is a strong resemblance to the Old Testament story of Hannah and the birth of Samuel (1 Samuel 1), and the identity in Hebrew of 'Anne' and 'Hannah' (both meaning 'grace') suggests that this may be the source of the legend and not merely an illuminating parallel. Other versions of the legend name Anne's father, a nomad called Akar, and claim that she was born in Nazareth, married Joachim at the age of 20 and gave birth to Mary aged 40. Joachim is supposed to have died soon after the birth of his grandson, Jesus Christ.

Development of the cult

Anne's cult is in evidence by the sixth century; Justinian dedicated a church to her in Constantinople, and relics from there were taken to Jerusalem and Rome. Her feast spread quickly from the continent to England and Ireland. There are records of a feast in honour of 'the conception of Anne' in 10th-century Naples, and this was observed shortly afterwards in Britain, probably beginning in Canterbury at the end of the 11th century.

As veneration of Mary became increasingly popular in the 12th century, so too did interest in her parents, with various churches throughout Europe laying claim to Anne's relics. She was especially popular as a patron of religious guilds in medieval England. The observance of her feast was made obligatory throughout England in response to a petition of 1382 by Pope Urban VI, and many have speculated that this was arranged to coincide fortuitously with the marriage of Richard II to Anne of Bohemia in the same year. The unhistorical basis of the cult has won it much criticism, most notably from Luther, but the feast was nonetheless extended to the universal church in 1584. A major reason for the startling popularity of her cult is that the relationship between Joachim and Anne served as a model for Christian marriage in a more accessible way than did that of Mary and Joseph.

Representation in art

Anne is frequently pictured holding Mary and Jesus (on her lap or in her arms), at her betrothal to Joachim, or teaching the young Mary to read Scripture. A famous picture by Dürer shows Anne and Joachim embracing at the Golden Gate after both had been divinely informed of the coming birth, and this is generally recognized as an iconographic representation of the conception of Mary.

Feast-day 26 July
Patron saint of miners

See illustration on following page.

*Virgin and Child with **St Anne** by Gerolamo dei Libri. National Gallery.*

Anselm

c.1033 Aosta — Canterbury 1109

The father of scholasticism

One of the most respected of theologians, who braved the displeasure of kings to defend the authority of the Church.

Anselm's first attempt to join a monastery at the age of 13 was foiled by his father, a nobleman of Lombardy. He left home in 1056 to study in Burgundy, living with his mother's family there. Hearing of the reputation of the monastery at Bec and of its friar Lanfranc, Anselm moved to Normandy and befriended the famous teacher, enrolling in his monastery in 1060. Here he studied Augustine and wrote many philosophical and theological works, including his famous ontological proof for the existence of God, becoming prior three years later when Lanfranc left for Caen.

Difficulties in England

In 1078 Anselm was named abbot of Bec, and as such visited England to inspect property belonging to the abbey. His move there came in c.1093, when he was elected archbishop of Canterbury to succeed Lanfranc who had died three years earlier: William II had kept the powerful ecclesiastical post empty until an illness made him fear for his life. Anselm's insistence on the pre-eminence of spiritual authority soon brought him into conflict with the more worldly rule of William, and in 1097 Anselm was exiled to Rome where he sought and obtained the full support of Pope Urban II. In exile he wrote his famous treatise on the Incarnation, *Cur deus homo*, and spoke convincingly at the Council of Bari on the procession of the Holy Spirit from the Son (*Filioque*), a contemporary theological contention.

When William died in 1100 Anselm returned to England, but soon conflicted with the new king, Henry I, opposing the investiture of laymen. Once again he was exiled to Rome in 1103, where Pope Paschal II worked out the terms of a compromise between the two intractable men by which the Church retained spiritual authority in investiture while the king enjoyed in practice the right of selection. Thus reconciled, the two worked amiably together, with Henry naming Anselm regent while he visited Normandy.

Scholarly influence

Anselm's prime concerns were the supremacy of ecclesiastical and spiritual authority, and the theological theory of scholasticism. This emphasized the harmonizing of faith and reason, working on the principles of Aristotle: he is considered the most important Christian writer from Augustus to Aquinas and was named a Doctor of the Church in 1720. His celebrated ontological argument is found in his *Proslogion* of 1078, and has remained a significant element in theological and philosophical debate on the existence of God ever since. Anselm also spoke for the abolition of slave trading and the importance of celibacy for priests.

Death and cult

He died in Canterbury on 21 April, and his secretary Eadmor of Canterbury wrote an affectionate and personal *Life*, which reveals Anselm as a gentle man despite his turbulent career. His cult was slow to grow, and was quickly overshadowed by that of Becket at Canterbury, but his influence is widely recognized. In art, his emblem is a ship.

Feast-day 21 April

Anskar

c.801 Picardy — Bremen 865

The apostle of the North

The first missionary to northern Europe, whose example remained influential though the results of his work seemed destroyed.

A youth of noble birth, Anskar received his education and became a monk at the Benedictine monastery of Corbie in Picardy; he was prompted to take his vows by a sobering vision of Charlemagne's death, and then he moved on to New Corbie (or Corvey) in Westphalia. By 826 he had begun his apostolate, preaching the gospel to the Danes after accompanying King Harold of Denmark there on his return from exile. His success prompted Bjorn, king of Sweden, to invite him to missionary work in his kingdom also, and Anskar was responsible for the first Christian church ever built in Sweden, at Birha. Some accounts claim that he was driven out of Denmark but achieved more success in Sweden.

Mission

Most authorities agree that in c.831 King Louis named him abbot of New Corbie and first archbishop of the newly-founded see of Hamburg, and that he was appointed papal legate to the Scandinavian countries by Pope Gregory IV. For the next 14 years he worked steadily at the difficult task of evangelizing among a strongly pagan people, organizing the work of mission, founding churches and even establishing a library, but all the ground he had gained seemed to be lost in 845, when invaders from the north swept down and razed Hamburg, overrunning Scandinavia and returning it to paganism; Anskar himself was almost killed in the attack. Afterwards he was made archbishop of the see of Bremen, which was then united with that of Hamburg, by Pope Nicholas I.

Return to Scandinavia

Anskar found it difficult to settle in Bremen, and as soon as the situation in Scandinavia improved he went back to carry on his missionary work as legate in 849. He found an influential convert in King Erik of Jutland. Although the environment was difficult and the people often hostile, Anskar won respect by his austerity (he wore a shirt of hair and lived on bread and water for much of the time), the miracles with which he was credited and his legendary generosity to the poor. He preached, founded educational establishments and campaigned against the slave trade, all with the same tireless persistence. His greatest impact was upon Denmark and northern Germany; after his death most other areas of his apostolate immediately lapsed back into paganism, where they remained until the arrival of St Sigfrid and other missionaries in the 11th century.

Cult

In art Anskar is usually shown wearing a fur pelisse, recalling his apostolate in the cold northern countries, and he occasionally holds the cathedral of Hamburg. His habit of inserting a short prayer at the foot of each psalm in his psalter began a form of devotion which gained widespread popularity.

Feast-day 3 February
Patron saint of Denmark

Anthelm

1107 Savoy — Belley 1178

Carthusian monk and bishop

Renowned for his uncompromising rule in both cloister and city, he was a central figure in Carthusian development.

As a young man, Anthelm was ordained as a priest at Belley in south-east France, but a visit to the Charterhouse at Portes so impressed him that he resigned his benefice and enrolled as a Carthusian monk at the age of 30. Just two years later, in 1139, he was appointed abbot at La Grande Chartreuse which had recently suffered damage, and under his leadership it flourished, becoming a worthy mother-house for the order. He improved both the physical and spiritual elements of the monastery, carrying out a programme of rebuilding, constructing a defensive wall and introducing an aqueduct in addition to his success in improving the relationship between the various charterhouses. These had previously been under the authority of local bishops, but Anthelm as minister-general united them more closely under a common rule.

It was under Anthelm that the Carthusian order really took on its distinctive character, and it was in his time too that La Grande Chartreuse produced such eminent ecclesiasts as St Hugh of Lincoln. Hugh always professed a great affection for his erstwhile teacher. Anthelm also commissioned John the Spaniard to draw up rules enabling women to enroll as Carthusians.

Move back to Belley

In 1152 Anthelm resigned his abbacy to live as a hermit, but he soon felt called to serve his order again; from 1154 to 1156, before returning to Grande Chartreuse, he was prior at Portes, the successor to Bernard himself. He was uncomfortable with the prosperity of the monastery, and set about distributing its assets freely to all in need. He was appointed bishop of Belley in 1163 by Pope Alexander III, whom he had supported against the antipope Victor IV, and despite his unwillingness to accept the post proved himself a fearless and energetic leader. He made widespread reforms among the clergy and was uncompromising in the shepherding of his flock, no matter how influential. He even excommunicated one Count Humbert III of Maurienne when one of his priests was killed attempting to rescue a fellow priest held prisoner by Humbert. Humbert appealed to the Pope who reversed Anthelm's edict: Anthelm removed himself from his see for a while in protest, arguing that Humbert was impenitent and therefore did not deserve restitution.

Death and cult

Anthelm was unable to go on what might have been his greatest mission, when requested by Pope Alexander to go as papal legate to England to reconcile Thomas Becket and Henry II. He spent his final years caring for lepers and the poor in Belley, and on his deathbed was visited by Humbert, repentant at last and seeking forgiveness. He died on 26 June, but in the humble way of his order his feast has only been celebrated by the Carthusians since 1607. His relics were translated in Belley in 1630. Representations of Anthelm in art show him with a lamp lit by a divine hand, or with a nobleman (ie Humbert) under his feet.

Feast-day 26 June

Antoninus of Florence

1389 Florence — Florence 1459

The people's prelate

Holiness and a deep concern for society made him a potent force in Florence, cradle of humanism and the Renaissance.

Son of a notary named Nicolo Pierozzi, the 16-year-old Antoninus enrolled as a Dominican under the leadership of the Prior of Santa Maria Novella in Florence, John Dominici. He spent his novitiate learning alongside Fra Angelico at Cortona and then moved to the new foundation at Fiesole, where he so impressed his masters that he was quickly appointed prior, first at Cortona and then back at Fiesole. He went on to the Dominican houses in Naples and Rome, as superior of the Minerva there in 1430, and was elected superior of the entire province.

On his return to Florence in 1436, Antonius founded his most famous monastery, San Marco, with the financial support of Cosimo de' Medici. It is famous for its frescoes by Fra Angelico, who painted a work of art in each individual monk's cell, and especially for the Annunciation scene on the main staircase. The monastery became a centre for Renaissance humanism and learning.

Life in Florence

Antoninus took a prominent role in the General Council of Florence in 1438–45, and in 1446 was elected archbishop of Florence by Eugenius IV. Unlike many of his contemporaries he lived an exemplary life of personal poverty, making frequent preaching tours on foot throughout his see, and using his authority to combat usury, magic and gambling and to provide practical help for the needy, such as a fellowship of St Martin for those ashamed to beg. He met the challenge of plague and earthquake by involving himself personally with the victims, encouraging the rest of his clergy to do the same. Cosimo de' Medici publicly announced that the preservation of Florence through these troubled years was due in no small part to the intercession of her miracle-working archbishop.

Antoninus also addressed himself to the new concerns of the age: his teaching on mercantile affairs and how they related to Christianity was vitally relevant to Florence in her period of great economic development, and he taught extensively on State duties to society. In his last years, Antoninus served as Florentine ambassador and was elected by Pius II to help in the task of reforming the papal court: Rome had early recognized his genius for combining holiness and personal integrity with an effective response to the fast-moving world of the Renaissance, and Pope Nicholas V had sought his advice on all manner of ecclesiastical and political matters.

Works and cult

The writings he left behind include several theological treatises, the most famous of which is his *Summa* of moral theology, and an early history of the world. He was canonized by the radical Pope Adrian VI in 1523, who was himself much concerned with reform and social justice, and his emblem in art is a pair of scales in which he weighs false merchandise against God's word.

Feast-day 10 May

Antony

251 Koman — Mount Kolzim 356

The founder of monasticism

Although he aimed at a life of seclusion, he attracted to himself the prototypical monastic community.

Born of wealthy Christian parents in Upper Egypt, Antony came into his inheritance on their death in c.269 and promptly gave it away to the needy, placed his sister in a convent and attached himself briefly to an old recluse before beginning to live as a hermit himself in a nearby cemetery. Here he lived an austere life of prayer, manual work and penance, undergoing famous temptations and trials of the flesh yet overcoming them all. His fame began to spread, and after 15 years he moved to an abandoned fort at Pispir where he lived for 20 years in complete solitude, eating only what others threw over the wall to him.

The first monastery

A group of disciples had inevitably gathered around his retreat; in 305 he emerged and organized a simple community. Each monk lived in prayer and penance under the general authority of Antony, coming together for worship, with communal work. He left for Alexandria in 311 to encourage the Christians there suffering under Maximinus, and on his return founded another monastery at Pispir before retiring again to the seclusion of Mount Kolzim near the Red Sea. This time he took with him a close disciple, Macarius. He visited Alexandria again in 355 to help in the fight against Arianism, working closely with his friend Athanasius, whose *Life* is our main source of information for Antony.

Death and cult

After his return to Mount Kolzim, he remained in his cave until his death on 17 January. In accordance with his wishes, he was buried secretly and his relics were not discovered until 561, when they were translated to Alexandria. Later translations have been claimed by Constantinople and La Motte. This latter is the home of the Order of Hospitallers of St Antony, founded in c.1100 to care for pilgrims. From these hospitallers, a familiar sight across Europe in the Middle Ages, come the emblem of the pig and the bell traditionally associated with Antony. Their pigs were allowed the privilege of freedom of the streets, and the order begged alms by ringing small bells, which were often used as protective charms. 'Tantony' is a diminutive applied to pigs or bells, the smallest of the litter or the softest of the peal.

Influence and iconography

Many people visited this remarkable saint during his life, out of veneration or just curiosity. He avoided the fanaticism and excess of many Desert Fathers, and although austere, was known for his sound teaching and personal warmth, a model for solitaries and monks ever since. Artists have developed the legends of Antony's temptations imaginatively, but early pieces often show Antony receiving St Paul the Hermit as a guest, together with the ravens that used to bring him half a loaf each day and on this occasion miraculously brought a full loaf. His emblems are a T-shaped staff and bell.

> **Feast-day** 17 January
> Patron saint of basket-makers, invoked against ergotism (St Antony's fire)

See illustration pxii.

Antony of Padua

1195 Lisbon — Arcella 1231

'The hammer of heretics'

*Known in his lifetime as a
magnificent preacher, this
popular saint is now invoked as
a wonder-worker.*

Son of a Portuguese knight, Antony grew up in Lisbon and was educated at the cathedral there. At 15 he enrolled with the nearby Canons Regular of St Augustine but left after only two years to finish his studies at Coimbra. After ordination in c.1220 he joined the Franciscans, wanting to emulate their martyrs in North Africa, and took the name of Antony in honour of the Egyptian saint. But illness compelled him to quit Morocco and the evangelizing of the Moors, and on the voyage back his ship was driven off course to Messina, Sicily. He travelled from there to Assisi, where the Franciscan General Chapter of 1221 was taking place.

A career in preaching

At the end of the Chapter, Antony was assigned to the small hermitage of San Paolo near Forli, and his enormous talent was first discovered when he was called on unexpectedly to speak at an ordination in Forli. Amazed by the power of his preaching, his provincial minister appointed him the first lector in theology of the Franciscans and commissioned him to preach throughout Italy. Thousands flocked to hear this short man denouncing sin and heresy with his resounding voice, crowds broke down in penitence, churches were too small to contain the hordes and he was obliged to speak in market places, when the townsfolk would frequently close up their businesses to go and hear him.

He was recalled after the death of St Francis to take on the position of minister provincial in Emilia or Romagna, and at the Chapter General in 1226 he was elected envoy to bring before Pope Gregory IX for settlement the questions that had arisen in the assembly. Antony took the opportunity to secure the Pope's permission to lay down his office and devote himself to preaching, primarily in Padua. Here he energetically denounced all social and moral wrong until in 1231 he became very ill.

Death and cult

He died at a Poor Clare convent on the outskirts of Padua, aged only 36, was canonized within the year and in 1946 was declared a Doctor of the Church by Pius XII. His shrine at Padua is notorious for miracles, and he is frequently known as 'the wonder-worker', especially as the patron saint of lost objects; one legend tells how a novice who secretly borrowed his psalter returned it in terror after a warning apparition. The 19th-century devotion 'St Antony's bread', alms given to the poor and hungry, reflects his social concern and exists as a fund today. Modern representations of St Antony often make reference to his vision of Jesus by showing the Christ-child seated on Antony's book, or to the legend that he once preached to fish, or with sheaves of corn recalling his traditional status as patron saint of harvests. As patron of lower animals he is often shown with a donkey.

Feast-day 13 June
Patron saint of Portugal, lost articles, the poor, lower animals and harvests

Apollonia

d. Alexandria 249

'That marvellous aged virgin'

Although she staunchly refused to deny her faith, the morality of Apollonia's voluntary death has been questioned by many.

During a riot in Alexandria in the last year of the reign of Emperor Philip, a mob hunted down and killed Christians in the town, looting their houses, torturing them to make them renounce their faith and murdering them. A detailed account was written by the bishop of the time, St Dionysius of Alexandria, who wrote about the persecution in a letter to Fabius, bishop of Antioch. We hear of atrocities such as those endured by the elderly Metras, who had splinters forced into his eyes before being stoned to death, and by Quinta, who was dragged by her heels over the cobblestones before being stoned in her turn. It is interesting in the light of these details that Dionysius asserts in his letter that none of the believers renounced their faith.

Death

One of the victims of the atrocities was an old deaconess, 'that marvellous aged virgin Apollonia' according to Dionysius. She was struck on the jaw so hard and so frequently that her teeth were knocked out, and a pyre was built outside the city on which to burn her alive if she refused to renounce her faith and join her torturers in their blasphemies. Apollonia begged for a moment's respite, then she seized her opportunity and leapt dramatically into the flames.

A controversial cult

Her cult began quickly in the West, with many dedications of churches and altars, but there is no evidence of an enduring Eastern cult despite the fact that her martyrdom took place in Alexandria. She is sometimes confused with another Apollonia, victim of Julian the Apostate, and a romantic impulse has frequently transformed her in art into a young and beautiful girl. Her usual emblem is a tooth, sometimes gilded and suspended on a neckchain or held by forceps to indicate its removal, and she is the patron saint of dentists; one dentistry journal in America is titled *The Apollonian.*

The manner of her death, whether her courageous leap was voluntary suicide or martyrdom, has for a long time been a talking point for theologians. Augustine argued that she must have acted from a specific prompting of the Holy Spirit in thus hastening her own death, since an uninspired leap would necessarily have been unlawful. Nevertheless, celebration of her feast has been confined to local churches only since 1970.

Feast-day 9 February
Patron saint of dentists, invoked against toothache

Arsenius

c.355 Rome — Troë c.450

The weeping monk

'I am often sorry for having spoken, but never for having held my tongue'.

Most of the details we have regarding Arsenius's early life are doubtful: it appears that he was born in Rome, became a deacon there and was later appointed tutor to the children of Emperor Theodosius I at his court in Constantinople on the recommendation of Pope Damasus I, who knew him to be learned and holy. He remained in this prestigious position for about 10 years, although it appears that his wisdom and his piety alike were to a large degree wasted upon Arcadius and Honorius, who proved a disgrace to their father and to their tutor in their adult life, and then resigned to become a monk with the desert community in Alexandria. After the death of Theodosius he withdrew to Skete where he learned about the life of a hermit from St John the Dwarf.

Discipline and compassion

After this apprenticeship, he lived in the strict austerity characteristic of the Desert Fathers, but in his case it was all the more remarkable since in order to pursue it he had rejected a substantial legacy left to him by a senatorial relative. Like other Desert Fathers too he is credited with a fine perception of the human condition and the gift of composing shrewd maxims on the need for self-discipline and holiness. He spoke particularly on the need to guard against over-hasty words and the benefits of taciturnity, and of the worthlessness of secular education. More than most of even this austere breed he seems to have been dedicated to isolation and self-mortification. It was said that he would pray with his arms uplifted from sunset until dawn, and that from the tiny measure of corn allocated to him each year he not only fed himself but even gave to others.

One interesting characteristic seems to have been his propensity to weep on every occasion, despite his rigorous standards of discipline. In addition to lamenting his own shortcomings, he found particular occasion to weep at the careers of his ex-pupils, and it was said that he wore his eyelashes away with tears.

Death

Barbarian raids on Skete in c.434 obliged Arsenius to quit his hermitage; he moved onto the rock of Troë in Memphis, then to Canapus (which he found too close to Alexandria for comfort), and finally back to Troë. He died there in c.450, and in an endearingly frank manner he confessed his own fear of death to his monks before passing away quietly and in confidence at the end. An unreliable *Life* was written some time later by St Theodore the Studite.

Feast-day 19 July

Athanasius

c.296 Alexandria — Alexandria 373

The champion of orthodoxy

Undaunted even by long and uncomfortable periods of exile, Athanasius spent his life battling against the influential forces of heresy.

Born to Christian parents in Alexandria and educated in theology there, Athanasius was ordained as a deacon and became secretary to Bishop Alexander in the city in c.318. At the Council of Nicaea in 325, Athanasius was present with his master when the heresy of Arianism was condemned and Arius himself excommunicated; Athanasius was to commit the rest of his life to defending the doctrine of the full divinity of Christ and the eternal authority of the Scriptures against this heresy.

Bishop of Alexandria

When Alexander died in c.328 Athanasius succeeded him and soon found himself battling against the Arian movement which was strong throughout the Mediterranean world, and especially in the imperial court. Emperor Constantine I was persuaded in 330 by Eusebius of Nicodemia to require Athanasius to readmit Arius to communion: the intractable bishop refused and a campaign was launched to discredit him. He was brought to trial in Constantinople for various alleged offences, and although cleared of them all he was then accused of murdering Arsenius, an Arian bishop. The charge was so ridiculous that Athanasius refused even to answer it, but he was called to council in Tyre by the emperor himself in 335. He was found guilty before a hostile court, and although

the emperor reversed the decision after speaking with Athanasius, he was later persuaded to uphold the conviction and the bishop was exiled in 336 to Trier in Germany.

Years of exile

After Constantine's death the next year Athanasius was recalled, only to be deposed when Eusebius again denounced him to Constantius, the son of Constantine ruling Alexandria. He spent seven years in exile in Rome, and was vindicated by a synod there before Pope Julian I. He returned to Alexandria in 345, after the death of the bishop who had replaced him, to be grudgingly reinstated then almost immediately exiled again by Constantius, who coerced Pope Liberius into acquiescence. Still firmly anti-Arian, Athanasius lived in the countryside around Alexandria until soldiers attacked his church one night and murdered many of his congregation. Athanasius fled to the protection of the desert monks and lived with them for six years, writing many of his most famous theological works.

Finally, in 361, Constantius's successor Julian the Apostate revoked all orders of banishment. Athanasius returned to Alexandria, but had to flee to the desert again when he came into conflict with Julian, who propagated paganism. Julian was killed in 363 and Athanasius was reinstated by his successor Jovian, but Jovian died after a tragically short reign of eight months and Athanasius was once again forced to flee when Emperor Valens exiled all orthodox bishops in 365. At last, four months later, the order was revoked and Athanasius returned to spend the rest of his life overseeing his church, preserving orthodoxy and enjoying the relative tranquillity after 17 years of fear and five separate periods of exile. He died on 2 May.

Works and cult

Athanasius wrote many influential works, including orthodox apologetics, his classic *Life of St Antony* and such major doctrinal works as the controversial *Contra Arianos*, and several letters to monks which still survive. The creed which bears his name is not his but is based upon his teaching, and it remains a central part of western Christian liturgy today. One of the great Greek Doctors of the Church, Athanasius is usually represented in his episcopal robes standing over a defeated heretic, holding an open book in his hand.

Feast-day 2 May

St Athanasius and the pagan, from The Fathers of the Church.

Augustine

354 Tagaste — Hippo 430

Greatest of the Latin Fathers

The conversion of Augustine was possibly the most significant in the history of the Catholic Church after that of St Paul.

A native of Roman North Africa, Aurelius Augustinus was brought up as a Christian by his mother, St Monica, although his father Patricius was a pagan Roman officer. At the age of 16 he left for Carthage to study rhetoric, hoping to become a lawyer, but then abandoned law to devote himself to literature, teaching and philosophical study. It was at this point too that he abandoned his Christianity and took a mistress. They lived together for 15 years and in 372 she bore him a son, Adeonatus.

Meanwhile Augustine's intellectual interests were developing as, inspired by reading Cicero's *Hortensius* (now lost), he became interested in philosophical thought; he studied Plato and soon moved on to Manichaeism, the doctrine that everything springs from the opposing principles of light and darkness. Much of his energy throughout his life was spent grappling with the problem of the existence of evil. He taught for some time in Carthage and Tagaste, and in 383 he moved to Rome to teach rhetoric. The next year he was appointed to the chair of rhetoric in Milan, but by now the appeal of secular philosophy was beginning to pall; after an unsatisfactory interview with a celebrated Manichaean bishop called Faustus, Augustine was becoming disillusioned with the theories of life which he had studied so hard.

Conversion

In Milan Augustine met Ambrose, the bishop of Milan, who introduced him to Christian Neoplatonism and whose preaching forced him to reconsider his lost faith. For a while he battled between the desire for worldly happiness and success and the call to a holy life. The spiritual conflict is revealed in all its anguish in his *Confessions*; finally however, after reading a Bible passage from Romans in his garden one evening, he experienced a firm spiritual certainty and turned back to God. He was baptized on the day before Easter in 387, along with a friend Alipius and his son Adeonatus.

Ordination and consecration

Later that year he returned to Africa where he founded a community organized along semi-monastic lines, based on prayer and study, and allowing also for lively discussion. His reputation spread beyond the community, and in 391 on a visit to hear Bishop Valerius speak in Hippo he was seized by the people and forcibly offered up for ordination. Valerius ordained him as priest and encouraged him to preach in the cathedral, an unusual privilege, but allowed him to keep the monastic lifestyle he loved. Only four years later he was appointed coadjutor to Valerius, and on the bishop's death the following year he succeeded to the full bishopric, which he held for the rest of his life. There is no doubt that Augustine was the leading figure in the African church of his day: he was a beloved and effective bishop, active in the care of his clergy and his community, personally involved in all areas of administration, both spiritual and temporal (he was known to give judgement in civil cases). A popular and influential monastic order was also set up along the principles laid down by Augustine's communities.

Works, doctrine and influence

It is Augustine's intellectual legacy, however, that secures his position as probably the greatest and most influential thinker of the Western Church. The tradition of Augustinianism, a doctrinal system and method of thinking based on that of Augustine, has proved one of the central impulses in theological and philosophical advances to the present day. He wrote a vast number of letters, sermons, treatises and devotional works, many of which still survive, and some of which were among the few works ever to be translated into Old English. The *Confessions*, a classic of spiritual autobiography and philosophical meditation, has inspired thousands, while his *De civitate dei*, powerfully contrasting the spiritual City of God with the crumbling Roman Empire of the day, stands monumentally as the first Christian philosophy of history. Other works deal authoritatively with Christian doctrine on grace, the Church, the Trinity, sex and marriage.

In answer to Manichaeism, the doctrine he had once studied which posited the existence of an evil force in conflict with that of good, darkness eternally opposed to light, Augustine asserted that God was the sole and good source of all creation, and that evil is a negative rather than a positive entity, the privation of good. Of the Church, he maintained that she was holy not through her members, who might be individually flawed, but through her purposes. In her relationship to secular power, he acknowledged the authority of the State only so long as it was based on a true recognition of God and was concerned with administering divine justice. He was always opposed to the death penalty.

Controversial teachings

On the issue of predestination many have found Augustine's teaching unacceptable. He held that the unmerited grace of God necessary for salvation is administered only by election, and that unbaptized infants who die are automatically damned. This stern vision of divine, inscrutable selection influenced many reformers, most notably Calvin, but has been strongly contested by theologians throughout history. His teaching that the sexual act is the means of transmission of original sin has also been questioned by more recent generations, but the marriage ceremony in the Book of Common Prayer draws heavily on Augustinian thought.

Death and cult

Augustine died at Hippo on 28 August, while the city was being besieged by Genseric's Vandal army. His cult quickly gained popularity; his relics were taken to Sardinia and later enshrined at Pavia, and his feast was celebrated universally. There are no known church dedications in medieval England, although they are common today.

In art, Augustine is frequently represented in his bishop's robes holding a book as one of the four Latin Doctors of the Church. The cathedral at Carlisle contains paintings of his life in the stalls, including pictures of him as a young man before conversion, at study or disputing with his mother. Because of his later penitence, his emblem is usually a broken, pierced or flaming heart.

Feast-day 28 August
Patron saint of theologians

St Augustine

Augustine of Canterbury (Austin)

d. c.604

The original archbishop of Canterbury

Leader of Gregory I's great mission to England, who decided upon Canterbury as the ecclesiastical centre of the country.

A native of Italy, Augustine studied under Felix, bishop of Messana, and enrolled as a monk in Rome at St Andrew, on the Celian hill. He became prior there, and in 596 was chosen by Pope Gregory the Great to lead an evangelistic mission to England. The 30 monks sent with him grew dispirited on the long journey, and in Gaul they were ready to turn back. Gregory intervened; he encouraged the monks and confirmed the authority of Augustine.

Work in England

The party finally landed at Thanet off the Kentish coast in 597, to be given a warm welcome by King Ethelbert of Kent, who was converted later that year. Ethelbert also offered them a house in Canterbury from where they began their mission, spending their time in daily devotion and discipline and in the central task of preaching. Augustine returned to the Continent to be consecrated bishop, and on returning to Britain decided to establish his see in Canterbury (in preference to the more obvious choice of London) and built Britain's first cathedral there. He had much success in converting the south of England (one famous legend claims that he once baptized more than 1000 people in one day) and soon reinforcements from Rome were called in to help in the work of consolidation, but in his efforts to cooperate with the Christians of Britain he was less successful. He tried to coordinate the bishops in a programme of evangelism but was insensitive in his approach, trying to impose Roman traditions on clergy familiar with long-established Celtic practice, and he largely failed to win their support at a conference at Aust, on the River Severn, in 603.

Death and cult

In addition to the cathedral at Canterbury, Augustine founded the nearby Benedictine monastery of St Peter and St Paul (now known as St Augustine), sees in Rochester and London, and a school in Canterbury. He died in 604, and his body was translated into St Peter and St Paul eight years later.

Although Augustine is sometimes known as 'The apostle to the English', it seems more appropriate to honour Gregory with this title, since Augustine was really carrying out in the field the vision and orders of his friend and superior. It was his impressive preaching, however, and the miracles frequently attached to his name, that made such a lasting impression on the people of the south of England. The earliest Anglo-Saxon laws surviving today were drawn up by Ethelbert, aided by Augustine, and it seems likely that a sixth-century manuscript known as the *Gospel of St Augustine*, now at Corpus Christi college, Cambridge, and traditionally used in the consecration of the archbishop of Canterbury, was brought to Kent by Augustine. In art he is often shown as a bishop baptizing a king.

Feast-day 27 September

Barbara

d. c.200

A romantic heroine

The legend of St Barbara made her one of the most popular saints of the medieval calendar, but it is now widely recognized as a romantic fiction.

Although some versions of her legend have Barbara killed during the persecutions of Maximus (c.303), there is no mention of her name in early martyrologies,and no sign of a cult until the fanciful *Acts* of the seventh century. Her popularity in Europe was due mainly to the *Golden Legend* of Jacobus de Voragine: according to this, Barbara was a beautiful young Syrian woman whose pagan father Dioscorus kept her imprisoned in a tower, away from the attentions of her many suitors. Barbara however much exasperated him by refusing to consider even the most eligible bachelors, and during his absence from home for a time compounded her obstinacy by becoming a Christian. She is said to have persuaded the workmen building a bathhouse for her father to alter the design which he had given them, in order to incorporate three rather than two windows, in honour of the Trinity. Barbara spent some time living a semi-eremitical life in the bathhouse, receiving baptism there from a local holy man.

Death

On his return, Dioscorus demanded of his workmen why his design for the bathhouse had been altered. Barbara was brought before him, and she calmly explained herself by saying that only three windows, symbolic of the one God in three persons, could truly admit light. Dioscorus was so enraged at his daughter's conversion and intransigence that he flew at her to kill her, but Barbara was miraculously whisked from his grasp. Undeterred, he dragged her before the authorities and had her condemned as a Christian to execution. She refused to apostatize, despite the severe beatings which she received in prison and the assurances of the judge that she had only to offer pagan sacrifice to be spared. It is said that she was strengthened and encouraged in her captivity by a vision of Christ. Dioscorus took upon himself the task of beheading her, taking her up a mountain to deal the blow, and on his way back down was himself killed by lightning. This is the origin of Barbara's association with death by lightning and, by extension, with sudden death by collapsing mines or cannonballs.

Cult

Her place of death has been variously assigned to Antioch, Heliopolis, Rome, Tuscany and, according to the Roman martyrology, Nicomedia. Not until after the ninth century do we find evidence of a widespread cult, but after this date its popularity grew at an astonishing rate, and she was listed as one of the Fourteen Holy Helpers. Her cult was officially suppressed in the Roman calendar of 1969 but her popularity and her frequent representation in art, as a princess with a tower, the palm of martyrdom or the chalice of happy death, has ensured her prominence in any study of important saints.

Feast-day 4 December
Patron saint of architects, builders, artillerymen, firemen, military engineers and miners, invoked against sudden death, lightning, fire and impenitence

---

Barnabas

First century

The companion of St Paul

Although not one of the Twelve, he is known as an apostle and especially honoured for his work with Paul in the early Church.

Our information about Barnabas comes mainly from biblical evidence, although there is much unreliable tradition concerning his subsequent doings. He was a Cypriot Jew originally named Joseph, but when he sold his possessions to live with the early Christian community in Jerusalem the apostles gave him the name 'Barnabas', meaning 'son of consolation'.

Work with Paul

After Paul's unexpected conversion, it was Barnabas who persuaded the nervous apostles to trust their old enemy. Barnabas was chosen to encourage and instruct the young church at Antioch, and feeling the need of assistance in this enormous task he brought Paul from Tarsus to help him. The two spent a year at Antioch preaching and establishing the practices of the growing church along apostolic lines, and it was during this time that the adherents of the new faith became known for the first time as 'Christians'.

From Antioch they went together on Paul's first missionary journey, beginning in Cyprus, with Barnabas's cousin, John Mark. On returning from this journey Paul and Barnabas opposed Peter and many of the Christians in Jerusalem over the issue of circumcision of Gentiles, resulting in the Apostles' Council of c.50 which ruled that Gentiles need not be circumcized before baptism. Barnabas proposed that John Mark accompany them on a second missionary journey, revisiting several of the same cities of Galatia: as Mark had left them in Perga on their first journey to return home, however, Paul objected. A breach between the two seems to have resulted, with Paul going on to Philippi and Corinth while Barnabas returned to Cyprus with John Mark.

After the *Acts*

Nothing more is known for certain, although some traditions claim that he went on to preach in Alexandria and Rome, becoming bishop in Milan before martyrdom by stoning in Salamis, the Cyprian port, in c.61. He is traditionally believed to have been reconciled with Paul before his death. Some of Paul's remarks in Galatians and Corinthians suggest that Barnabas's apostolate may indeed have extended beyond his native island, but it is unlikely that he was connected with Milan. The Milanese church dedicated to him, however, gave its name to the Order of Barnabites founded there by Antony Zaccaria in 1530.

Works and cult

The apocryphal *Epistle of Barnabas* is now widely accepted as the work of an Alexandrian Christian of the late first century, and the *Acts of Barnabas*, once believed to be John Mark's, have been identified as fifth century. In ecclesiastical art Barnabas is shown as a middle-aged, bearded apostle, often holding a book and an olive branch, and frequently in company with Paul. The tradition of invoking his protection from hailstorms presumably arises from his association with death by stoning.

Feast-day 11 June
Patron saint of Cyprus, invoked against hailstorms and as a peacemaker

Bartholomew

First century

The enigmatic apostle

Although his fate has always fired the imagination of artists, the facts of his life are uncertain and even his name is controversial.

Virtually all that is known of Bartholomew is that he was called to be one of the 12 apostles of Christ. In John's Gospel Jesus describes Nathanael rather than Bartholomew as, 'A true Israelite, in whom there is nothing false' and John claims he came from Cana; most modern scholars accept that they are in fact the same apostle. Both are mentioned specifically in the company of Philip, and after the ascension John lists Nathanael overtly in his list of the disciples, omitting Bartholomew. The name Bartholomew means 'Son of Tolomai', so the explanation could well be that this was a patronymic rather than a real name.

Apart from this scant biblical evidence nothing is known of his background, nor anything of his movements subsequent to Jesus's death and resurrection. The Roman martyrology follows the tradition of ascribing to him an apostolate in India and Armenia, where he is said to have been martyred by flaying and then beheading on the orders of King Astyages. The spot of his death is traditionally identified as Derbend, on the Caspian Sea. Other traditions hold that he preached in Mesopotamia, Persia and Egypt before his death. The situation is complicated by the indefinite use of the name 'India' to refer to a vast area generally east or south of the Mediterranean. Eusebius comments that St Pantaenus, entering India at the beginning of the third century, discovered natives who were acquainted with the gospel and who produced a Hebrew Gospel of Matthew which they claimed to be that of Bartholomew, but because of the loose geographical reference this tradition is of little help in ascertaining the exact location of Bartholomew's apostolate.

Cult and iconography

His supposed relics are believed to have been translated to the island of Lipara, on to Beneventum, and finally to Rome where they are still thought to remain in St Bartholomew's church on the Tiber. His popularity in England was no doubt increased as a result of a gift of Bartholomew's arm, given to Canterbury in the 11th century by Cnut's queen, Emma. Another reason for his undoubted popularity (there were 165 ancient churches dedicated to him in England alone) was his manner of death: his emblem in art is a flaying knife but he is often shown with his own flayed skin. The subject was a challenging and irresistible one for many artists. Unsurprisingly, he has come to be known as the patron saint of tanners and all workers with leather, including such associated trades as shoemaking, bookbinding and dyeing.

> **Feast-day** 24 August
> Patron saint of Florentine salt and cheese merchants, tanners and leather-workers, invoked against nervous diseases and twitching

Basil the Great

c.329 Caesarea — Caesarea 379

Patriarch of Eastern monks

An eloquent and passionate Doctor of the Church, whose influence has permeated all monasticism.

Basil's family was a wealthy, respected and an extraordinarily pious one: in addition to Basil himself, his grandmother, parents and three siblings are all venerated as saints. Basil was educated in the schools of Caesarea, Constantinople and Athens, where he studied alongside Gregory of Nazianzus and Julian, later the apostate Emperor. He taught rhetoric in Caesarea for a while but soon followed his family in the religious life, visiting monasteries in Spain, Egypt and Palestine before settling as a hermit on the shores of the river Iris at Annesi, Pontus, in 358. He quickly attracted a number of companions, including his friend Gregory, and became the founder of the first monastery in Asia Minor, laying down the principles on which Orthodox monasticism has operated ever since.

Public life

Neither his ordination in 363 nor the invitation of Julian the Apostate to join him at court tempted Basil to leave his community in Pontus, but when Gregory appealed for help in his fight against Arianism in 365 he responded promptly and took administrative responsibility in Caesarea under Archbishop Eusebius whom he succeeded in 370, receiving authority over 50 bishops in Pontus. Basil's main conflict now was with Emperor Valens in Byzantium, a notorious Arian much given to the persecution of orthodox Christians, who demanded that Basil comply with his heterodoxy. Basil remained firm even in direct opposition to Roman civil authority and Valens eventually withdrew from Caesarea.

Basil's concerns did not end with the preservation of sound doctrine and the assertion of spiritual over temporal authority: he was much involved in work with the poor and sick, active in the rehabilitation of thieves and prostitutes, and built a new town, Basilia, complete with church, well-equipped hospital and guest-hospice with trained medical staff and artisans. He emphasized the importance of preaching, drawing enormous crowds to his own powerful sermons, and he was among the first to recognize the value of classical education to the Christian intellect. He belongs to the inclusive Christian tradition, appreciating and valuing the best of secular culture and integrating it vitally within the context of an orthodox faith.

Death and cult

He died on 1 January, aged only 49 but worn-out by illness, austerity and hard work, and his funeral was attended by vast crowds of mourners. His letters reveal some of the reasons for his popularity: he was a truly likeable man, sincere, practical and intelligent, if somewhat headstrong. In art his emblem is a supernatural fire, often with a dove also, and in the West he is frequently shown along with the other Doctors of the Greek Church. In the East he is venerated as the first of the Three Holy Hierarchs. In his Rule Benedict acknowledged Basil's influence, and his magnificent work on the Holy Spirit remains an unsurpassed classic of Catholic theology.

Feast-day 2 January
Patron saint of Russia

Bathild

England — Paris 680

Slave-girl, queen and the humblest of nuns

She demonstrated extraordinary qualities of good sense, humility and piety in an equally extraordinary life.

Anglo-Saxon Bathild was captured by pirates in 641 and sold into slavery in the household of Erchinoald, mayor of the imperial palace. King Clovis II of the western Franks soon noticed this beautiful and capable young Englishwoman, who had risen to a position of responsibility and trust within her master's household, and in 649 he wedded her.

Queen and regent

In their short marriage of only eight years Bathild bore Clovis three sons, all future kings: Clotaire III, Childeric II and Thierry III. After Clovis's death in 657 Bathild acted as regent for the five-year-old Clotaire and proved herself worthy of her new role, ably defending the waning Merovingian power against the ascendant Frankish kings. She ruled intelligently and compassionately, ransoming many captives, fighting the slave-trade of which she had herself been a victim, and energetically promoting the activities of the church. Among the many monasteries which she endowed were St Denis, Corbie and Chelles.

The English writer Eddius (the biographer of St Wilfrid) claims that she was responsible for the assassination of Bishop Annemund of Lyons and others for political reasons, but this seems unlikely and is unsupported by other authorities. It seems probable that Eddius simply mistook the name, as indeed he mistook the name of Annemund himself, confusing him with his brother, Dalfinus. Although authorities such as William of Malmesbury and, to an extent, Bede, have followed Eddius, many other important sources have rejected the accusation. It has been suggested that the confusion might involve the Frankish queen Brunhilda, who died in 613.

Last years and death

A revolution led by nobles at the palace in 665 forced Bathild to quit the regency and withdraw to her convent at Chelles, where she spent the rest of her life quietly under obedience to the abbess there, distinguished only by an attitude even more humble than that of her sisters. Several sources claim that she had long wished to retire here, and that the revolution was nothing more than a spur to her own inclination. She died in the convent after a long and painful illness, borne in patience. After her death Chelles, her most famous foundation, was to produce many of the most renowned of the Anglo-Saxon nuns.

Cult

After her canonization by Pope Nicholas I, Bathild's cult won popularity more readily in France than in her native England. We are fortunate in possessing an authentic text of her *Life*, written by a contemporary, and much reference is made to her in the less reliable *Life of St Eligius*, wrongly attributed to St Ouen. In art her emblem is a ladder extending towards heaven, playing upon the felicitous French pun of *Chelles – échelle*. Bathild herself is shown as a crowned nun, often performing menial tasks such as sweeping, or giving money to the poor.

Feast-day 30 January
Patron saint of children

Bede, the Venerable

673 Northumberland — Jarrow 735

The father of English history

Although he confined his life's work to the library at Jarrow, Bede's writings have been both example and inspiration for every succeeding generation of historians.

Our information about Bede comes almost entirely from a short autobiographical entry at the end of the *Historica Ecclesiastica* and from the account of his death by the monk Cuthbert. He was sent as a young child to be educated at the monasteries of Wearmouth and Jarrow, where he studied under St Benedict Biscop and St Ceolfrith. He enrolled as a monk at Jarrow in 682 and was to spend the rest of his life there, travelling very little and little concerned with affairs of state or indeed any affairs beyond the churches and monasteries of Northumbria. He was a model brother, whose self-discipline, devotion and application were as notable as his scholarly achievements.

He was ordained in c.703 by St John of Beverly: 'Venerable' was a title commonly given to priests in the day and since monks were seldom ordained it became attached to Bede's name as a distinguishing feature. It was considered especially appropriate as a tribute to the saint's great learning, and was formally approved in 853 at the Council of Aachen.

Works

Within the confines of his monastery, Bede's love of study and writing flourished and brought forth a remarkable literary harvest.

He completed 25 works of biblical commentary, which he regarded as his most important work, several lives of the saints, scientific and theological treatises including a theory of music and several hymns, and works of orthography and chronology.

It is as a historian however that he is best remembered; his *Historica Ecclesiastica*, finished in 731, gives an account of the development of Christianity in England until Bede's day and is the single most valuable source for the history of the period, written in a highly readable style. In it Bede demonstrates a remarkably responsible historical approach, citing authorities and presenting, comparing and evaluating evidence, although it is inevitably limited as a historical document in some ways. Bede was also the first historian to use the convention 'AD', signifying *anno Domini*. Unfortunately, his vernacular writings and translations, believed to have been among the first writings in Old English, are now lost.

Death and cult

His death was recorded by the monk Cuthbert, who tells how Bede pressed on with his translation of John's Gospel, dictating the last sentence just before his death, and how he died singing a Gloria. A cult began within five years of his death, with miracles reported at his relics, but there are few ancient dedications. After Pope Leo XIII recognized him as the only English Doctor of the Church in 1899, several modern churches and schools were dedicated to him. He is shown in art studying peacefully among his books, often illuminated by light from heaven. Bede is also the only Englishman mentioned by Dante in his *Paradiso*.

Feast-day 25 May

Benedict

c.480 Nursia — Monte-Cassino c.547

The founder of western monasticism

His famous Rule, fusing prayer and labour with community life, became the blueprint for monastic developments throughout Europe.

Born of a well-to-do family, Benedict spent his childhood in Nursia with his twin sister St Scholastica. Sent to complete his education in Rome, the young Benedict was so appalled at the corruption there that he fled the city. He lived for a time at the village of Enfide, about 30 miles from Rome, but achieved notoriety there when he miraculously made whole a sieve which had been borrowed and broken by his nurse. To truly abandon the world, he realized that he would have to become a solitary. He became a hermit in the mountains of Subiaco (now the Sacro Speca), and he was fed by a monk, Romanus, who supposedly let food down to him in a basket. To quench the fleshly temptations to which he was victim he developed such extreme practices as rolling naked in thorns.

The fame of this holy, cave-dwelling solitary spread until he was invited to take up abbotship at a monastery in Vicovaro. Benedict reluctantly accepted, but the monks there soon regretted their invitation when faced with his unswervingly strict rule, and it is said that they tried to poison him. The attempt was discovered when Benedict made the sign of the cross over his cup, as was his custom, and it shattered into pieces. Without anger, Benedict left the community.

Move to Monte-Cassino

Back in Subiaco, Benedict's piety attracted a large number of disciples whom he organized into a community of 12 small monasteries, emphasizing retreat and manual work. The monks had as yet no formal rule, but based their way of life on the example of Benedict himself. A famous story told by Gregory of Nyssa involves a brawny Goth who took the habit with Benedict's community and set about his task of clearing undergrowth from the grounds with such gusto that the head of his newly-acquired hedge-hook flew off and landed in the lake. The new monk was aghast, but when Benedict heard of his misfortune he miraculously made the iron head float and reattach itself to the shaft.

Subiaco became famous as a centre of spiritual discipline, but in c.525 Benedict left suddenly, perhaps because of the discrediting rumours spread by a jealous nearby cleric, Florentius, whose attempts to compromise the monks by exposing them to temptation were endangering the purity of their souls. Whatever the reason, Benedict arrived in Monte-Cassino where he demolished the pagan temple and in c.530 he began work on the great abbey there which was to become the cradle of western monasticism. Unlike remote Subiaco, the abbey at Monte-Cassino attracted many visitors including ecclesiasts, secular leaders and laymen in search of sanctity.

The Benedictine Rule

It was here that he completed the final version of his famous Rule, incorporating the traditions of such great Christian writers as Basil and Cassian with Benedict's own sober common sense, emphasizing obedience, community life and moderation. The main duties for the Benedictine monk were prayer, reading and manual work, and the Rule avoids excessive individual asceticism (it is said that when Benedict heard of a well-intentioned hermit near Monte-Cassino who had chained his foot to a rock

45

near his cave, he sent him a reproof, instructing him to bind himself with the chains of Christ rather than a more literal one of iron). It therefore proved a practical and flexible model for monasteries throughout the West, even enforced by imperial decree in the eighth century. One of its most radical and valuable features was the respect accorded to menial work: manual labour was recognized as not only productive but a dignified means of serving God. In addition to overseeing his monastery, Benedict advised both spiritual and secular leaders of the day, though he himself (like most monks) was never ordained, and worked for the benefit of the needy of the area.

Although we know little of Benedict's sister Scholastica, beyond the fact that she is said to have consecrated herself to God from an early age, she and Benedict met annually. Tradition holds that on one occasion, when Benedict had refused her entreaties to stay and talk with her for longer, she brought down by her prayers such a violent storm that he was obliged to remain with her, and three days later she died.

Death and cult

Benedict died at the monastery on 21 March, traditionally in prayer, supported upright by his brethren before the altar, having taken communion. During his life he had been attributed with countless miracles and the gift of prophecy and insight, and it is said that at the end he foresaw his own death and directed his monks to dig his grave six days before he passed away. This foreknowledge and calm acceptance is presumably the source of the tradition by which

he is invoked by the dying. He was buried at Monte-Cassino beside Scholastica, and although Fleurs has claimed possession of his relics from the seventh century, Monte-Cassino has always vigorously denied the claim. As Benedict's Rule gained popularity, especially in the reforms of Cluny in the 10th century, so his cult became more widespread, and he was proclaimed patron saint of Europe by Pope Paul VI in 1964.

Our information about the life of this central figure in western Christianity is drawn almost exclusively from Book II of the *Dialogues* of Gregory the Great, based on the eye-witness accounts of Benedict's disciples, which was popularized on the Continent by inclusion in Jacobus de Voragine's *Golden Legend*. The *Dialogues* take the form of non-chronological sketches of various deeds by Benedict for instruction and emulation rather than a systematic biography.

In addition to his influence on monasticism, stories such as the miraculous mending of the sieve endeared him to the common folk, and he is usually depicted with a broken utensil, or with the broken cup and serpent, representing poison, recalling the attempt to kill him that was miraculously foiled. He is also shown in the Benedictine cowl, holding his Rule or a rod of discipline.

Feast-day 11 July
Patron saint of Europe, coppersmiths and schoolchildren, invoked against fever and poison, and by the dying and servants who have broken their master's belongings

St Benedict by Hans Memling. *Uffizi, Florence*

Benedict Biscop

628 Northumbria — Wearmouth 690

The founder of Wearmouth and Jarrow

His passion for Roman liturgy and learning set the standard for later English monasteries and inspired his protégé, the Venerable Bede.

The early life of Benedict Baducing, as he was christened, was spent as courtier to King Oswiu of Northumbria, but in 653 he left to pursue the spiritual life. He did not immediately enrol as a monk, but went first to Rome on pilgrimage to visit the shrines of the apostles, accompanied by St Wilfrid, and soon returned for a second visit, this time taking with him Alcfrith, son of Oswiu. It was on the way back from this trip in 666 that he took his vows as a monk at Saint-Honorat, Lérins, and took the name Benedict. He stayed there as novice for two years before journeying back to Rome. Benedict returned to Britain in 669 in the company of the new Archbishop of Canterbury, St Theodore, and he became abbot of St Peter and St Paul there for two years.

Wearmouth and Jarrow

By now he felt ready to establish his own foundation so, after visiting Rome again to collect the necessary relics, works of art and manuscripts, he founded a monastery dedicated to St Peter at Wearmouth in 674, on land given by King Egfrith of Northumbria. Its Romanesque style was unique among British monasteries at the time; Benedict had even brought in French workmen to supply his abbey with a lead roof and glass windows. His Rule for the new monastery was based largely on that of the original Benedict himself.

After a fifth journey to Rome in which he reassured Pope Agatho as to the healthily orthodox state of the English church, Benedict returned with an enormous collection of manuscripts and also with the abbot of St Martin's at Rome, John, who taught the English monks the uncial hand, an elegant rounded script for manuscripts, and the correct chants for the Roman liturgy. Soon afterwards he founded a second monastery, only six miles away but this time on the Tyne rather than the Wear, called Jarrow, dedicated to St Paul. This too was built on land given by Egfrith, and the sister foundations became renowned as centres of learning and Roman practice, with an enormous collection of books and art unrivalled in Britain. Benedict's library later made possible the work of Bede, whom he received into his monastery as a young child and who was later to write his *Life* and a sermon for his feast-day.

Death and cult

In his last years, Benedict delegated the abbacy of his monasteries and he spent the three years before his death paralyzed and confined to bed. Soon after his death a local cult sprang up, supported by Bede, which became more widespread after the translation of his relics to Thorney in c.980. In art he is portrayed by the waters of the Tyne, together with his two monasteries, and often in company with Bede.

Feast-day 12 January
Patron saint of painters and musicians

Benedict of Aniane

c.750 — Inde 821

The second Benedict

Like Benedict before him, he turned from a solitary life of austerity to a monastic reform incorporating community life, learning and art, which changed the face of Western monasticism.

As a youth, Benedict son of Aigulf of Maguelone served as cup-bearer in the imperial courts of Pepin and Charlemagne, and fought in the army at Lombardy, until his conversion to Christianity at the age of about 20. Leaving the court he enrolled as a Benedictine monk at Saint-Seine near Dijon but found the regime there too lax for his liking. He left after three years to live as a hermit on the bank of the river Aniane in Languedoc.

A reforming force

Gradually Benedict attracted a number of eremetical followers and established a community, where life was centred around productive manual labour, transcribing manuscripts, poverty, austerity and solitude. He developed his foundation closely along the lines of the original Benedictine Rule, and worked in close collaboration with Louis the Pious to establish such stable Benedictine reform throughout France. Louis built a monastery for him at Inde (later called Cornelimunster), near Aachen, and effectively placed him as director of monasticism in Europe.

In 817 Benedict presided over a council of abbots at Aachen, at which he codified the legislation for reform in his *Capitulare monasticum*. This was added to the original

Rule of Benedict and imposed on monasteries throughout the empire; the guidelines contained within it emphasized the need for poverty, chastity and obedience, a standardized form for the Divine Office and for living conditions of the monks, and the constitutional appointment of abbots who were themselves monks to counter the lay ownership so prevalent at the time. Benedict felt strongly that the monks should be able to study, teach and write, and so should be free to hand menial tasks over to serfs, and he emphasized too the central place of the liturgy in monastic life, insisting on a daily conventual Mass. As it stood, however, the plan he had presented at Aachen had been impractical in its attempt to impose uniformity on a vast number of houses. Many minor details in which he had hoped to impose consistent practice had to be dropped to ensure the adoption of the rule throughout the empire, and in the process it appears that his original austerity may have been significantly mitigated.

Death and works

After a long illness, Benedict died at his monastery in Inde. Although his systematic, centralized reforms were later ignored by many, and he lacked the luminous spirituality of the original Benedict, his practical impact on his order is unquestionable. In addition to this central work of reform, for which he has been called the restorer of Western monasticism, Benedict made an extensive study of other monastic rules which he compiled in his *Codex regularum*, and he demonstrated the centrality of Benedict's rule by showing its correspondence with the teachings of ancient church fathers in his *Concordia regularum*.

Feast-day 11 February

49

Bernadette

1844 Lourdes — Nevers 1879

The visionary of Lourdes

The visions of this uneducated peasant girl made known to the world the most famous healing waters in Christendom.

Marie Bernarde Soubrious was born on 7 January, the first child of a poverty-stricken miller named François Soubrious and his young wife Louise. Given the diminutive pet name Bernardette as a child, she suffered from asthma, poverty and a lack of education. Her delicate health was not improved by a bout of cholera, contracted during the epidemic of 1854, nor by the insanitary conditions of the dark, damp basement in which she lived. But at the age of 14, on 11 February 1858, Bernadette experienced a vision of the Virgin Mary while collecting firewood on the bank of the river Gave near Lourdes. Over the next six months she saw a series of 18 visions, in which 'the Lady', who identified herself as 'the Immaculate Conception', indicated a nearby spring from which she told Bernardette to drink: opinion is divided as to whether this was a forgotten spring or one created miraculously. She also directed Bernadette to erect a chapel on the site; beyond this the content of the visions was mostly concerned with the importance of prayer and penance.

Development of Lourdes

Bernadette's claims were subjected to enormous scepticism. She was questioned exhaustively by church and state authorities but, in spite of her youth and her intellectual simplicity, her story was unshakeable. Unlike many visionaries Bernadette was a stable character not given to emotional outbursts, and those investigating the claims were forced to acknowledge her disinterestedness and veracity. The incessant attention and questioning was a mental and physical ordeal for the sensitive girl, whose asthma was worsened by the fatigue of cross-examination. Finally however the visions were ecclesiastically approved, and work began to make the site of the visions one of the largest pilgrimage sites the Christian world has ever known. The spring has regularly produced 27 000 gallons of water each week since its discovery, and countless miracles of healing have been reported in its waters and at the shrine there.

Later life and death

Bernadette herself retired to the convent of the Sisters of Charity at Nevers in 1866, wishing only to escape the unwanted publicity and the equal measures of suspicion, curiosity and enthusiasm with which she was regarded. She was not involved with the development of Lourdes, and did not even attend the consecration of the basilica there in 1876, but spent the rest of her life patiently suffering ill health, proving a quiet and self-effacing nun renowned for her simple piety until she died aged only 35. She was beatified in 1925, and when she was canonized by Pope Pius XI in 1933 it was not so much for her visions as for the integrity and humility of her life. She is listed in the official records of the Church as Marie Bernarde, but to the faithful who honour and invoke her she is always known by her pet name, Bernadette.

Feast-day 16 April

Bernard of Clairvaux

1090 Fontaines — Clairvaux 1153

The last of the Fathers of the Church

Pre-scholastic in his theology, eloquent, passionate and sometimes unreasonable, Bernard's impact extended far beyond the Cistercian order which he revived.

The son of a nobleman of Burgundy, Bernard was born in the family castle near Dijon and educated in Châtillon-sur-Seine. As a young man he was known for his wit and charm, living a brilliant but dissipated life, but in 1113 he joined the original Cistercian monastery at Cîteaux, along with four of his brothers and 27 other companions whom he persuaded to join him. The recently founded order was floundering, but this large novitiate revived it, and in 1115 Cîteaux sent out Bernard as abbot with 12 other monks to form a daughter house at Langres. Unsurprisingly, the inexperienced leader made mistakes (he was initially over-strict with his monks in conditions of severe poverty), but he soon took steps to put these right, and his reputation for holiness drew unprecedented numbers of applicants to the monastery. Its name was changed from Vallée d'Absinthe to Clairvaux, and it in its turn founded a further 68 Cistercian monasteries, including several in Britain.

Influence in public life

Bernard's influence spread beyond his monastery as he became advisor to spiritual and secular leaders. He devised the Rule for the Order of Templars, knights dedicated to the defence of the church and the care of pilgrims and the sick, and supported it strongly at the Synod of Troyes. He was vocal too in ecclesiastical politics, powerfully defending the election of Pope Innocent II in 1130, and outspoken in his attacks on what he perceived as heresy, forcing Abelard and his rationalistic faith into retirement at the Council of Sens. His charisma won him many loyal friends, but he undoubtedly also made many enemies. He energetically supported the Second Crusade against the Turks, but when the venture ended in disaster he blamed the lack of purity and commitment of the soldiers.

Works

Deeply emotive in places, especially in devotion to the Virgin, Bernard's works proved to be a huge influence on medieval spirituality. His treatise *On the love of God* and his sermons *On the Song of Songs* have remained classic works. His popular name, 'Doctor Mellifluous', reflects the sweet, affective nature of his teaching. His success as leader of a monastery and effective founder of an order came through an instinctive blending of mysticism and practical economic development, the kind of synthesis that characterizes his letter to a former monk Pope Eugenius III, dealing with both holy mysteries and the duties of papal office, *De consideratione*.

Death and cult

Bernard died at Clairvaux on 20 August, and his unofficial cult was formally sanctioned by canonization in 1174. He was named a Doctor of the Church in 1830 by Pius VIII. In art, his emblem is a beehive, symbolizing eloquence, and he is often shown with the Virgin Mary.

Feast-day 20 August
Patron saint of Gibraltar, beekeepers and wax-melters

Bernardino of Siena

1380 Massa di Carrara — Aquila 1444

The people's preacher

Primarily a preacher, his commitment to reform reshaped the Franciscan order.

Bernardino degli Albezzeschi, whose father was govenor of his native city, was orphaned at the age of seven and brought up by an aunt. In 1400, when Siena was stricken by plague, Bernardino and his friends ran the local *La Scala* hospital which would otherwise have shut down for lack of staff when it was needed most. After the epidemic, he nursed his aunt, now bedridden and sick, until her death.

A powerful preacher

In c.1404 Bernardino joined the Franciscans, as a solitary first at Colombaio near Siena and then at Fiesole, near Florence. He later became known as an outstanding preacher: beginning in Milan in 1417 he took his impassioned message throughout Italy on foot. His lengthy sermons called his listeners to penitence, poverty and devotion to Jesus's name, urging them to abstain from gambling and debauchery. Although weak when he began, his voice soon developed an extraordinary resonance, capable of rousing a vast crowd to the extremes of emotion. Bernardino attributed this to the Virgin, and is himself traditionally invoked against hoarseness.

His sermons usually ended with a call for devotion to the name of Jesus, with Bernardino holding up a badge bearing the letters IHS (from the Greek form of Jesus's name) to illustrate his point, and he is now regarded as the patron saint of advertising. It is said that one former maker of playing cards, hard hit by Bernardino's strictures against gambling, recouped his losses by manufacturing copies of this badge. Bernardino's theology was questioned by those envious of his popularity, and even by the University of Bologna, but he was finally vindicated by Pope Martin V.

Franciscan reform

In 1427 he was offered the see of Siena and later those of Ferrara and Urbino: he rejected all three. He did however agree to become vicar-general of the friars Observant in 1438, and their numbers soared in consequence. He recalled the monks to a stricter observance of the original Rule and established schools of theology at Perugia and Monteripido to promote sound doctrine and discipline. His *Statutes for Observants*, which first codified their practice and organized them as a unit, was probably written c.1440.

Death and cult

Bernardino preferred the itinerant preaching life, and in 1443 he resigned his administrative post. He set out from Massa di Carrara on a last journey in 1444, preaching as he journeyed towards Naples, but his strength gave out at Aquila in Abruzzi; he died there on 20 May and miracles were reported at his tomb. He was canonized by Pope Nicholas V in 1450 and his cult was quickly popularized throughout Europe by the expanding friars Observant. He is represented as a short elderly Franciscan, usually holding his tablet inscribed IHS, and sometimes with three mitres at his feet symbolizing the rejected bishoprics.

Feast-day 20 May
Patron saint of advertisers, invoked against hoarseness

Blaise (Blase, Blasius)

d. c.316

The patron saint of sore throats

His unreliable legend has made him popular as intercessor for one of our most common complaints.

Although he probably existed as an Armenian bishop and martyr, all our evidence about Blaise is unreliable; there is no evidence of a cult earlier than the eighth century and the Greek and Roman *Lives* that survive are pious accounts of marvels and unthinkable tortures in which little consideration is given to historical accuracy. It is probable that he was the bishop of Sebastea in Cappadocia, and that he was executed in the persecutions of the early fourth century, possibly under the Emperor Licinius. The unreliable *Acts* of St Eustratius record that Blaise received this saint's relics with honour after his martyrdom under Diocletian, and that he fulfilled all the wishes expressed in Eustratius's will.

A fugitive bishop

According to his unreliable legend, Blaise was born of wealthy, noble Christian parents and was consecrated as bishop of Sebastea while still very young. When the persecutions began he withdrew to live in a cave as a hermit, where he healed wild animals. Sought out by a woman whose son was choking to death on a fishbone, Blaise miraculously healed the boy. But he was eventually discovered by hunters of the emperor out searching for wild beasts for entertainment in the amphitheatre: they were astonished to find Blaise surrounded by animals and yet unharmed by them. They took him before Agricolaus, governor of Cappadocia and Lesser Armenia, found him guilty of being a Christian and had him imprisoned.

Death and cult

Blaise refused to recant and underwent horrific tortures for his faith; he is thought to have been torn with iron wool-combs before his execution by beheading, hence he is regarded as the patron saint of wool-combers and his iconographic emblem is a comb. He is also usually shown with two candles (sometimes only one), recalling the legend that while in prison he was visited by the woman whose son he had healed, who brought him food and candles. This is also the basis for Blaise's patronage of those suffering from throat diseases, and of the blessing of St Blaise, begun in the 16th century and still practised today, in which two candles are placed on the throat of the sufferer. Other representations have him as a hermit tending wild animals, or healing the choking boy. He is known as one of the Fourteen Holy Helpers.

> **Feast-day** 3 February
> Patron saint of wool-combers, invoked against throat diseases

Bonaventure

1221 Bagnoregio — Lyons 1274

The seraphic doctor

His diligence and common sense in reforming the Franciscan order have led many to call him its second founder.

Legend has it that Giovanni di Fidanza, born near Orvieto in Tuscany to a noble physician father, received the name Bonaventure from St Francis of Assisi himself, who had miraculously cured him as a young child.

Early life

Bonaventure enrolled with the Franciscans in 1243 and quickly became known as one of their most promising novices. He was sent to study at University in Paris and went on to become Master of the Franciscan school there in 1253. A contemporary of Thomas Aquinas, his theology owed rather less to Aristotle and emphasized the affective aspect of faith over the purely rational (he is widely recognized as a mystical rather than a dogmatic theologian); the two received their doctorate in theology together in 1257. Both too were involved in defending the mendicant (begging) monastic orders against their critics; largely thanks to Bonaventure's treatise *On the poverty of Christ* the mendicant orders received the approbation and protection of Pope Alexander IV in 1256.

Reformation and the Council of Lyons

Aged only 36, Bonaventure was appointed minister-general of the Franciscans. This was a time of crisis for the order, which was suffering from poor organization, complacency and internal divisions; by his brilliant administration and moderate approach he achieved such lasting success that he is known as the order's second founder. He corrected the extremist tendency to exalt poverty above all else, emphasizing more than did Francis the importance of study and therefore the legitimacy of owning books, but he held firmly to the original Franciscan ideals of detachment, simplicity, poverty and work.

He refused his appointment to the archbishopric of York by Clement IV in 1265, but was compelled to obey in 1273 when Gregory X elected him cardinal bishop of Albano with a command against disobedience (although he kept the papal envoy waiting while he finished washing up dishes at the monastery). He was directed by Gregory to draw up the agenda for the fourteenth General Council of Lyons and played a prominent part there in securing the reunion of the Latin and Greek churches. He preached at the mass of reconciliation, but died soon afterwards on 15 July and so did not see the union repudiated shortly afterwards by Constantinople.

Works and cult

Bonaventure's intellectual legacy is impressive: his *Life of St Francis* was the official biography of the Order and he also wrote many treatises including his famous commentary on Peter Lombard's *Sentences*, important spiritual works such as the *Breviloquium* and the *Itinerarium mentis ad deum*, biblical commentary and hundreds of sermons. In his own day however he was better known for his humble simplicity and courtesy. There are no signs of an early cult, but he was canonized in 1482 by Sixtus IV and nominated Doctor of the Church in 1587. In art he is shown as a cardinal in Franciscan robes, usually reading or writing.

Feast-day 15 July

Boniface

c.680 Crediton — Friesland 754

The apostle to the Germans

An Englishman with a burning sense of mission, who with unfailing energy blazed a trail through pagan Europe.

An Anglo-Saxon peasant born in Devonshire and christened Wynfrith, the young Boniface (as he later called himself) attended the Benedictine school in Exeter and later at Nursling in the diocese of Winchester. He became director of the abbey school there, and wrote the first Latin grammar ever produced in England, was ordained at the age of 30 and spent some years teaching and preaching in the area with much success. Well-known and well-respected, he was selected as envoy to the archbishop of Canterbury by King Ine of Wessex.

The call to mission

But in 716 Boniface decided to leave England for the mission field; he followed Wilfred and Willibrord into Frisia but was soon forced to return after conflict with the strong pagan tribes there. He was offered the post of abbot in Nursling in 717, but he was committed to mission and left the next year, this time with a clear mission and the papal blessing from Gregory II.

He was directed to Bavaria and Hesse, but discovering on the way that the situation in Frisia had improved, he stopped there as assistant to Willibrord for three years before travelling on to Hesse, where he preached with much success. He was consecrated bishop back in Rome in 722 and then returned to Hesse, protected by special pledge of Charles Martel. His success in Hesse was increased dramatically when he publicly destroyed the sacred Oak of Thor at Geismar without suffering retribution, and his emblem in art is an axe. In Thuringia he founded a monastery at Ohrdruf, helped by other English monks, and in 731 was created metropolitan of Germany beyond the Rhine. He established his own archbishopric at Mainz and devoted himself to radical reformation of the church.

In 738, after Charles Martel's defeat of the Saxons in Westphalia, Boniface wrote a famous letter urging the English to help him in this new opportunity for evangelism, reminding them of their common Germanic background. He continued founding monasteries and bishoprics throughout Germany, including Bavaria where he was sent as papal legate in 738, and supervised the reformation of the church in France together with Charles's sons.

Death and cult

By now an old man, he handed over responsibility for reform and administration to his followers and returned to Frisia and his original mission. He reclaimed much of the country from paganism and entered into the unevangelized north-east, present-day Holland, where he and his companions were attacked by pagans on 5 June. Boniface's body was buried in the abbey he had founded at Fulda, now the centre of his cult; he is widely venerated in Germany and Holland but little-known in Britain, despite his contemporaries' belief that he was a special patron of England. Modern historians have recognized his enormous influence in European history, for his missionary and monastic activities and also for his extensive alliances with Popes and emperors.

Feast-day 5 June
Patron saint of brewers and tailors

Brendan the Navigator

c.486 Kerry — Annaghdown c.577

The travelling abbot of Clonfert

Although Brendan's historical existence is not in doubt and he is one of Ireland's most famous saints, much of his life is lost in legend.

The son of Findlugh of Tralee, Brendan was fostered as a child by the famous nun Ita and educated at St Jarlath's abbey school in Tuam by the bishop of Kerry, St Erc. Given this religious background, it is hardly surprising that he went on to become a monk himself. He was ordained by Erc in 512 and set about founding monasteries throughout Ireland, including Clonfert (in 559) which became an important missionary centre of about 3000 monks and survived until the 16th century, Annaghdown, Inishadroum and Ardfert. He also travelled extensively in Scotland, befriending Columba in Argyll according to Adomnan, and very probably in Wales and beyond, but it is impossible to detail the events of his life with any real certainty. He probably died while on a visit to his sister Brig in Annaghdown.

Brendan's great influence in southern Ireland is attested by the significant number of place names which are named after him, most famously Mount Brandon on the Dingle Peninsula. From the ninth century onwards there is evidence of a strong cult of St Brendan in Ireland, and he was popular too in Wales, Scotland and Brittany.

The *Navigation of Brendan*

The stories of Brendan's wide travelling gave rise to the *Navigation of Brendan*, a 10th- or 11th-century visionary romance written in Latin which describes Brendan's seven-year voyage to a 'Land of Promise' in the west, identified by some as the Hebrides and Northern Isles, by others as Iceland, and by some as the Canary Islands or even North America. An expedition by Tim Severin in 1976–7, aimed at duplicating the voyage in a hide-covered curragh, succeeded in reaching Newfoundland via Iceland and Greenland, which would seem to agree with the journey described in the epic. Most scholars however accept the work as a charming and romantic fiction in a well-attested genre, whilst recognizing its popularity and influence in the Middle Ages. Matthew Arnold's poem 'St Brandan' retells the story, and the saint is a popular figure in art, standing aboard ship giving mass while the fish crowd round to listen.

Feast-day 16 May
Patron saint of sailors and travellers

Brice (Britius)

Tourraine — Tours 444

Bishop of Tours

A difficult and insubordinate prelate in his youth, Brice later changed his ways.

Brice was educated as a monk at the monastery of St Martin of Tours at Marmoutier but as he became a priest and deacon he appears to have been contemptuous of his master, making sweeping criticisms which he was unable to substantiate when challenged, such as accusations of insanity or senile superstition. It is said that Martin regarded his troublesome deacon as a trial from God rather than as a colleague. Nevertheless, Martin prophesied that Brice would succeed him as bishop of Tours and this prediction came true on his death in 397.

A controversial bishop

Brice's episcopate was a long and troubled one; his enemies, of whom the abrasive ecclesiast made many, had much ammunition with which to oppose him, and some they made up themselves. He was accused of laxity, neglect of his duties and even adultery. Brice appealed to the Pope against this last charge and was eventually vindicated by a papal enquiry (Gregory of Tours alleges that he proved his innocence with a miracle), but he spent seven years as an exile in Rome while an administrator was appointed to govern his see. These years appear to have worked a change in Brice; perhaps sobered by the strength of feeling against him, he repented of his irresponsible behaviour and completely reformed his life.

A reformed man

On his return to Tours (after the death of Armentius, the administrator who had ruled in his absence) Brice was a changed man: committed, self-disciplined, humble and full of energy for reform. He set about establishing various religious foundations and showed such devotion in performing his duties that by the time of his death he was considered to have more than compensated for his earlier failings and was popularly venerated as a saint.

Cult

The link with the popular Martin of Tours did much to further Brice's cult in Europe, especially in Italy and England: his is a common name in many ancient English calendars. Certainly in art he is often shown with St Martin, but his more usual iconographic emblem is the fire or hot coals which he carries in his hand or vestments.

One of the most famous historical events to take place on St Brice's feast day was the command of King Æthelred the Unready that all Danes in England should be slaughtered in 1002; this was the infamous Massacre of St Brice's day, which precipitated the invasion of Swein the following year.

Feast-day 13 November

Bridget

1303 Sweden — 1373 Rome

Founder of the Bridgettines

Famous as a foundress, visionary and mystical writer, Bridget was also a fearless commentator on the events of her day.

Daughter of Berger Persson, the governor of Upland, Bridget was sent to an aunt in Aspen when her mother died in c.1315. At the age of 14 she married the 18-year-old nobleman Ulf Gudmarsson; they lived happily for 28 years, producing eight children (including the future St Catherine of Vadstena). In 1335 Bridget was called to the court of King Magnus II as chief lady-in-waiting to his new queen, Blanche of Namur. Bridget's visions prompted her to rebuke the royals for their dissipated lifestyle, but although they liked and respected her they refused to act on her warnings.

From court to cloister

After a pilgrimage to the shrine of St Olaf at Trondheim, Norway, in c.1340, Bridget quit the court completely, leaving with her husband on another pilgrimage, to Compostela, Spain. But Ulf died in 1344 at the Cistercian monastery at Alvastra, and Bridget spent some time as a penitent there in mourning for his death. In 1344 or 1346, with a generous endowment from Magnus, she founded the Order of the Most Holy Saviour, the Bridgettines, at Vadstena by Lake Vattern. The monastery was primarily for women and it became a centre of Swedish spirituality, with its emphasis on simplicity of lifestyle and the importance of study.

> **Feast-day** 23 July
> Patron saint of Sweden

The energetic visionary

Bridget's visions, of Christ's life and passion and also of contemporary happenings, sometimes led her into dangerous outspokenness: she condemned Magnus's crusade against the Letts and Estonians, denounced Pope Urban V and his successor Gregory XI for not returning the papal court from Avignon to Rome, and urged Clement VI to intervene to secure a peace between France and England.

She left for Rome in 1349 seeking approval for her Order and spent the rest of her life away from Sweden, on pilgrimage or in Italy. She was renowned for her devotion in visiting shrines and for caring for pilgrims and the needy, and for the visions which continued throughout her life. Although she dictated many of them, the documents we have appear to have been extensively edited, and their veracity is difficult to determine.

Death and cult

Bridget was deeply troubled in later life by the adulterous affair between her son Charles and Joanna I of Naples, which began on a pilgrimage to the Holy Land with his mother and ended with his death by fever only weeks later. She herself died in Rome on 23 July, on her return from Jerusalem, and her relics were translated to Sweden the next year. Her daughter St Catherine of Vadstena obtained final official approval for the Order, which at its peak boasted 70 houses.

Bridget was canonized in 1391, despite some controversy centring around her *Revelations*, revered for her piety rather than her visions. In art she appears as an abbess, dressed in the Bridgettine robes with a cross on her forehead, holding a book and a pilgrim's staff.

Brigid (Bride)

c.453 Faughart — Kildare c.523

The Mary of the Gael

Second only to St Patrick in the love of the Irish and credited with countless miracles and blessings, she was foundress of the first convent in Ireland.

Difficult though it is to disentangle the factual information about Brigid's life from the rich tapestry of folklore spun around it, it seems probable that she was born into a peasant family near Dundalk in Ireland, of parents baptized by St Patrick himself. She became a nun at an early age, probably professed by St Mel of Armagh, and after spending some time near Croghan Hill with seven companions she followed Mel to Meath in c.468. The central achievement of her life came in c.470, when she founded the first convent in Ireland at Kildare. The foundation was a double monastery, with Brigid as abbess of the convent, and in time it became a centre for Irish spirituality and learning around which the cathedral town of Kildare grew up. Brigid is credited also with the founding of a school of art there.

Death and cult

Although the miracles attributed to her are sometimes fantastic, it seems likely that the compassion, charity and strength which characterize them all were real attributes of the historical Brigid. She is known as the Mary of the Gael from a vision of Bishop Ibor, who supposedly saw a vision of the Virgin the day before seeing Brigid and

pronounced them identical. Brigid died at Kildare and was buried there, but her relics were reburied at Downpatrick, along with those of Patrick, during invasions by the Danes. Place names and churches throughout Britain testify to the extent of her cult, most notably St Bride's Bay in Dyfed, Wales, and the church on Fleet Street in London. In art she is shown as an abbess, usually holding a lamp or candle and often with a cow nearby recalling the legend that the cows she kept as a nun once produced milk three times in one day for the benefit of her visitors.

A poetic passage in the *Book of Lismore* testifies to her special position in the Irish religious tradition: 'It is she that helpeth everyone who is in danger: it is she that abateth the pestilences: it is she that quelleth the rage and the storm of the sea. She is the prophetess of Christ: she is the Queen of the South: she is the Mary of the Gael.' Her importance during her own day, however, has been exaggerated; one popular tradition holds that she was consecrated as a bishop by Ibor, which is almost certainly untrue, and it is sometimes claimed that the abbots and abbesses of Kildare enjoyed supremacy over the whole of Ireland, another fiction which has given much credibility to the expansion of Brigid's cult and the proliferation of her *Lives*. She was formally named a patron of Ireland in 1962.

Feast-day 1 February
Patron saint of Ireland (after St Patrick), poets, blacksmiths, healers, cattle, dairymaids, midwives, newborn babies and fugitives

Bruno

c.1030 Cologne — Calabria 1101

Founder of the Carthusian order

The order which he founded, though small, proved a great force for spiritual reform throughout Europe.

Born into a noble family of Cologne, Bruno was sent to be educated at the famous cathedral school in Rheims. He returned to Cologne after his studies to be ordained and was appointed canon at St Cunibert's in c.1055, but he left the next year to return to Rheims as professor of theology and grammar and remained there for nearly 20 years, teaching such illustrious pupils as the future Pope Urban II.

The move to Grenoble

In 1074, Archbishop Manasses obtained for him the post of chancellor of Rheims, but only two years later Bruno was one of a council of clerics who denounced the loose-living Manasses as unfit for his position. In the face of Manasses's virulent anger, Bruno prudently fled the city and although the people of Rheims clamoured for him to succeed as archbishop he chose instead a life of seclusion, becoming a hermit under the authority of St Robert of Molesmes (later founder of Cîteaux). He moved on in c.1084 with six companions to found a monastery at Grenoble based on the precepts of solitude, austerity and manual labour on land in the untamed mountains of the Grande Chartreuse given by the bishop St Hugh of Grenoble. This is the source of the name given to all Carthusian communities, 'Charterhouse'. The monks spent much time in prayer and penitence,

and in the transcribing of holy books. Bruno later became confessor to Hugh, and the prayerful, simple principles on which the monastery was run soon made it popular with new recruits and famous throughout the area.

The second foundation

So successful was it that in 1090, much against his will, Bruno was called to Rome by Urban II as his adviser in church affairs and clergy reform. Urban also offered him the archbishopric of Reggio, but Bruno managed to persuade his former pupil to allow him the seclusion he craved, and the next year he left Rome with the Pope's blessing to found a community, St Mary's, at Della Torre in Calabria. He never saw his brethren in France again, but a letter of encouragement he wrote to them has survived, and their prior Landuin visited Bruno to draw up more formalized rules of the order. Bruno developed a close friendship with Robert Guiscard, a count of Sicily, whose brother Roger gave the land at Della Torre.

Death and cult

Bruno died at Della Torre on 6 October, and has never been officially canonized since the seeking of public honour runs contrary to the Carthusian spirit. But in 1514 Pope Leo X gave permission to the order to celebrate the feast, and this equivalent canonization was extended to the universal Church in 1674. His emblem in art is a ray of light, which illuminates the saint and the book which he holds.

Feast-day 6 October

Caedmon

d. c.680

The father of English sacred poetry

The first sacred Anglo-Saxon poet, whose gift for simple poetry and song brought religion within reach of the common people of his day.

All our information about Caedmon comes from the writings of Bede. He was a cowherd attached to Whitby Abbey during the rule of St Hilda until he one night suddenly received or discovered within himself the gift of song and poetry. Bede poetically tells us that he was called in a dream to 'sing of the Creation'.

He joined the monastery as a lay brother and applied himself to the study of Scripture, and with his new-found knowledge he began to compose a vast cycle of vernacular poems which prefigured the later mystery plays, spanning the creation and the stories of Jewish history in Genesis, the entry of the Jews into the Promised Land, the life and Passion of Christ and the Last Judgement, encouraged always by Hilda and his fellow monks. Unfortunately for us only a few lines of his poetry survive, transcribed in the vernacular and in Latin in an early manuscript of Bede's *Historica Ecclesiastica*.

Death and influence

Known for his holiness and generosity as well as his gift for poetry, Caedmon seems to have foreseen his death and died with great dignity, despite his humble birth. His influence in propagating Scripture and doctrine in the form of the vernacular song must have been invaluable in an age when few could read and write and even fewer understood the Latin used by ecclesiasts.

> **Feast-day** 11 February

> **Caedmon's Hymn**
> Praise we the Lord
> of Heaven's kingdom,
> God's might and His wisdom.
> Father of glory,
> Lord everlasting,
> wonders has He made.
> First he built
> for the children of earth
> heaven as their roof:
> guardian of mankind,
> He created this world, our home,
> the Lord everlasting,
> Almighty God.
>
> Translated by Sally Purcell. From *Everyman's Book of English Verse*, ed John Wain, (Dent 1981)

Cajetan

Vicenza 1480 — 1547 Naples

Reformer and founder of the Theatines

His outstanding work in reforming the corrupt clergy of his day has too often gone unrecognized.

Cajetan's background promised great things for his career: born into the line of the Counts of Thiene he was educated at university in Padua, where he achieved notable success in theology and law, and went on to become senator in Vicenza and then protonotary in Rome, appointed by Pope Julius II in 1506. While performing his ecclesiastical and legal duties in Rome, he put his energies into a project closer to his heart—the revival of the priests' congregation, the Confraternity of Divine Love. On Julius's death in 1513 he resigned his office, rejecting the bright future awaiting him in the field of administration, in order to devote himself more fully to caring for the needy and to the reformation of a demoralized clergy.

After his ordination in 1516, Cajetan returned to Vicenza to work with the Oratory of St Jerome, helping the poor and nursing the sick and incurable, and he founded a similar house in Verona before going on to continue his charitable work in Venice.

The Theatine order

In 1523, together with Pietro Caraffa (later the fanatical and unpopular Pope Paul IV), he founded a community of clergy who were to be engaged in practical pastoral work and care for the sick and poor. Cajetan hoped that these congregations would restore apostolic values among a notoriously corrupt clergy, and encouraged the priests to trust wholly in the providence of God and to make careful study of the Bible and Christian doctrinal writings. The priests were known as Theatines, from the Latin form of Caraffa's see, Chiete.

The success of the project was slow, and it is remarkable that it survived at all, especially as the attack on Rome by Charles V in 1527 destroyed the community's house. The order relocated to Naples, where it gained ground slowly but steadily. Caraffa had been appointed provost-general in 1524, but in 1530 Cajetan was elected superior for three years. At the end of this time Caraffa was re-elected and Cajetan moved on to Verona and finally Naples, where he defended the bishops' reforms and attacked the widespread heresies of the area. He also founded the *montes pietatis* there, pawn shops run not for profit and exploitation but to help the poor.

Death and cult

Cajetan died in Naples on 7 August and he was canonized in 1671. He is remembered as a great and tireless reformer, who anticipated many of the resolutions of the Council of Trent, although the order which he helped to found is usually eclipsed by the more famous (and more highly-organized) Jesuits of Ignatius Loyola. The subsequent unpopularity of Caraffa did little to promote the order's reputation.

Feast-day 7 August

Callistus I

d. c.222 Rome

The slave who became Pope

An man of extraordinary ability and humanity, Callistus's belief in the mercy of God conflicted tragically with the severe doctrine of the day.

Callistus began his chequered career as slave in Rome to a Christian master, Carpophorus, who recognized his great natural ability and placed him in charge of a bank containing his own money and that of other Christians. Somehow the money was lost and Callistus fled Rome in panic, only to be caught in Portus and sentenced to the treadmill. Luckily for him the bank's creditors requested his release, but he was swiftly rearrested for brawling in the synagogue, perhaps in pursuit of the lost money. This time he was scourged and sent to work in the Sardinian mines, but his luck held and he was released along with other Christians at the intercession of Marcia, mistress of the Emperor Commodus.

The convict becomes Pope

His next charge, which he administered more successfully, was a Christian cemetery on the Appian way (now known as the Cemetery of Callistus) which housed the mortal remains of most of Rome's bishops, among others. Along with this post came deaconship from Pope Zephyrinus, who so appreciated the talents of his protégé that he welcomed Callistus as a close friend and advisor.

On Zephyrinus's death in 217 Callistus was elected his successor, although he was denounced by his rival candidate Hippolytus as a Sabelian (in fact Callistus had condemned Sabelius and his Monarchian heresies), and an altogether unsuitable Pope because of his laxity towards repentant sinners. Callistus's policies were indeed so lenient as to outrage the rigorists: he readmitted repentant murderers and adulterers to communion, retained bishops who repented of mortal sins, and flew in the face of Roman civil law by recognizing marriages between free women and slaves. This may have been due in part to his own background, but it seems probable that he was sensitive too to the plight of Christian women in Rome's patriarchal society, who might otherwise be forced to take non-Christian husbands from their own class.

Death and cult

The controversy led to schism in the church, with the rigorists led by Hippolytus, who set himself up as an antipope. Callistus seems to have been killed in a riot (there is no record of any official persecution at the time), and has been venerated as a martyr since the fourth century. He himself is buried on the Aurelian Way, not in the cemetery that bears his name. Most of our information about Callistus comes from the unfriendly pen of the thwarted Hippolytus or that of another critic, Tertullian, but it is nevertheless possible to appreciate his great qualities despite their enmity.

Feast-day 14 October

Canute

c.1043 — Odense 1086

King of Denmark

Venerated as a martyr in Denmark, his attempt on the English throne was thwarted by rebellion at home.

The illegitimate son of Swein Estrithson (the nephew of King Cnut of England), Canute succeeded his brother Harold to the throne of Denmark in 1081 to become Canute IV. Six years earlier he had made his first attempt to win the crown of England from William the Conqueror, coming to the aid of three rebellious earls, but he had succeeded only in invading York before he was defeated and driven out.

For several years Canute contented himself with his Danish kingdom: he married Adela (the sister of Count Robert of Flanders) and set about building churches and strengthening the position of the clergy in a land now at least nominally Christian after the evangelistic efforts of English missionaries. One of his most famous foundations was Roskilde church, a great edifice which became the traditional burial place for Danish monarchs.

Failed invasion

In 1085 Canute prepared a second, more wholehearted attack on England to secure the crown which he believed was rightfully his, gathering together a huge fleet drawing on the resources of friendly Norway and Flanders. In England, William the Conqueror was clearly worried by the threat. He withdrew supplies from the coast and brought in large numbers of mercenary fighters. The planned invasion had to be abandoned however when Canute faced a widespread rebellion led by his brother Olaf: his subjects were dissatisfied with heavy taxation and the jarls had many unsettled disputes. Canute fled to Odense but was pursued, and finally captured in the church of St Alban there. The rebels allowed him to take the sacraments of the Penance and the Eucharist before killing him as he knelt at the altar, along with 18 of his followers.

Cult

The circumstances of his death were such that, rightly or wrongly, Canute came to be regarded as a martyr, and veneration for him was increased by the restlessness of Anglo-Saxons in Norman England and by the miracles reported at his tomb. His relics were duly enshrined, and his cult was approved by Pope Paschal II in 1101 at the request of King Eric III of Denmark. In art he is usually represented as a Scandinavian king (often barefoot) with his royal insignia and the sword or dagger with which he was killed, occasionally in company with St Carlo Borromeo. Although the date of his death was 10 July, and this date was celebrated by the mother house of Odense, Evesham, his feast in the universal calendar is 19 January.

Feast-day 19 January

Carlo Borromeo

1538 Arona — Milan 1584

The pattern for prelates

A key figure for reform in the Counter-Reformation, whose devotion to his see of Milan won the hearts of his people there.

Carlo, son of Count Gilbert Borromeo, was born on 2 October at the family castle of Arona on Lake Maggiore. He was educated at the Benedictine abbey at Arona before going on to further education in Paris and Milan, where despite his speech impediment he proved a hard-working, intelligent and devout pupil. By the age of 22, with a doctorate in civil and canon law, he was appointed secretary of state, administrator of Milan and cardinal by his uncle, Pius IV, despite the fact that he had not even been ordained as a priest. Because many of these prestigious duties necessitated his residence in Rome, Borromeo appointed a deputy to govern in Milan. He acted as legate for Pius on many occasions, and in keeping with his position in society he kept a large and lavish household. This extravagance disturbed him, and he considered quitting to become a monk, but was persuaded to wait for an opportunity to live in Milan.

In the meantime, he was one of the motivating forces in initiating the final part of the famous Council of Trent, which had been suspended in 1552. His influence can be seen in many of the decrees for reform which it passed, especially in the *Catechismus Romanus*, in the composing of which he played a prominent part. In 1563 he was

ordained and consecrated bishop of Milan, but delayed his appointment because of commitments to the catechism and other liturgical reforms resulting from the Council.

Reform in Milan

When he finally arrived in his diocese in 1566, having gained permission to move from Rome from Pius's successor Pius V, he found it desperately in need of the very reforms which he had advocated at Trent. He set about improving moral and educational standards among the clergy, living humbly himself as an example, and distributing his wealth to the needy. The administration was reorganized and regular visitations begun; he began religious education for lay people in 'Sunday schools' and founded many seminaries such as the Helvetic college in Milan (1570). Also in 1570 famine struck, followed six years later by plague; through both disasters Carlo organized and participated in relief work with the victims.

Death and cult

Carlo's reforming zeal made him many enemies, but all attempts to remove him from his post and even to assassinate him failed. He continued working tirelessly in his diocese until his dedication and commitment wore him out by the age of 46, and he died on 3 November. He is buried in the cathedral there; a popular cult developed almost immediately and he was canonized in 1610. He was loved and respected not only for his practical reforming measures, which were many and important, but for his love of learning and the arts and his personal humility and unselfishness.

Feast-day 4 November

Catherine of Alexandria

c.290 Alexandria — c.310

'The bride of Christ'

It is unlikely that the saint who gave her name to the 'Catherine wheel' ever existed, but her exotic legend has captured the imagination of the pious throughout the ages.

Legend has it that Catherine was born of a wealthy, possibly even a royal, family in Alexandria, and that after her conversion by a vision at the age of about 18 she denounced the emperor Maxentius for his persecution of the Christians. Thinking to silence this upstart girl, the emperor confronted her with 50 pagan philosophers; instead of exposing the fallacies of her faith through reason, however, they were unable to answer her arguments (some accounts say they were all converted) and the furious Maxentius had them executed. He then tried to bribe Catherine into silence with the offer of a royal marriage, and was further enraged when she refused, calmly declaring herself 'the bride of Christ'.

Torture and death

Catherine was imprisoned, but not silenced. On returning home from a camp inspection one day Maxentius found that his wife, his chief soldier Porphyrius and 200 of his imperial guard had been converted to Christianity. By now almost insane with anger, Maxentius executed them and prepared a spiked wheel on which Catherine was to be broken, but he was thwarted again when

the wheel burst leaving Catherine unharmed, although several spectators were killed by flying splinters. Finally he had the troublesome saint beheaded, at which it is said milk rather than blood ran from her veins.

The various traditions are unanimous that the saint's body was miraculously translated to Mount Sinai by angels, where Emperor Justinian built a monastery for hermits in 527. The monastery has borne the name of St Catherine since the eighth or ninth century, and her shrine is displayed there. It is thought that monks returning from pilgrimage may have brought these precious relics back to their monastery in the eighth century.

A popular cult

From this spectacular legend, and flourishing especially in the devout and credulous Middle Ages, the cult of Catherine swept the Christian world. There are countless church dedications, many cycles of her life in murals and stained glass survive in Britain, and she is frequently depicted in paintings, tapestries and manuscripts, identified by the wheel of her martyrdom or shown confounding the pagan philosophers. The obvious association of her legend with learning and Christian apologetics has led to Catherine's patronage of various related groups; the link with libraries may also be due to the famous ancient library at Alexandria.

Feast-day 25 November
Patron saint of philosophers, preachers, librarians, young girls and craftsmen working with a wheel (eg potters, spinners etc)

St Catherine of Alexandria. Italian School National Gallery.

Catherine of Siena

1347 Siena — Rome 1380

One of the greatest Christian mystics

The advisor and critic of Popes, whose devout mysticism endeared her to her native Italy.

Giacomo Benincasa, a dyer of Siena, had 25 children of whom Catherine was the youngest, a high-spirited and good-looking girl much given to penitential prayer who steadfastly refused her parents' entreaties to marry. At the age of 16 she became a Dominican tertiary, living at home and spending much time in prayer and solitude. It was now that she first experienced visions, divine ones of Christ and his saints, and diabolical ones in periods of spiritual aridity.

After this preparative time she began work in a hospital, nursing patients with advanced cancer or leprosy. She gradually attracted a group of disciples, but the attention given to her supernatural gifts was not all positive; she was at one stage brought before the General Chapter of the Dominicans at Florence and accused of being a fraud. The charge was dismissed.

The outspoken mystic

Catherine and her disciples travelled widely, calling their listeners to respond to the love of God with repentance, reform and commitment, and they are credited with several dramatic conversions. In an attempt to further communicate her ideals Catherine dictated her mystical *Dialogue* and several other devotional works and letters addressed to people of every social rank (she herself was illiterate).

In 1375, the year in which she is said to have received the stigmata in ecstasy, Catherine entered the world of public affairs. She attempted, unsuccessfully, to arbitrate a peace between rebellious Florence and the Pope, and prevailed upon Pope Gregory XI to return his court from Avignon to Rome the following year. The next Pope, Urban VI, faced opposition from a rival Pope Clement VII in Avignon who commanded the loyalty of several European leaders, the beginning of the Great Schism. Catherine wrote to these leaders urging them to recognize only Urban, but she also rebuked Urban for his insensitivity and harshness. Recognizing her integrity, he invited her to work for him and she threw herself wholeheartedly into the task of raising support for the Pope in Rome.

Death and cult

On 21 April she suffered a paralytic stroke: eight days later she died, and it is said that the marks of the stigmata became clearly visible. Her friend and confessor Raymond of Capua (later master-general of the Dominicans) wrote her biography, which promoted popular veneration until her canonization by Pope Pius II in 1461, and her cult grew through the diffusion of her writings and the support of the Dominicans. Her body lies in Sta Maria sopra Minerva in Rome, near to that of Fra Angelico, but her head is claimed by Siena.

She was named patron saint of Italy in 1939 and declared a Doctor of the Church by Pope Paul VI in 1970. In art she is represented with the stigmata holding a lily and a book, occasionally wearing a crown of thorns.

Feast-day 29 April
Patron saint of Italy

*The Marriage of **St Catherine of Siena** by Lorenzo d'Alessandro da Sanseverino. National Gallery.*

Cecilia

Second or third century

The virgin martyr of music

Her influence on later ages as virgin martyr and patron saint of music is entirely disproportionate to the historical veracity of her legend.

Estimations of Cecilia's dates range from the second to the fourth centuries, but it seems likely that if she existed at all it was during the persecutions of Emperor Alexander Severus in the early third century. Her legend was unknown until the fifth century, when it quickly became the basis for one of the most popular cults of the Church.

According to this legend, Cecilia was born into a Christian patrician family in Rome and early consecrated her virginity to God. Against her will she was betrothed to one Valerian, and on her wedding night told him of her vow and persuaded him to respect it. Valerian and his brother Tiburtius were converted by her example, and devoted themselves to charity. Discovered burying the bodies of Christian martyrs, they were duly brought to trial themselves and on refusing to offer pagan sacrifices were executed, along with a soldier called Maximus converted by their fortitude. All three are now venerated as saints.

Death and cult

Cecilia was apprehended burying their bodies and she in her turn was brought before the prefect, Almachius. Almachius tried to overthrow her faith by debate; when this failed he gave orders that she was to be suffocated in her own bathroom. Although the furnaces below the house were stoked to an insufferable heat, Cecilia was miraculously unharmed and Almachius sent a soldier to despatch her by beheading. Unfortunately for Cecilia, the soldier proved to be an incompetent executioner; three blows failed to kill her and she lingered on for three agonized days, still singing to God as the legend records, before finally dying. After her death her house became a church, possibly the Sta Cecilia in Rome's Trastevere quarter, and her body was buried in the Cemetery of Callistus.

Her supposed relics, along with those of Valerian and Tibertius, lie in the church of St Cecilia in Trastevere, translated there by Pope Paschal I in c.820. At its rebuilding in 1599 her body was discovered to be incorrupt (although it disintegrated in air), and a replica of a statue made by Maderna of her body now marks her original tomb in the Cemetery of Callistus.

Perhaps the most familiar version of Cecilia's legend is that immortalized by Chaucer in the *Canterbury Tales*, as told by the Second Nun. Other famous dedications include Raphael's painting at Bologna, Dryden's 'Song for St Cecilia's Day' and Pope's 'Ode for Music on St Cecilia's Day'. Her status as patron of music and musicians appears to date from the 16th century, and is based on the account of her wedding day when, instead of listening to the festive music, Cecilia sat apart and 'sang in her heart to the Lord'. She is usually represented with an organ, lute or other musical instrument, but ancient art shows her without an emblem.

Feast-day 22 November
Patron saint of poets, singers, music and musicians

Chad (Ceadda)

Northumbria — Lichfield 672

First bishop of Mercia

Despite some controversy over his consecration, he was an exemplary and popular bishop renowned for his humility.

Chad was born and educated in Northumbria, studying along with his brother St Cedd under Aidan at Lindisfarne. As part of his monastic training, he spent some time working in Ireland under St Egbert at Rathmelsigi, and on his return succeeded his brother to become abbot of the monastery founded by Cedd at Lastingham in Yorkshire in 664.

Two bishoprics

Two years later, with a dire shortage of bishops in Britain, Chad was appointed bishop of York by King Oswiu. As Oswiu's son Alcfrith had appointed St Wilfrid to the same post, however, there was great confusion when Wilfrid arrived back in the country. Wilfrid tactfully retired to Ripon, but Archbishop Theodore intervened and declared Chad's consecration invalid. Wilfrid was restored, but Chad accepted the ruling with such good grace that Theodore, impressed by his humility and holiness, made good his consecration and had him appointed bishop of Mercia, a new and important position in an area newly open to Christianity.

In Mercia Chad established the see of Lichfield, following the organizational guidelines laid down by Theodore's council at Hertford. He founded a monastery at Barrow in Lincolnshire, on land given by the king of the Mercians, Wulfhere, together with a retreat near his church in Lichfield and an abbey in Bardney. Bede records that his life as bishop was characterized by 'great holiness of life', and it is said that in his humility he travelled everywhere on foot until forced to ride a horse by the insistence of Theodore.

Death and cult

Chad died on 2 March and was buried in Lichfield at the church of St Mary. According to Bede he was popularly regarded as a saint straight away, and his first shrine included an opening through which handfuls of the dust could be collected, to be mixed with water and given to heal sick men and animals. The Roman Catholic cathedral in Birmingham claims to possess some bones of Chad, but the shrine in Lichfield was destroyed shortly after the Reformation. Dedications in Britain, both ancient and modern, are common, concentrated mainly in the Midlands. His popularity both in his own time and throughout Christian history is due largely to his own pleasant nature. Both Bede and Eddius commend him for his outstanding qualities of humility, piety and integrity.

His representation in art is usually linked with Lichfield cathedral, and he is frequently shown holding a vine branch. One legend connects him with the two sons of Wulfhere, Wulfhad and Ruffin, whom he converted to Christianity and baptized and who were subsequently put to the sword by their apostatized father. The legend is highly unreliable, but some representations of Chad show him converting the two princes, led to him by a hart while out hunting.

Feast-day 2 March

Christopher

Third century

The Christ-bearer

One of the most popular of saints, traditionally invoked by the pious and the doubter alike for protection when travelling.

Christopher's martyrdom, traditionally held to have taken place at Lycia in Asia Minor during the persecutions of Decius, is the only fact known about him. The early classical legends associated with his name developed through the Middle Ages into the story popularized by the *Golden Legend*, and based on the saint's name, meaning 'Christ-bearer', according to which Christopher was a fearsome-looking giant who, being so powerful himself, vowed only to serve the most powerful of masters. At first he believed this to be Satan, but on realizing that the Devil was afraid of Christ, he pledged his allegiance to the latter.

Searching how best to serve his new master, he met a hermit who instructed him to perform Christian service by living alone by a ford and carrying travellers across the river on his massive back. One of his passengers, a small child, grew so heavy that half way across the river Christopher feared they would both be drowned, despite his great strength. The child then revealed himself as Christ, and explained to the exhausted giant that he had just carried the creator of the world and all the weight of its sin on his back. To verify these words, he told Christopher to plant his staff in the ground where the next day it would sprout leaves and flowers.

Death and cult

After this experience, Christopher is believed to have preached in Lycia with great success until his imprisonment. While in prison, two women were sent to seduce him but rather than weakening he is supposed to have converted his temptresses. He underwent various tortures, including being shot by arrows, but according to legend the arrows turned on his captors, one of whom was wounded in the eye and later healed by Christopher's blood. Finally he was beheaded, and his enormous body dragged through the city's streets.

Because of his role as protector, Christopher has become the patron of all travellers, and motorists especially in modern times. It was believed that anyone who saw a picture of St Christopher would not die that day; hence the popularity of his representation on particularly conspicuous church walls, and the custom of carrying a medallion bearing his image when on a journey. He is most frequently shown carrying the Christ-child across the river.

Although the cult has always been immensely popular, it has been widely condemned as superstition from the time of Erasmus's *Praise of Folly*. After the 17th century, occurrences of his image decrease, but with the advent of motorized transport and air travel, with their new dangers, his cult has widely revived. There was much popular opposition in 1969 when his feast was reduced to the status of a local cult.

> **Feast-day** 25 July
> Patron saint of travellers, especially motorists and sailors

*St **Christopher** carrying the Christ-child, with St Rocco and St Sebastian by Lorezo Lotto. Loreto.*

Clare

1194 Assisi — Assisi 1253

Founder of the 'Poor Clares'

After St Francis, her devotion and idealism were the driving force behind the development of the Franciscans.

Born into the noble Offreducia family, Clare dismayed her parents when she refused to marry at the age of 12 and horrified them six years later when, after hearing a Lenten sermon of St Francis, she ran away from home to take the veil from him at Portiuncula, renouncing all her possessions; Francis put her under the care of the Benedictine nuns at St Paul's convent in Bastia. The strenuous attempts of her family to persuade her to return home proved fruitless, and in fact soon after her removal to Sant' Angelo di Pazo, Clare was joined by her younger sister Agnes, who also took the veil from St Francis. It is said that their father sent a dozen men to forcibly fetch Agnes back, but Clare's prayers made her sister so heavy that they could not shift her.

The community of poverty

In 1215 Francis offered Clare a house next to the church of St Damiano in Assisi, and she became abbess of the first community of women living under the Franciscan rule, whose poverty and austerity were unique among nuns of the day. After the death of her father, Clare was joined by her mother, another sister Beatrice, and members of the wealthy Ubaldini family of Florence. She obtained a special dispensation from Pope Innocent III ensuring absolute poverty, without ownership of any land or buildings and living entirely by alms, and

the *privilegium paupertatis* was granted in 1228 by Pope Gregory IX and extended to Perugia and Florence in addition to San Damiano. The Poor Clare order, as it became known, soon spread throughout Europe (especially Spain). Some houses accepted a modified vow of poverty formalized by Pope Urban IV in 1263, allowing ownership of land, and were known as Urbanists. Clare herself was adamant that her order should continue to enjoy absolute poverty.

She spent her entire life at the convent at Assisi, famous for her holiness, contemplation and wisdom, advisor to many influential church leaders. After the death of Francis in 1226 she perpetuated many of his ideals, and by her prayers she twice saved Assisi from the armies of Emperor Frederick II: they fled at the sight of Clare holding the Sacrament at the city walls. Many representations show her holding a monstrance, or trampling a turban or scimitar (the defeated armies numbered several Saracens among their ranks).

Death and cult

After 27 years of poor health, Clare died in 1255 and was canonized two years later by Alexander IV. Her order, although haunted by disputes over poverty until its reformation by St Colette in the 15th century, continues today as a mainly contemplative one, preserving the ideals that inspired both Clare and Francis. A legend that she once clearly saw a Christmas service which she could not attend because of illness led to her patronage of television by an apostolic letter of 1958.

> **Feast-day** 11 August
> Patron saint of television

Clement I

d. c.101

The first of the apostolic fathers

An early successor of St Peter, whose reputation did much to establish the authority of Rome.

St Peter was succeeded as bishop of Rome by Linus and Cletus, and according to legend Cletus's successor in c.91 was a freedman of the imperial household. The Emperor Trajan however found the extensive apostolic activity of the new bishop intensely galling, and according to the fourth century *Acts* Clement was sentenced to labour in the Crimea. Undaunted, he is said to have created a spring there and preached with such success to the miners that 75 new churches were built among the Christian community. At this, the imperial displeasure was roused to such a pitch that Clement found himself lashed to an anchor and drowned. Seven hundred years later Cyril and Methodius, the apostles to the Slavs, claimed to have discovered the pieces of his body together with the anchor, and the relics were translated to the church of San Clemente in Rome in 868, where eighth-century frescoes survive depicting scenes from the life of the saint and the translation of his relics.

Feast-day 23 November

Epistle to the Corinthian church

Although most of these details are untrustworthy, it is generally accepted that Clement is the author of a letter to the church in Corinth, which was suffering a schism, written in c.95. This is the earliest known example of Rome intervening authoritatively in the affairs of another apostolic church and administering admonition, suggesting the pre-eminence of Rome in ecclesiastical affairs by the end of the first century. The letter also contains useful information on the deaths of Peter and Paul at Rome. Apparently the intervention was not resented by the Corinthians, and the original was reread at the liturgy there in 170.

Cult

The sensational *Acts* gave rise to the popular representation of Clement with an anchor as his emblem, often surrounded by fish. He is also patron of Trinity House (formerly the Guild of the Holy Trinity and St Clement) in London, controlling lighthouses and lightships, and he gave his name too to St Clement's Isle, Mount Bay. The most famous church dedication is that of St Clement Danes in London, where the parish emblem is an anchor, immortalized in the nursery rhyme 'Oranges and Lemons', which in turn has recently given rise to the name of the popular soft drink called St Clements, a mixture of fresh orange juice and bitter lemon.

Columba (Colmcille)

c.521 Gartan — Iona 597

'Pilgrim for Christ'

The central figure of Celtic Christianity.

Born in Co Donegal, of the Irish royal clan of Niall, Columba was educated at Molville (where he became deacon), Leinster and under St Finnian at Clonard, where he was probably ordained before going on to Glasnevin. When Glasnevin was struck by plague in 543 the monastery was disbanded, and Columba spent the next 15 years or so travelling through Ireland, founding monasteries (most notably at Derry in 546), preaching and converting, until a dispute arose with St Finnian over the possession of a transcript made by Columba of a copy of St Jerome's psalter owned by Finnian. In what may be the first recorded case of copyright legislation, King Diarmaid ruled in favour of Finnian. Columba incited Clan Niall to fight Diarmaid's troops at the battle of Cuildeimhne: his men won the day, but there was massive bloodshed. Some say that it was Columba's remorse which drove him to mission in Scotland.

Scotland

Columba sailed for Iona in 563 with 12 companions and founded his most famous monastery, the centre of Celtic Christianity. From this base he set about his task of converting the Picts; his most celebrated success came near Inverness where he made a great impression on King Brude by driving a monster from the Ness. He is also attributed with the conversion of the Irish king, Aidan of Dalriada.

Columba remained in Scotland, mainly at Iona, for the rest of his life, but revisited Ireland on several occasions. He attended the Synod of Druim Cetta in c.580 and argued successfully for the exemption of women from military service and the importance of bards in Irish Christian culture. It seems likely that Christianity was known in Scotland before Columba's arrival, and his direct influence was limited mainly to the western, Irish areas. He founded so many churches in the Hebrides that he gained the Gaelic name Colmcille, 'Colm of the Churches'. The importance of his monastery at Iona and the influence of his followers as factors in the development of western Christianity, however, cannot be overstated. The monastic traditions of Iona were respected throughout Europe, and widely followed until the Benedictine order gained almost universal prominence, and Celtic practices dominated monastic and ecclesiastical life in Scotland, Ireland and Northumberland until the adoption of Roman practices in Cuthbert's time and beyond.

Death and influence

The main source of information about Columba is Adomnan's famous *Life*, an uncritical list of miracles, visions and prophecies which portrays Columba as an imposing personality, austere and passionate. Columba was also a competent and prolific scribe, and, especially in his last years, spent much time transcribing books, some of which survive today. He died at Iona on 9 June and was buried there until Viking raids on the island necessitated the translation of his relics to Dunkeld in 849, where his shrine quickly became a popular destination for pilgrims. His warrior background increased his popularity, and he was frequently invoked in battle.

Feast-day 9 June

Columban
c.543 Leinster — Bobbio 615

The younger Columba

Probably the most influential of the Irish monks in Gaul, and founder of several monasteries.

Despite his mother's objections, Columban dedicated himself to the religious life from an early age. His family were noble and he probably received an excellent education before deciding to become a monk, a decision traditionally believed to have been made after an experience of severe carnal temptation. He lived first as a disciple of Sinell (a follower of Finnian), on an island in Lough Erne called Cluain Inis, and then went on to Bangor as a disciple of St Comgall. After many years, in c.590, he obtained permission from Comgall to leave with 12 companions on a mission to Gaul, one of the many Irish monks to enter voluntary exile on the Continent.

Conflict of traditions

The Irish group founded three centres of monasticism, Annegray, Luxeuil and Fontaine, but their distinctive practices inevitably provoked criticism from the Frankish bishops. The rule was inflexibly Celtic, the monks observing the Celtic method of calculating Easter in preference to that of Rome, and they refused to recognize the authority of bishops. Columban defended himself in letters to Pope Gregory the Great and later to Boniface, respectfully acknowledging the papal supremacy but arguing that in Ireland the Christian tradition had been upheld without contamination, whereas this was not the case in other countries. A synod was convened at Chalons in 603, to which Columban was summoned to defend himself, but he refused to attend. He wrote instead, pleading for toleration for the traditions of the Celtic communities.

Columban made more powerful enemies for himself when he denounced Theoderic II of Burgundy for his immorality, refusing to baptize his illegitimate children. The king was furious, as was his formidable grandmother, Queen Brunhilda; by royal edict Columban and his monks were expelled from the country in 610. On the journey back to Ireland Columban was shipwrecked; he was given the protection of King Clotaire II of Neustria and King Theodcbert at Metz, Austrasia, and he and his monks began to evangelize the Alemanic people around Bregenz, Lake Constance. They encountered fierce opposition but were making some headway when in 612 Burgundy conquered Neustria and they found themselves in what was now Theoderic's territory. The monks fled to Lombardy, where they were welcomed at the court of the Arian king Agiloff.

Death and influence

Columban then founded a monastery at Bobbio, participating in the building himself. It became the greatest centre for monasticism and spiritual life in the area and it was there that he died on 23 November. He left behind several works, including a summary of his Rule, poetry, letters and sermons, and a treatise against the Arian heresy. His Rule proved influential but in its original form was almost impractically strict, incorporating for example corporal punishment to ensure discipline, and it was later superseded by that of Benedict. His emblem in art is a bear.

Feast-day 21 November

Cornelius

Rome — Civita Vecchia 253

Pope and martyr

He remained fearless in his humane concern for sound doctrine, despite the difficult and dangerous days in which he lived.

Nothing is known of Cornelius's early life, but when St Fabian was martyred in 250 Cornelius was elected his successor as Pope, after a gap of a year. This delay was due mainly to the continued persecutions of Decius, but it also reflected deep division within the Church itself. The main controversy centred on the issue of repentant apostates; one party, led by the Roman priest Novitian, held that apostasy was an unforgivable sin and that the Church could not and should not welcome lapsed but repentant sinners back into communion. The issue was of desperate importance because of the number of people who had lapsed during the persecutions, but it also concerned those who had comitted such sins as murder or adultery.

Cornelius rejected this harsh teaching, and following the line of St Cyprian of Carthage he claimed that the Church had authority to admit apostates and sinners to reconciliation as long as suitable penance was performed. This issue too was significant; many priests had been over-lax, failing to emphasize sufficiently the need for true penitence in those who had lapsed and were now seeking reconciliation.

Novitian set himself up as rival bishop of Rome, the first of the antipopes, but his doctrine was defeated at councils in Carthage and Rome and he himself was excommunicated.

Death and cult

Cornelius's victory was shortlived however; persecution flared up again under Emperor Gallus in 253 and he was banished to Civita Vecchia (Centumcellae), where he died soon afterwards. Some traditions claim that he was beheaded, but it seems more likely that his death was caused by harsh conditions in exile. Whatever the details of his death, he has been venerated as a martyr from the time of Cyprian onwards. On his tomb in Rome is inscribed 'Cornelius Martyr' and a painting of his famous ally Cyprian on the wall of the crypt dates from the eighth century.

Several surviving examples of the correspondence between Cyprian and Cornelius, some written while Cornelius suffered in exile, testify to the likeable and generous character of the Pope, and his earnestness to preserve sound doctrine. In the Roman martyrology Cornelius is closely associated with Cyprian, and they share a feast-day. In art he is usually represented in papal vestments, holding a triple cross or a horn, or occasionally with bulls, and this association has led to his patronage of cattle and other domestic animals.

Feast-day 16 September
Patron saint of cattle and domestic animals, invoked against earache, epilepsy, fever and twitching

Crispin and Crispinian

d. c.287

The shoemaking brothers

They owe their fame largely to Shakespeare's version of the battle of Agincourt, fought on their feast-day in 1415.

Although they are thought to have been martyred in Rome, the cult of these two saints has historically been centred around Soissons in France since the sixth century, perhaps as a result of a translation. One late and unreliable legend recounts how these two noble Roman brothers came along with St Quintinus as missionaries to Gaul, where they made their living as shoemakers to avoid draining the resources of the local Christians, and were eventually martyred there. Other, equally unreliable traditions hold that they fled to Faversham in England at the height of Roman persecution, where they made their shoes in a house built on the site of the present Swan Inn on Preston Street, which was a centre for pilgrimage until the 17th century. Faversham commemorates them with an altar in the parish church, and it is this English tradition which

probably lies behind the famous patriotic invocation in Shakespeare's *Henry V* (Act I, scene iii), since the battle of Agincourt was fought on their feast-day.

Death and cult

An elaboration on the legend of their martyrdom in Soissons has them brought before one Rictiovarus, a notorious hater of Christians (whose existence is doubted by many modern scholars), who tortured them in an effort to make them recant. Not only was he unsuccessful in his attempt on their faith, he was also unable to kill the pair who were miraculously protected against the worst methods of execution he could devise. Boiling, drowning and burning were all equally ineffective in taking the lives of the two brothers. Humiliated and distraught, Rictiovarus committed suicide and the martyrs were then successfully executed on the command of the emperor Maximian. It seems more likely that Crispin and Crispinian were martyred in Rome and their relics later translated to France where St Eloi later rebuilt their shrine and encouraged devotion.

As the patron saints of shoemakers and leather-workers, their emblem in art is a shoe or last. Many artists developed the legends of the torture to produce graphic works in which the two staunchly face cudgels, flaying, and boiling oil while their persecutors are destroyed by heavenly fire.

See illustration on following page.

> **Feast-day** 25 October
> Patron saints of shoemakers, cobblers and leather-workers

St. Crispin and St. Crispinian

PATRONS OF THE GENTLE CRAFT.

" Our shoes were sow'd with merry notes,
And by our mirth expell'd all moan ;
Like nightingales, from whose sweet throats
Most pleasant tunes are nightly blown :
The Gentle Craft is fittest then
For poor distressed gentlemen !"

St. Hugh's Song.

St Crispin and St Crispinian

Cuthbert

634 Lauderdale — Inner Farne 687

'The wonder-worker of Britain'

*One of the best-loved British
saints, especially dear to his
native Northumbria, Cuthbert
was renowned for his compassion
and his love of peace in
a divided age.*

Most of our information about Cuthbert is
from the authoritative pen of Bede, confirmed by supplementary sources.
Orphaned as a child and brought up by a
foster-mother, Cuthbert spent his teenage
years as a shepherd until one night he saw
a vision of a soul being transported to
heaven. When he heard a few days later the
news of Aidan's death he recognized his
vocation and in 651 entered Melrose Abbey, under the abbotship of Eata and the
special care of St Boswell, where he remained a monk for 13 years. He made
countless missionary journeys in the surrounding area; the town of Kirkcudbright
('church of Cuthbert') in Dumfries and
Galloway testifies to the extent of his
influence.

Uncertain days

In 661 King Alcfrith invited Eata to found a
monastery in Ripon. The abbot took
Cuthbert with him as guest-master, and the
hospitable saint is said to have welcomed all
visitors as though they were Christ himself.
But when conflict arose over the Roman
and Celtic traditions of the dating of Easter,
Eata and Cuthbert returned to Melrose,
where Cuthbert was made prior, and Eata
was replaced at Ripon by St Wilfrid.

Wilfrid spoke strongly for the Roman

tradition at the Synod of Whitby in 664,
citing St Peter as his authority, and King
Oswiu was so impressed that he decided in
Rome's favour. Colman of Lindisfarne resigned his see in protest and retired to
Ireland; Eata took his place and Cuthbert
went with him to become prior of Lindisfarne for the next 12 years. In this fraught
and partisan environment, Cuthbert's
peaceful nature and diplomacy were tested
as he sought to reconcile the quarrelling
monks in addition to continuing his missionary work. He frequently escaped to a
nearby islet (now called St Cuthbert's Island) for tranquillity, but the fame of his
holiness was such that at low tide he was still
beset by pilgrims seeking healing, teaching
and comfort. In his moments of solitude he
befriended the island's eider ducks, now
popularly known as St Cuthbert's ducks
and more affectionately in the North East
as 'cuddy's chickens'. It seems appropriate
that today the Farne Islands are known for
their famous bird sanctuary.

Later life and death

Cuthbert's privacy was shattered when, at
the Synod of Twyford in 684, he was elected
bishop of Hexham by King Egfrith and the
clergy. Cuthbert was unwilling to leave his
island hermitage for the large Northumbrian see, but at the personal urging of the
King he was consecrated at York on Easter
Day, 685. However he went straight from
there to meet Eata at Melrose, and arranged to swap sees with him for the more
secluded and familiar Lindisfarne. He spent
his last two years diligently administering
his diocese and caring for the victims of the
plague that swept it, performing miracles of
healing and prophecy. But two months
before his death he finally regained the
tranquillity of Inner Farne, where he died
on 20 March, 687. His last words, addressed
to his brethren, are recorded by Bede:

'always keep peace and divine charity among yourselves'.

Cult

His body was returned to Lindisfarne for burial, and when it was elevated to an above-ground shrine 11 years later, it was found to be incorrupt. Together with the miracles of healing reported at the shrine, this was a great stimulus to veneration. After the Danes attacked Lindisfarne in 875, the remaining monks wandered the Borders searching for a safe home for their shrines and relics. They finally settled at Durham in 955, where they built a Saxon church over Cuthbert's shrine. The relics were translated into the new Norman cathedral on the site in 1104 and again pronounced incorrupt. Cuthbert's body seems to have decayed only after the Reformation, along with the Christian unity that he so cherished. His relics are still in Durham cathedral, where a special collect is read on his feast-day.

Many churches in England (especially in the North) and several in Scotland are dedicated to Cuthbert, and he is remembered in the stall paintings in Carlisle cathedral and in the Cuthbert window of the late Middle Ages in York. He is often represented carrying the head of King Oswald, said to have been buried with him, or with otters or eider ducks at his feet.

Cuthbert was renowned for his great physical and moral strength, his gifts of healing and consolation, and above all for his single-minded service to God expressed in warm concern for his fellow creatures.

Feast-day 20 March

St Cuthbert and his two brethren return to the land of the Picts, from The Life and Miracles of St Cuthbert. *British Museum.*

Cyprian

c.200 Carthage — Carthage 258

Bishop of Carthage

A late convert to Christianity, who nevertheless achieved much in the church of his day and died a martyr's death.

Until the age of about 46, Cyprian enjoyed a successful career in Carthage as orator, teacher of rhetoric, and lawyer. But after his conversion to Christianity he turned his attention and his studies exclusively to the Bible and Christian writings, being especially influenced by Tertullian. He was soon ordained as a priest, and was popularly elected bishop of Carthage in 248. The following year Decius began his fierce persecution of Christians and Cyprian went into hiding, a move condemned by many but one which allowed him to supervise his see rather more effectively than he might from a prison, by means of letters written to encourage and instruct the Christians there.

Controversy in the Church

When he returned in 251 it was to find that many Christians had apostatized during the persecutions, and that they were being readmitted to the church without any penance by Novatus, a priest in schism. At the other extreme, the antipope Novitian taught that an apostate could never be readmitted to the church. With Pope Cornelius, Cyprian advocated a middle course by which the lapsed could be reconciled after suitable penance. He called a council at Carthage in 251 to formalize the terms for receiving back the *lapsi* and to confirm the supremacy of the Pope. It was here that he first read his *De unitate ecclesiae*,

a call for unity and understanding in the church. Soon after his return to Carthage, however, the city was struck by plague and although Cyprian organized and led relief efforts for the victims, many pagans blamed the visitation on him and upon the ascendancy of the church. Cyprian wrote his *De mortalite* to comfort his stricken city.

In the controversy on the validity of baptism by heretics or apostates, Cyprian led the rigorist opposition of the African church to Pope Stephen I. Subsequent church doctrine has ruled against him, accepting that the faith of the one being baptized confers legitimacy, but Cyprian nevertheless won his place in the canon of saints by his martyrdom a few years later.

Death and cult

During the persecutions of Valerian Cyprian was tried and exiled to Curubis, and on the appointment of a new proconsul was retried. Once again he reaffirmed his faith, refusing to sacrifice to pagan gods, and he was led away to be beheaded on 14 September.

During his life Cyprian inspired great devotion among his flock, and the accounts we have of him, including a biography by Pontius, show him as a conscientious pastor, greatly concerned with the condition of the church as a whole and of each individual under his care. His writings are many and varied, making a valuable early contribution to the great tradition of Latin Christian literature. He is sometimes confused with Cyprian of Antioch, the converted magician, hence the Common Prayer Book lists his day as 26 September.

Feast-day 16 September

Cyril and Methodius

c.826 Thessalonica — Rome 869
c.815 Thessalonica — Moravia 885

The apostles of the Slavs

*Their influence on Slavonic
Christianity and literature
was enormous.*

These two brothers were born in Thessalonica of a senatorial family. Cyril (christened Constantine) was educated at the University of Constantinople, where he studied under Photius and later succeeded him as teacher, being nicknamed 'the Philosopher'. His older brother Methodius went on from Constantinople to become provincial govenor of a Slav colony in Opsikion.

In 861 the two were sent by Emperor Michael III to evangelize the Khazars in Russia, and achieved great success by quickly learning the local language. Methodius became abbot of a Greek monastery on his return, but in 863 the Duke of Moravia, Rostislav, requested missionaries who could teach his people in the vernacular. Remembering their familiarity with the Slavonic language Photius, now patriarch of Constantinople, appointed Cyril and Methodius.

Literary influence

One of their most significant achievements was the invention of the 'glagolithic' alphabet, the basis of the Cyrillic alphabet which was probably the work of a later disciple, and they are thus regarded as the founders of Slavonic literature. They translated much Scripture and liturgy into Slavonic and through their diligence converted many Slavs where German missionaries before them had failed. They did however encounter opposition from German bishops and missionaries who felt themselves snubbed and questioned the

brothers' use of the vernacular for the Roman liturgy. In the midst of political and religious controversy Cyril and Methodius either withdrew or were recalled to Rome. They brought with them relics of St Clement and were received with honours by the new Pope, Adrian II, who vindicated their methods.

It was only on becoming a monk that Cyril took the name by which he is usually known, but he died shortly afterwards and was buried in San Clemente in Rome, where his funeral is commemorated in a fresco. Methodius was consecrated as bishop of Moravia but was imprisoned for two years on his return because of continued opposition from German bishops. He was released at the Pope's intervention, but cautioned to discontinue his controversial use of vernacular liturgy. His enemies were as fierce as ever, and in 879 he was again called to Rome to answer charges of heterodoxy. Pope John VIII cleared him of the charges, confirmed his appointment as archbishop of Simium and Moravia, and gave papal permission to celebrate the Mass in Slavonic.

Cult

Methodius returned to his see until his death, encountering opposition until the end. The feast-day of the brothers was extended to the universal church in 1880 by Leo XIII, and Pope Paul II named them patrons of Europe along with Benedict. In recent years they have been recognized as pioneers in evangelism and the use of the vernacular in liturgy. In art the brothers are shown holding between them a church, often surrounded by their Slavonic converts.

Feast-day 14 February
Patron saints of Europe

Cyril of Alexandria

c.376 Alexandria — Alexandria 444

Bishop and theologian

A volatile and often over-hasty bishop, his contributions to orthodox doctrine were nevertheless invaluable.

Little is known of Cyril's early life beyond the fact that he was a nephew of Theophilus of Alexandria, took part in the deposition of St John Chrysostom as a young priest, and on his uncle's death in 412 succeeded him as archbishop of Alexandria.

Although he used his authority to battle for orthodoxy, he appears to have acted insensitively and over-hastily on some occasions. He closed down the churches of the Novatians, attacked the Neoplatonists and in 415 expelled all Jews from the city. When opposed by the imperial prefect Orestes, Cyril quarrelled with him bitterly and roused his monks against him, with the tragic result that his followers lynched Orestes's friend Hypatia, a respected Neoplatonist philosopher, in the belief that she had prejudiced him against their leader. Although this crime may have been performed without Cyril's knowledge, it was certainly done in his name.

Defence of orthodoxy

Cyril's claim to sanctity rests in his spirited and uncompromising defence of the unity of Christ's person, against the heresy of Nestorius who claimed that Christ contained within himself two distinct natures, human and divine. Cyril persuaded Pope Celestine I to call a council at Rome to investigate this teaching; Nestorius was pronounced a heretic and threatened with excommunication. When he refused to capitulate the Council of Ephesus was convened (431). Cyril presided and denounced the absent Nestorius, whose doctrine was condemned by all those present, influenced no doubt by the theological and rhetorical skill of Cyril himself.

The matter was not allowed to rest there; Archbishop John of Antioch and about 40 of his followers, who were convinced of Nestorius's innocence, arrived in Ephesus too late for the council and convened their own at which they denounced Cyril. In some confusion by now, Emperor Theodosius II had both Nestorius and Cyril arrested but released the latter after a deputation of legates confirmed the papal ruling that Nestorius had been condemned and Cyril pronounced innocent. Two years later Nestorius was exiled, after John and Cyril concurred on his heresy.

Works and cult

From then until his death Cyril applied himself to theological and doctrinal writings, clarifying issues such as the Incarnation and the Trinity, which were to prove invaluable in the church as a means of resisting heresy. He was undoubtedly a great theologian, who wrote precisely and with convincing reasoning, but his tendency to misrepresent the arguments of his opponents has been much criticized by modern scholars. In addition to these treatises he wrote commentaries on the Pentateuch, Mark and Luke, a defence of the faith against Julian the Apostate, and several sermons and letters. Pope Leo XIII declared him a Doctor of the Church in 1882; he has always been greatly venerated in the Eastern church and is shown in art as a venerable bishop holding a book and pointing skywards.

Feast-day 27 June

Cyril of Jerusalem

c.315 Jerusalem — Jerusalem 386

Bishop of Jerusalem

Despite his attempts to remain neutral in the Arian debate, his life was characterized by controversy.

Born and brought up in Jerusalem, of well-to-do Christian parents, Cyril was ordained by St Maximus and placed in charge of catechumens, whom he taught for several years. In Lent of 347 he delivered his 23 famous *Katéchésis*, succinct and memorable instruction for those about to receive baptism or, after Easter, having just received it.

Thrice exiled

He was appointed bishop of Jerusalem in c.351 after the death of Maximus and almost immediately was obliged to defend his authority when Acacius, Arian metropolitan of Caesarea, claimed precedence over him. The furious Acacius called a council of bishops sympathetic to Arianism which condemned Cyril for selling church property in order to provide for the poor during a famine, and in c.358, on the authority of the emperor, Cyril was banished from Jerusalem and went to live in Tarsus. He was recalled in 359 after the Council of Seleucia, which also deposed Acacius, but was again expelled thanks to Acacius's influence with the emperor Constantius. When Constantius died and was succeeded by

Julian the Apostate in 361 Cyril was again recalled, only to be exiled for a third time in 367 when Emperor Valens revoked Julian's recalling of all exiled clergy. In all he spent about 16 years of his 35-year episcopate in exile.

Later life and cult

When Cyril returned to Jerusalem from banishment for the last time after the death of Valens it was to find a city scarred by controversy and corruption, and he dedicated the rest of his episcopate to its restoration. Even now however he was not free from controversy: in 379 the concerned members of the Council of Antioch sent St Gregory of Nyssa to discover the state of the diocese of Jerusalem. Their concern stemmed from the apparent hesitation of Cyril in accepting the word *homoousios*, one of the central elements of the Nicene Creed. Some have speculated that Cyril had in fact some sympathy with the Arian cause, but Gregory reported that despite the desperate condition of the Jerusalem see, its bishop was fully orthodox. At the General Council of Constantinople in 381 Cyril happily accepted the term *homoousios* in the revised Nicene Creed, and it seems likely that his query had been linguistic rather than heterodox in any way, despite his tolerance of some leaders with Arian tendencies. He died an old man, and has been revered as a Doctor of the Church since 1882.

Feast-day 18 March

Daniel the Stylite

409 Maratha — near Constantinople 493

Successor to Simeon Stylites

Another famous pillar saint, whose dramatic example deeply influenced his age.

The son of Christian parents in Mesopotamia, Daniel entered a nearby monastery at the age of 12. He spent the next 30 years there, during which time he accompanied his abbot to Antioch. On the journey they visited St Simeon Stylites, aloft on his pillar at Telanissus, and Daniel was inspired. When the abbot died some time later Daniel refused the abbacy, going instead to revisit Simeon. He stayed there for two weeks and joined Simeon on his platform to receive instruction.

He continued journeying, intending to make a pilgrimage to the Holy Land, but was forestalled by political unrest in the area. Instead he settled as a hermit at Philempora near Constantinople, living for nine years in an abandoned temple thought to be inhabited by devilish spirits. Daniel's only link with the world was through a small window; inside the temple he was reputed to be hideously tormented by the demons. The healing of the patriarch Anatolius, suffering from a long and serious disease, was attributed to his prayers and his fame began to spread.

The pillar saint

When Simeon the Stylite died in 459 Daniel inherited the saint's cloak and his lifestyle. He lived on a series of pillars for the next 33 years: the first, which he erected himself just outside Constantinople, provided inadequate protection from the elements, and the emperor intervened to supply a platform raised on two joined pillars with a rail and shelter. Daniel refused to descend even for ordination: the archbishop conducted the service at the base of the pillar and ascended by a ladder to give the new priest communion. He became famous for his wisdom and his miracles of healing and prophecy (he foresaw a serious fire in Constantinople in 465), and his sermons attracted vast crowds of listeners. In spite of his extreme way of life, Daniel's teaching was simple and practical: he encouraged his hearers to love God and each other, to care for the needy, and to avoid sin, specifically gambling and debauchery.

Only once did Daniel descend from his pillar; to rebuke Basilicus for usurping the emperor Zeno. He had to be carried in a chair, since he was by now unable to walk, and he was refused an audience by Basilicus. Zeno was however restored soon afterwards, and immediately went to thank his old ally.

Death and cult

A week before his death Daniel preached his final sermon, an inspired discourse on Creation and Redemption. The patriarch Euphemius ascended the pillar to give him the viaticum before he died, and the saint's body was finally brought down, bent and unkempt from his long years of exposure, to be buried at the foot of his pillar.

Although many are deeply suspicious of the stylite practice, there can be no doubt of Daniel's personal piety and integrity. He inspired many to holiness although few were called to emulate him.

Feast-day 11 December

David of Scotland

c.1085 — Carlisle 1153

The great Scottish king

*His reign marked a time of
religious and social
reorganization in Scotland and
an awakening national identity.*

The sixth and last son of Malcolm III of
Scotland (known as Malcolm Canmore)
and St Margaret, David was sent at the age
of nine to be educated at the Norman court
of England along with his sister Matilda,
who later married King Henry I of England.
When his elder brother Alexander succeeded to the throne in 1107, the young
David became prince of Cumbria, which
included the Lothian region, and secured
the title of earl of Huntingdon by marrying
Matilda, whose father St Waldef was earl
of Northumbria. In 1124 he ascended to
the Scottish throne, and aimed at securing
Northumbria, to which he had some claim
by marriage. To complicate matters further, in 1127 he pledged along with other
English noblemen to acknowledge the claim
of another Matilda, the daughter of David's
sister and King Henry I, to the English
throne.

However in 1135 Stephen succeeded in
England, and the relatively cordial terms
on which Scotland and England had previously stood took an immediate turn for the
worse. David attacked and held most of the
Border castles and demanded Carlisle,
Doncaster and Huntingdon for his son
Henry. The next year he also claimed Northumberland, and in 1138 led an invasion of
the north of England with an army aug-
mented by Scandinavian and German
forces, and the infamous Picts of Galloway.
He was defeated at Standard by Stephen's
troops but managed to secure favourable

terms by the treaty of Durham in 1139,
receiving Northumberland for his son as he
had wished and establishing his court at
Carlisle.

Development in Scotland

From now on David concerned himself less
with civil war and more with Scottish affairs,
replacing Celtic tribal traditions of land
ownership with a feudal system, encouraging trade in developing Scottish towns,
introducing an Anglo-Norman legal system
and setting up the office of Chancellor. He
also improved the Scottish church, strengthening links with Rome and resisting the
attempts of the English church to impose
its jurisdiction in Scottish ecclesiastical affairs, and founding many new sees,
churches and monasteries. He was popularly admired for his justice, generosity and
holiness, and the description of him by St
Ailred, who served in his court as a young
man, emphasizes his humility, practicality,
chastity and love of justice, although he was
widely condemned for failing to control his
troops when they committed atrocities in
the north of England. It is said that David
created the Scotland that was to stand against
Edward I of England.

Death and cult

David died at his court on 24 May, and his
grave at Dunfermline became the centre of
his cult until the Reformation. The cult
revived when his name was inserted into the
calendar of the Scottish saints by Archbishop Laud and several churches have
since been dedicated to him, although he
has never been officially canonized.

Feast-day 24 May

David of Wales

c.520 Pembrokeshire — Menevia c.589

The patron saint of Wales

Known as 'The Waterman' for his abstinence and austerity, David's missionary activity formed the basis of Welsh monasticism.

Little is known of the historical David, a monk from Pembrokeshire. Most of our information comes from the earliest *Life* of c.1090, written by Rhygyvarch, the son of Julien, bishop of St David's, which is more concerned with vindicating the claim of his father's bishopric to independence from the Norman authority of Canterbury than with presenting an accurate biography. Rhygyvarch informs us that David was the son of a chief of Cardigan, Sant, his mother was St Non, and he was educated first at Hen Vynyw then for 10 years as a pupil of the scribe Paulinus (whose sight he is reputed to have restored after it was lost with weeping) studying scripture on an island.

Monastery and mission

He then embarked on a lifetime of missionary work, founding about 12 monasteries including Glastonbury and Menevia (later St David's) where the regime of the monks, based on the Egyptian monastic model, was especially strict. They performed harsh austerities and hard manual labour, keeping no cattle to help them plough, in addition to much studying and living mainly in silence on a frugal diet of vegetables, bread and water. David gained the nickname *Aquaticus*, 'Waterman', from the reputation for abstinence which soon attached to

his community. It may also refer to his penchant for immersing himself entirely in cold water as a means of subduing the flesh. St Gildas strongly criticized David's rule as being more ascetic than Christian.

His fame spread until he was summoned to speak at the Synod of Brefi in c.550, where he so impressed the assembly by his preaching that he was unanimously elected archbishop, with authority over the whole of Wales. This detail is almost certainly a fabrication designed to invest Julien's see with metropolitan status. Equally fictitious are the legends that he was consecrated archbishop while on pilgrimage in Jerusalem, and that he established a formal Welsh church with himself as primate.

Death and cult

David died an old man at his monastery in Menevia. His cult was approved by Pope Callistus II in c.1120, and the relics translated to a shrine in the cathedral at St David's in 1131 and again in 1275 at the rebuilding of the cathedral which was largely financed by offerings at the shrine.

There are many dedications in South Wales and several throughout south-west England, and through the monks who visited Menevia he is said to have had a great influence on Irish monasticism also. The conventional nickname for a Welshman, Taffy, comes from the alternative spelling 'Dafydd', but the well-attested custom of wearing a leek or daffodil on his feast-day, 'begun upon an honourable request' according to Shakespeare's Flewellyn in *Henry V*, has never been convincingly explained.

> **Feast-day** 1 March
> Patron saint of Wales

Denis (Dionysius)

d. Montmartre c.250

First bishop of Paris

The cult of France's patron saint has suffered from attempts to identify him with other religious figures.

An Italian by birth, Denis was sent to Gaul as a missionary from Rome in the middle of the third century. On his arrival in Paris he taught effectively and established a centre for Christianity on an island in the Seine, but his success aroused opposition from the Roman authorities (the persecutions of Valerian were now at their height) and he was arrested along with two companions, a priest named Rusticus and Eleutherius, a deacon. The three are believed to have been beheaded on the hill now known as Montmartre, 'hill of martyrs'.

Confusion of identity

This was the basis of the legend recounted by Gregory of Tours in the sixth century, but by the mid ninth century confusion had arisen between three different historical figures called Dionysius: the original martyr was identified with Dionysius the Areopagite, a Christian Neoplatonist of the fifth century, and with a Greek disciple of St Paul mentioned in Acts 17: 34 who had been converted in Athens by Paul's sermon on the Unknown God. To accommodate this elaboration, it was held that this Dionysius was sent to Gaul at the end of the first century by Pope Clement I and he was attributed with the much later writings of an unknown mystic wrongly identified as Dionysius the Areopagite. This tortuous conflation was propagated by the abbot of St Denis, Hilduin, and greatly increased the popularity of Denis's cult throughout Europe.

Cult

A further elaboration of the legend claimed that Denis was a *cephalophore*, a martyr believed to have carried his own head to his burial place (in this case the site of the abbey of St Denis) after execution. This is the basis of the most common representations of St Denis, shown carrying his head on a book before him or preparing to catch it as he is beheaded. After the bodies of Denis, Rusticus and Eleutherius were recovered from the Seine they were supposedly buried in a tomb over which the abbey of St Denis was built, which became the burial ground for a line of French kings.

> **Feast-day** 9 October
> Patron saint of France, invoked against headaches, frenzy and strife

Dominic

1170 Calaruega — Bologna 1221

Founder of the Dominicans

His concern for mission led to the foundation of one of the most widely-respected and influential monastic orders.

Born in Old Castile, Spain, Dominic was educated by his uncle, an archpriest, and then at the University of Palencia, where he was probably ordained and became a canon regular at Osma cathedral in 1199. He was appointed prior of the chapter, and followed the strict Benedictine rule, giving himself over to prayer and penitence.

In c.1204 Dominic left the community with his bishop Diego de Avezedo on a mission to the Albigensian heretics of Languedoc. Here, removed from contemplation to the challenge of the mission field, Dominic developed his gift for reasoned preaching and displayed his genius for organization by establishing in 1206 a house of holy and austere nuns to receive the converts and to function as a base for preaching. He attached to this nunnery a house for preaching friars, who combined an exemplary lifestyle with learning and discussion.

The peaceful work of conversion was interrupted in 1208 when some Albigensians murdered the papal legate, Peter of Castelnau, drawing on themselves the wrath of Rome. Pope Innocent III declared a crusade against them which raged violently for seven years, and although Dominic tried to carry on with his missionary work in the wake of the bloodshed, he met with little success.

Feast-day 8 August
Patron saint of astronomers

The Dominican order

The leader of the Pope's troops, Count Simon IV of Montfort, gave Dominic a castle in recently-conquered Casseneuil in 1214 in which Dominic, with six followers, founded his Friars Preachers, which received canonical approval from the bishop of Toulouse the next year. In 1216 he received approval from Pope Honorius III, on condition that the order should follow an existing Rule. Dominic chose that of Augustine, which lent itself well to modification to suit his vision of an order of holy men devoted to learning, practical poverty and above all to missionary preaching. His order was the first to omit manual labour, and the Divine Office was chanted more quickly and simply than in many others.

Over the next few years, Dominic worked tirelessly to establish his order throughout Europe, with great success. His formula of intelligent and learned preaching from a monastic background fulfilled a deeply-felt need in the medieval world, fusing the intellectual with the everyday.

Death and cult

The first General Chapter of the Dominicans was held in Bologna in 1220, and the following year Dominic died there after an aborted preaching tour in Hungary. Veneration began quickly after his death; he was canonized in 1234 and a tomb was built about 30 years later by Nicolas Pisano, to be later embellished by others including Michelangelo. His emblem in art is a dog, from a pun on the Latin *domini canis*, Dominicans. The dog holds in its mouth a torch, symbolizing truth, and is often accompanied by a lily, star or book. Occasionally Dominic is shown receiving a rosary from the Virgin, from a tradition that he first invented it.

Dubricius (Dyfrig, Devereux)

d. c.612

'Chief of the Church in Britain'

One of the most important of the early saints of South Wales, around whose name innumerable and improbable legends grew up.

We have little reliable information, although a wealth of apocryphal detail, about this popular saint. He was probably born at Medley near Hereford and went on to become a monk, whose first foundation was at nearby Ariconium (modern Archenfeld). Later foundations included Henllan and Moccas (in the Wye Valley), which attracted countless novitiates, and having studied there for some time he moved on to found and populate new monasteries and churches. Dedications in Powys and Somerset suggest that his influence reached far beyond his immediate locality, and this view of his importance is supported by the seventh-century *Life of Samson*, which names Dubricius, titled bishop, as the figure supervising Samson's ordination and consecration. It seems clear that he was particularly influential in south-east Wales and Herefordshire, where he worked mainly from his monastic foundations. The village of Saint Devereux in Herefordshire takes its name from a corruption of St Dyfrig. As an old man Dubricius retired to Bardsey Island, where he died peacefully.

Cult

Many unreliable details have become attached to his legend: he was believed to be the first bishop of Llandaff and archbishop of Caerlon-on-Usk, who handed over his metropolitan status to David at the Synod of Brefi, clearly an anachronism, although it is likely that he and St Deinol were the ones who persuaded David to attend the Council. The translation of his relics to Llandaff in 1120 did much to popularize his cult. Geoffrey of Monmouth, who is not renowned for his accuracy, reports that it was Dubricius who crowned Arthur King of Britain and Tennyson takes up the legend in his *Idylls of the King*, Dyfrig is the High King in *The Coming of Arthur*. In art he is represented holding two croziers and the archbishop's cross.

The Coming of Arthur: Tennyson's *Idylls of the King*

And Lancelot past away among the flowers,
(For then was latter April) and returned
Among the flowers, in May, with
   Guinevere.
To whom arrived, by Dubric the high saint,
Chief of the Church in Britain, and before
The stateliest of her altar-shrines, the King
That morn was married, while in stainless
   white [...]
And Arthur said, 'Behold, thy doom is
   mine.
Let chance what will, I love thee to the
   death!'
To whom the Queen replied with drooping
   eyes,
'King and my Lord, I love thee to the
   death!'
And holy Dubric spread his hands and
   spake,
'Reign ye, and live and love, and make the
   world
Other, and may thy Queen be one with
   thee,
And all this Order of thy Table Round
Fulfil the boundless purpose of their king!'

Dunstan

909 Baltonsborough — Canterbury 988

Reviver of monasticism in Britain

Statesman, archbishop and reformer, Dunstan stands as the central and formative figure of the tenth century.

Born into a noble family with royal connections, Dunstan was educated by Irish monks in nearby Glastonbury and as a youth spent time in the household of his uncle Athelm, archbishop of Canterbury, and in the court of King Athelstan. Driven out of the court on slanderous charges of studying magic and paganism, he faced a crisis in his life. For a while he wavered between the attractions of married or monastic life, but a serious illness decided him: on recovering he took monastic vows and was ordained as a priest by Alphege, bishop of Winchester, along with his friend Ethelwold.

For a few years he lived as a hermit near Glastonbury, practising the handcrafts that he loved, until at Athelstan's death the young Edmund succeeded to the throne, and Dunstan was recalled as his advisor. Once again he was the victim of slander, but his disgrace was revoked after Edmund narrowly escaped death at Cheddar Gorge. He had vowed to redress the wrongs done to Dunstan if his life were spared, and on returning safely home he duly appointed him abbot of Glastonbury. It was the beginning of the rebirth of English monastic life, after the Scandinavian invasions had all but quenched it.

Monastic reform

Dunstan set about rebuilding and enlarging the abbey and training the monks in the strict Benedictine Rule, greatly aided by Ethelwold. Edmund was killed in 946 and succeeded by Edred, who put a substantial part of the royal treasury into Dunstan's keeping. But Edred was quickly succeeded by Edwy, who resented Dunstan's outspoken criticism and exiled him to the Continent. Here he visited the reformed monastery at Ghent, the first direct contact between British and continental monastic revivals.

After popular revolt, Edwy's younger brother Edgar was chosen as king and installed Dunstan as bishop of Worcester then London, and finally archbishop of Canterbury. He worked closely with the king to revive English monasticism, through personal involvement and through the inspiration he gave to others. The *Regularis concordia*, drawn up by Ethelwold but clearly inspired by Dunstan, formulated the practical means for applying Benedict's rule and with its emphasis on royal protection for monasteries served to unify church and state throughout England. Dunstan's modified coronation rite for Edgar remains the basis of the modern service.

Death and cult

During the reign of Æthelred the Unready, the elderly Dunstan retired somewhat from state affairs and spent more time at Canterbury, teaching and preaching right until his death. A cult soon began and gained in popularity, becoming nationwide by the early 12th century.

He is traditionally regarded as a craftsman, and several bells, organs, tools and pictures are claimed to be his. He is often shown in art holding the devil by the nose with a pair of tongs, or plying his harp or his goldsmith's tools.

Feast-day 19 May
Patron saint of goldsmiths, jewellers, locksmiths, blacksmiths, musicians and the blind

Dympna

d. Gheel ninth century

Patron saint of the insane

An Irish princess murdered by her father, who was the inspiration for a compassionate and effective approach to mental illness.

When the bodies of an unknown couple were discovered at Gheel (to the east of Antwerp in northern Belgium), together with an inscription of the name Dympna, and miraculous cures were reported at the site, the popular folk-tale that grew up around them soon became regarded as a saint's *Life*. According to this tale, Dympna was the daughter of a pagan Celtic chief and a Christian mother. After her mother's death, Dympna was forced to flee with her confessor St Gerebernus, first to Antwerp and then on to nearby Gheel, to avoid the incestuous attentions of her father. There they lived peacefully as solitaries, but Dympna's father succeeded in tracking them down by tracing the coins they had spent, and demanded that she return home with him. When Dympna refused, he murdered the girl and her confessor on the spot. The bodies were buried there, and at their translation in the 13th century several miracles of healing of insanity and epilepsy were reported.

Cult

A cathedral was built in Dympna's honour in the town, and as the saint's reputation for healing spread it became a centre of pilgrimage for the mentally ill. The pilgrims were housed originally in a sick-room built for the purpose next to the church, but as their numbers increased over the centuries this limited accommodation proved inadequate. By the 14th century the townsfolk of Gheel were accustomed to opening their homes to give hospitality to those who had travelled for healing. In 1850 the government formalized this arrangement under medical supervision, and the hospital system which thus evolved has proved one of the most famous and effective institutions of its kind in the world. Its special concern is the integration of the mentally ill with society, for example by boarding out patients in private homes in the area.

In art Dympna is usually shown as a princess with a sword holding a devil on a leash, and often with St Gerebernus.

> **Feast-day** 15 May
> Patron saint of the insane, invoked against mental illness and epilepsy

Edmund

841 East Anglia — Hellesdon 870

Martyr-king of East Anglia

Fuelled by his status as a hero-figure and by the increasing importance of his abbey, Edmund's cult has remained exceptionally popular in England.

An Anglo-Saxon who had been brought up as a Christian, Edmund is traditionally believed to have been chosen king of East Anglia while still a youth, as the adopted heir of the famous Offa of Mercia. He ruled wisely and peacefully for several years, but disaster came with the invasion of Ingwar from Denmark in 865. In 870 Ingwar led his enormous army down into East Anglia, capturing Thetford in Norfolk. Edmund set out against them with as great an army as he could muster, but he proved no match for the 'Great Army' of the Vikings. His troops were defeated, and he himself captured at Hoxne in Suffolk and imprisoned. His captors demanded that he renounce his Christianity and pay tribute of land and homage to Ingwar, both of which Edmund staunchly refused to perform, despite horrific torture.

Various legends purport to tell the manner of his death: some claim that he was scourged, tied to a tree and shot until he bristled with arrows, then beheaded, others have speculated that he was offered as a pagan Viking sacrifice, or simply beheaded.

Development of the cult

Whatever the manner of his death, Edmund was quickly revered as a martyr and English folk-hero in the best traditions of Anglo-Saxon Christian provincialism. He was buried in a small chapel at Hellesdon in Norfolk, and in c.915 his body was pronounced incorrupt. It was translated to Bedricsworth, which later became known as Bury St Edmunds, where a great Benedictine abbey was founded in 1020 by King Cnut. The abbey at Bury soon became one of the most powerful in England, and Edmund's cult gained widespread popularity in the Middle Ages, with many church dedications, especially in southern England.

When the Norman cathedral was erected on the site Edmund's remains were translated into a new shrine in 1095, and a further translation in 1198 was immortalized by Jocelin of Brakelond's description, later translated and considered by Thomas Carlyle in *Past and Present* (Book II, chapter 13). Some controversy has arisen over a claim that his relics were taken to France by French soldiers defeated at the Battle of Lincoln in 1217, and that they now rest at Saint-Sernin, Toulouse. Although the French offered to return them in 1912, many scholars protested that the authentic relics remained at Bury and the translation was never performed.

In art, Edmund's emblem is usually an arrow or occasionally the wolf which was believed to have guarded his head after execution. He is also famously portrayed on the Wilton Diptych along with Edward the Confessor, as the patron of England who presents Richard II to the Virgin Mary and Child.

Feast-day 20 November
Patron saint of Richard II, invoked against plague

See illustration on following page.

*The Wilton Diptych (left panel) showing **St Edmund**, St Edward the Confessor (see p99), Richard II and a pilgrim. National Gallery.*

Edmund Arrowsmith

1585 Haydock — Lancaster 1628

Jesuit priest and martyr

Undaunted by the persecution of Catholics in his day, Arrowsmith worked fearlessly as a priest in his native Lancashire and died as unshakeable as he had been in life.

Christened Brian Arrowsmith, son of a yeoman farmer, Edmund always used his confirmation name in adult life. At the time anti-Catholic feeling ran high in England, and both his mother Margery Gerard and his father Robert had suffered imprisonment for their faith. When Edmund began to study theology under an elderly priest in England, therefore, they judged it safer to send him to the English college at Douai on the Continent to allow him to pursue his calling unmolested.

He was ordained in 1612 and joined the mission to England the following year, returning to Lancashire where he began to preach vociferously without regard to the threat to his life from anti-Catholic government forces, provoking one of his friends to joke that he had better always carry some salt in his pocket to ward off all the evil luck he was calling down on himself.

Feast-day 25 October

Persecution and death

He ministered to the Catholics of the area for 10 years before being arrested in 1622 and brought before the Anglican bishop of Chester. However as James I was engaged at that time in pursuing a Spanish marriage for his son, it would therefore have been impolitic for him to appear intolerant to Catholics and Arrowsmith was released along with other imprisoned priests without further incident. In 1624 he joined the Jesuits at the Clerkenwell novitiate in London and resumed his duties as priest.

But his forthright integrity again got him into trouble; he was betrayed to the authorities by a young Catholic named Holden, who was smarting under Arrowsmith's rebuke for his incestuous marriage, and in August 1628 he was brought before Sir Henry Yelverton at Lancaster Assizes and condemned as a priest. The court sentenced him to be hung, drawn and quartered, but he was kept chained for two days without food, constantly taunted to renounce his faith and escape death. He refused to apostatize, and was executed at Lancaster on 28 August. His last words were reputedly 'Bone Jesu'.

Cult

He was beatified by Pope Pius XI in 1929, and in 1970 was canonized by Paul IV as one of the Forty Martyrs of England and Wales. His hand is preserved at St Oswald's church in Ashton-in-Makerfield, near Wigan, and several apparently miraculous cures have been reported there.

Edmund of Abingdon

c.1175 Abingdon —Soissy 1240

Critic of the king

The first Oxford master and the last archbishop of Canterbury to be canonized.

Born in Berkshire on 30 November, Edmund was the eldest son of the wealthy merchant Reginald Rich, who later became a monk. His son was renowned for his piety from an early age; educated at the universities of Oxford and Paris, he returned after graduation to teach art and mathematics at Oxford. Ordained after receiving his doctorate in theology, he went on to teach that subject at Oxford and soon became known for his preaching and personal holiness. In c.1222 he was appointed canon and treasurer of Salisbury cathedral, which was then in the process of construction.

By now his reputation for integrity and articulacy was such that in 1227 Pope Gregory XI commissioned him to preach throughout England in favour of the Sixth Crusade against the Saracens. He had clearly become something of a favourite with the Pope, and in the fraught elections for the archbishopric of Canterbury, in which Gregory rejected three proposed candidates, the position was finally given to Edmund, despite the latter's objections.

Conflict with the king

As archbishop Edmund also became advisor to King Henry III, and successfully performed several diplomatic missions, including arbitration between the king and his nobles in 1234–6 which averted civil war. Although he did not greatly enjoy the administration and diplomacy which came with his new post, Edmund threw himself wholeheartedly into the task of ecclesiastical reform. He gathered around him holy and capable men such as Richard of Chichester, held uncompromisingly to his rights of visitation and resisted the intrusion of court politics into the running of the church, protesting loudly against Henry's appointment of a papal legate for England. His intransigence brought him into conflict with the monastic chapter of Canterbury who, supported by Henry, resisted his authority: in 1238 he excommunicated 17 of the monks of Christ Church, an action condemned by Henry and revoked by the papal legate, Cardinal Otto.

Death and cult

Further disputes arose between Edmund and Henry. The archbishop condemned Henry's practice of leaving sees vacant while collecting their revenue for the crown, and in 1240 he left England again, possibly for the papal court, but died at Soissy, near the Cistercian abbey at Pontigny, where he was buried.

Despite his troubled rule, Edmund's personal goodness and holiness cannot be doubted, and neither too can his good intentions. He left behind a simple but comprehensive programme for spiritual growth, the *Speculum ecclesiae*, originally written for monks, which gained much popularity among the laity in the following centuries. He was canonized in 1246 and for many years his shrine was a popular destination for pilgrims. The cult spread in southern England, with the dedication of St Edmund Hall at Oxford which was believed by many to be built over his tomb. In art he is usually shown praying before the Virgin with a vision of the Christ-child.

> **Feast-day** 16 November

Edward the Confessor

1003 Islip — Westminster 1066

Last of the Old English kings

Called 'the Confessor' because of his extraordinary piety, Edward was also a well-loved and capable ruler.

The son of King Æthelred the Unready and Emma, sister of a Norman duke, the young Edward was educated first in Ely. At the Danish invasion of 1013 he was sent with his mother to Normandy where he remained after the death of his father and his mother's return to England to marry Cnut, now king of England. Their son, Harthacnut, named his half-brother as his successor, and on his death Edward was recalled to England and ascended the throne in 1042. Two years later he married Edith, daughter of the powerful Earl Godwin, whose support had been instrumental in securing his throne but whose Saxon loyalties were later to conflict with Edward's own Norman preferences. The marriage was childless, and was popularly believed to have been unconsummated as a result of Edward's saintly chastity. There is no evidence for this unlikely proposition.

Edward's rule was peaceful and prosperous; he was popular with the poor for his generosity, gentleness and sound government, for example the remission of cripplingly heavy taxes. He faced opposition from nobles with firmness, however. He banished Godwin in 1051, and when he arrived back with an armed fleet from Flanders, met him in person and established acceptable terms to avoid revolt. He also exiled one of Godwin's sons, Tostig, after a rebellion in his earldom of Northumbria, and he is said to have named Godwin's

other son Harold as his successor. Confusion over the rival claims of Harold and William of Normandy led to the Norman Conquest after Edward's death.

Death and cult

Near the end of his life Edward rebuilt St Peter's abbey at Westminster, site of the modern Westminster Abbey in which English monarchs are traditionally coronated and buried. Edward spent vast sums on the Romanesque church, but was too ill to attend its consecration. He was buried there and there his body has remained up to the present day.

There was some hesitation of the part of both Normans and Saxons before Edward's cult was popularly accepted, the Normans claiming rightful inheritance and the Saxons celebrating his lineage. Official canonization came in 1161, and the relics were translated to a shrine in the abbey on 13 October 1163. During the Middle Ages Edward was widely regarded as the patron of England, together with Edmund of East Anglia, until overtaken in popularity by the warrior St George.

It is said that English pilgrims in the Holy Land were met by an old man called John the Apostle, who gave them a ring which he had received from Edward as a beggar near Westminster Cathedral two years earlier and directed them to warn the king of his impending death. This legend is the basis for the popular representations of Edward in art, giving a ring to a pilgrim. From 1163 his principal feast-day has been the date of his translation.

Feast-day 13 October

See illustration on p96.

Egwin

d. Evesham 717

Founder of Evesham

Famed for the legend of the fish who ate the key.

Our earliest information about Egwin comes from an 11th-century *Life*, which may however draw on earlier material, as it claims to do. According to this, Egwin was descended from the Mercian kings and related to the king of Mercia at the time, Ethelred.

Bishop of Worcester

Committed to a religious life from his youth, he was appointed bishop of Worcester in c.692. He seems to have made enemies within his diocese, and this rebellious faction took their case against him before the archbishop of Canterbury and the king, claiming that Egwin had been too severe with his clergy and perhaps making other, unspecified charges. Feelings ran so high that Egwin was obliged to quit his diocese; he set off on a penitential pilgrimage to clear his name at Rome, with his feet locked in chains. He threw the key to his fetters into the river Avon, and it is said that later, when in Rome, he bought a fish at the market and discovered the key inside it. The legend is reminiscent of much popular folklore, with elements drawn from Greek and European traditions. He succeeded in obtaining vindication from the Pope, and returned triumphant to his see.

Leaving aside the fantastic legend of the fish, Egwin's most outstanding achievement was the foundation of Evesham abbey. It was traditionally believed to have been inspired by a vision of the Virgin in a field by the Avon, first seen by a local herdsman. After a refounding in 975, this was to become one of the greatest and most influential Benedictine monasteries in the country. Some scholars have questioned Egwin's role in its foundation, and have suggested that Evesham was in fact one of the seven unidentified monasteries in Mercia founded by Wilfrid.

Death and cult

In c.709 Egwin made a second pilgrimage to Rome in the company of Conrad, King of Mercia, and King Offa of the East Saxons. He died and was buried at Evesham; in c.1077 his relics were taken on an extensive tour around the south of England by the monks there in an attempt to raise money for urgently needed repairs and expansion as the community developed beyond the capacity of the existing buildings. On this journey miracles were reported in every place visited by the saint's relics, and the doubts expressed by Norman ecclesiasts such as Lanfranc as to the authenticity of this dubious Anglo-Saxon cult were effectively silenced. Egwin is usually represented in art with a fish and the key which was discovered inside it.

Feast-day 30 December

Elizabeth of Hungary

1207 Sáros — Marburg 1231

The queen who served beggars

One of Germany's most loved saints, Elizabeth's private tragedy spurred her on to a life of self-sacrifice and unqualified service.

As befitted a daughter of King Andrew II of Hungary, a suitable marriage had been arranged for Elizabeth in her infancy and at the age of four she was taken to live at the court of Landgrave Herman I of Thuringia, as fiancée to his son Louis (later Louis IV). The marriage of political expedience proved to be a love-match too, and when the two were married 10 years later, after the succession of Louis, they appear to have been extraordinarily happy. They lived comfortably at the Wartburg castle near Eisenach with their three children, and Elizabeth was able to give full reign to her impulsively generous nature in building hospitals, giving money to the poor, and caring for the needy and especially for orphans.

A holy grief

Elizabeth's idyllic world was shattered when news came that her husband had died of plague at Otranto while on Crusade with Frederick II. She was distraught with grief, but worse was to come. According to legend, her brother-in-law evicted her from Wartburg, accusing her of mismanaging her husband's estates through wasteful charity. However her move from there came about, it is clear that after making provision for her children Elizabeth enrolled as a Franciscan tertiary at Marburg in Hesse (she had promised Louis she would never marry again) and devoted the rest of her life to the relief of the needy.

She built a hostel near her own humble house and worked tirelessly, spurred on always by the brutal direction of her spiritual advisor Conrad of Marburg, who had learned his brand of spiritual discipline in the inquisition of heretics. The ruthless regime he inflicted upon her is infamous; in addition to the austerities she practised upon herself he forced her to part with the two ladies-in-waiting she had known since childhood, replacing them with harsh companions, and frequently slapped and beat her himself.

Death and cult

Despite his brutality Elizabeth refused an offer to return to Hungary, preferring instead to pour out her life in meeting the needs of others. She spent her time in menial tasks, cleaning and making clothes for the poor and fishing to feed them. Her spirit remained unbowed by Conrad's sadistic treatment (she claimed that she rose after his chastisement like grass in the rain), but her physical condition was so weakened that she died aged only 24. She was canonized soon after by Gregory IX, in 1235, and the following year her relics were translated to the church of St Elizabeth at Marburg. The shrine was a popular destination for pilgrims until it was removed by the Lutheran Philip of Hesse in 1539.

Elizabeth's romantic history captured the imagination of artists, and she is frequently depicted wearing her crown and sheltering or tending beggars.

Feast-day 17 November
Patron saint of bakers, beggars, Sisters of Mercy, charities and lace-makers, invoked against toothache

Elizabeth of Portugal

1271 — Estremoz 1336

The peacemaker

Known as Isabel in Portugal, she sought peace, holiness and justice in a personal and public world of strife.

Named after her grand-aunt Elizabeth of Hungary, Elizabeth was the daughter of King Peter III of Aragon. At the age of only 12 she was married to King Denis of Portugal, and as queen she became known and loved for her piety, social concern and generosity, establishing educational and religious establishments to meet the needs she saw around her. These included a hospital, a hostel for women in need or in danger and an orphanage; in addition she provided shelter for pilgrims and money for alms to the poor. Her own marriage was unhappy: despite Denis's undoubted capabilities as a ruler he was a jealous, unfaithful and inconsiderate husband. They had two children, and Elizabeth was forced to spend much of her time in the trying position of peacemaker between Denis and their rebellious son Alfonso who had attempted an armed coup. She was also called upon to heal dissensions among various other members of her royal family. The task was a delicate one: Elizabeth found herself expelled from court at one stage and exiled to

a fortress when Denis accused her of supporting Alfonso against him.

God's servant

Denis died in 1325 after a long illness, through which Elizabeth nursed him, and at the last he appears to have repented of his treatment of her. With her husband gone, Elizabeth's first thought was to join the order of Poor Clares. She went on pilgrimage to Compostela, but was persuaded instead to become a Franciscan tertiary. She spent the rest of her life in retirement near the Poor Clare convent which she had founded at Coimbra, living simply and devoting herself to serving the needs of the surrounding community.

She performed one last, great service for the cause of peace in the year of her death when her son, now Alfonso IV, led his troops against Alfonso XI of Castile. Elizabeth went onto the battlefield and succeeded in reconciling the two leaders and averting bloodshed, but the effort finally exhausted her and she died soon afterwards on 4 July. Her body was returned to the convent in Coimbra; she was buried there and miracles quickly began to be associated with her tomb. Her local cult was approved by Leo X in 1516, and in 1626 she was canonized by Pope Urban VIII.

Her emblem in art is the rose, either worn in a crown or carried in wintertime, from a legend that the bread she carried would miraculously turn to roses. She is often confused with her more famous namesake, Elizabeth of Hungary; indeed their legends have many points of similarity.

Eloi (Eligius)

c.588 Chaptel — Noyon c.658

The apostle of Flanders

A master-craftsman who was also a beloved bishop, a tireless social reformer and an advisor to kings.

Born near Limoges in Gaul of Gallo-Roman parents, he was apprenticed by his metal-working father to a goldsmith named Abbo, master of the mint at Limoges. Having learnt his trade Eloi worked under the royal treasurer Bobon and gained a name for himself as a goldsmith of exceptional skill who was unusually economical with his materials. This thriftiness attracted the attention of King Clotaire II who took him into his personal service on learning that he had managed to make two exquisite thrones out of the gold allocated for only one. He became master of the mint in Paris and was commissioned by both Clotaire and his successor, Dagobert I, to work on various royal projects such as shrines, crosses, chalices and plaques. In 629 Dagobert selected him as his chief counsellor, and he was entrusted with several important missions of state.

Episcopacy

Naturally Eloi gained great personal wealth from his sudden elevation: this he used to help the needy, free slaves and establish a number of churches and other foundations. In 640 he was ordained as a priest and the following year was consecrated bishop of Noyon and Tournai. He now devoted his prodigious energy and talents to pastoral and evangelistic work, preaching very successfully in Flanders and around Tournai, and working too in Frisia, despite opposition from the pagan leaders. He continued to found monasteries, including those at Noyon, Paris and Solignac. Throughout his life he was regarded with the greatest respect and affection; St Bathild too looked to him for counsel when she was acting as regent in Gaul, and it is probably due to his intervention, at least in part, that the Council of Chaldon passed its decrees on the rights of slaves and the responsibilities of their owners.

Death and cult

He died in his monastery at Noyon, a popular figure whose craftsmanship and holiness alike were revered. No one piece of work can now be identified positively as Eloi's, although many are traditionally attributed to him, including the famous chalice of Chelles which was lost during the French Revolution. His cult became so widespread in the Middle Ages that even Chaucer's Prioress swears 'by St Eloi'. Not surprisingly he was claimed as patron by metalworkers, and goldsmiths in particular; his emblems in art are more frequently a hammer, anvil and horseshoe than the goldsmith's hammer, although this does occur, because of a legend which tells how he detached the leg of a horse in order to shoe it more easily and then restored it to the animal. After his intercession was claimed to have healed the horse of a monk of Noyon, he has been traditionally regarded as a patron of veterinarians and horses. He is occasionally shown, like Dunstan, grasping the Devil's nose with a pair of pincers.

Feast-day 1 December
Patron saint of smiths and metalworkers

Erasmus (Elmo)

d. Formiae c.303

The sailor's friend

Although he is traditionally invoked for protection by sailors, the reason why is far from clear.

Although there is a wealth of legendary accretions, few historical facts are known about this popular saint. He was a bishop of Formiae in the Campagna in Italy and was probably martyred during the persecutions of Diocletian. By confusion with another martyr, one Erasmus of Antioch, his legend claims that he was a Syrian who fled to Mount Lebanon during the persecutions to live as a solitary. His hiding place was discovered and he was brought before the Emperor, beaten, covered in pitch and set ablaze. Miraculously he survived unhurt, and was imprisoned only to be released by an angel and taken to preach in Illyricum. Here he carried on with his work of preaching and teaching. The number of his converts was so great that he was soon discovered anew and underwent more torture. Once again he was delivered by an angel, this time to Formiae, where he died of his wounds.

As Erasmus had proved immune to the various tortures to which he had been subjected in the past, a popular legend developed which claimed that a new and particularly grisly death had been devised for him. The saint was cut open at the stomach and his entrails were wound out while he was still alive. This torture legend is the source of his patronage of those suffering from stomach pains. His relics were supposedly translated to Gaeta when Formiae was attacked by Saracens in 842, and he is invoked as patron there.

St Elmo's fire

His emblem in art is a windlass; this has been variously explained as a symbol of his patronage of sailors, which grew from a legend that he was unafraid of a violent storm, refusing to stop preaching even when a thunderbolt landed beside him, or as the instrument of torture with which his entrails were wound out which was then mistaken for a nautical capstan, whence his patronage of sailors began. The phenomenon of lights which sometimes appear at the mastheads of ships after a storm, caused by electrical discharge, was known as St Elmo's fire by Neapolitan sailors, since it was believed to be a sign of the saint's protection through the time of danger.

Cult

Erasmus's cult was widespread throughout Europe, with hagiographers embellishing the legend throughout the Middle Ages, and he was named as one of the Fourteen Holy Helpers in the 15th century.

Feast-day 2 June
Patron saint of sailors, invoked against birth-pains, colic and danger at sea

---

Ethelbert

c.560 — Canterbury 616

The first Christian Anglo-Saxon king

The influential and dynamic king of Kent, whose cooperation made possible the work of Augustine at Canterbury.

Although he had actually been defeated by the Wessex king Ceawlin at the battle of Wimbledon in 568, Ethelbert succeeded in retaining and even expanding his power in Kent and the surrounding areas, and his overlordship was recognized to some degree by most of the country below the Humber. When Augustine and his monks landed on Kentish soil in 597, they were greeted at Thanet by Ethelbert and his Frankish wife Bertha, who was herself a Christian. Bertha had brought with her to England her chaplain Liudhard, but despite the claims of some legends they seem to have played little part in the conversion of their people. Ethelbert was at first guarded in his reception of the missionaries; according to Bede he insisted that a conference take place in the open air for fear of witchcraft.

On hearing their message for the first time he rejected it for himself, preferring to keep loyal to the pagan faith of his ancestors, but as a gesture of goodwill in recognition of their sincerity he offered them a house at Canterbury, which became the centre for their preaching there. Even allowing for exaggeration, it appears that many of his subjects were actually converted before their king: Gregory the Great wrote a letter in 601 congratulating and encouraging Ethelbert on his conversion but this was after a letter to Eulogius of Alexandria in which he declared that 10 000 English converts had been made.

The Christian king

From now on Ethelbert committed himself to sharing in the work of the missionaries, helping to found Christ Church abbey (later the cathedral) and the monastery of St Peter and St Paul (later St Augustine's) at Canterbury, and the church of St Andrew at Rochester, but he believed strongly in the necessity of personal conviction and never tried to impose his new faith on his subjects. He is said to have been instrumental in bringing about the conversion of Sabert, king of the East Saxons, and building the first church of St Paul in London on his land. Aided by Augustine, Ethelbert wrote the earliest extant Anglo-Saxon code of law which includes measures to protect clergy and churches by demanding high compensation for any damage caused to them.

Death and cult

He died on 24 February and was buried in a chapel in his monastery of St Peter and St Paul. Although it seems likely that a local cult began soon after his death, he is only listed on calendars from the 13th century, and since 24 February is the feast day of St Matthias, he is usually listed on 25 February.

Feast-day 25 February

Etheldreda (Audrey)

c.630 Exning — Ely 679

Queen and abbess

After two unsuccessful marriages,

she found brief happiness

as a nun.

The five sisters born to Anna, King of the East Angles in Suffolk, are all honoured as saints: Etheldreda, Sexburga, Erconwald, Ethelburga and Withburga. Probably the most famous however is Etheldreda, who commands an astonishing number of ancient dedications and calendars and who is celebrated in a lengthy poem by the Venerable Bede.

As a young girl she was married to Prince Tonbert of the Gryvii but it appears that the marriage, which lasted only three years, was never consummated. After Tonbert's early death Etheldreda spent five years in solitude on the island of Ely, which had been her dowry. Another match was arranged for her in 660, a politically advantageous union with the 15-year-old king of Northumbria, Egfrith. Egfrith agreed that Etheldreda might retain her virginity, but after 12 years he grew weary of the brother–sister relationship and demanded from his wife normal conjugal relations. Etheldreda sought the advice of St Wilfrid, bishop of Northumbria, who approved her decision, and with the reluctant consent of Egfrith the marriage was dissolved and in 672 Etheldreda entered the convent at Coldingham under the direction of her aunt, Ebbe. The next year she founded a double monastery at Ely, on the site of the present-day cathedral, and restored the old church there which had been destroyed by pagan Mercians.

Death and cult

Etheldreda spent the remaining seven years of her life in the monastery, living a life of penance, austerity and prayer. Other members of her family joined her there, and after her death she was succeeded by her sister Sexburga. Etheldreda died of a plague which struck down several other nuns in the community; she developed a tumour on her neck which she claimed was punishment for her younger, more frivolous days when she had adorned herself with necklaces.

She was buried at Ely, and it was reported that her body was discovered, 17 years later, to be incorrupt and the tumour on her neck healed. Her relics were translated into a shrine by Sexburga in 695, which soon became a popular centre for pilgrimage with many miracles attributed to her intercession as her cult developed.

The shrine was destroyed at the Reformation but St Etheldreda's church in London claims to possess some relics, and her hand, discovered near Arundel in 1811 and thought to have been hidden by a recusant, is claimed by St Etheldreda's Roman Catholic church in Ely. In art she is depicted crowned, holding a staff which may be budding and sometimes a book. The word 'tawdry', meaning cheap and showy, and the obsolete 'tawdry-lace', which referred to a silk necktie, is a corruption of 'St Audrey'. This is said by some to refer to the frivolous necklaces on which Etheldreda blamed her tumour, but it may simply refer to the cheap jewellery sold at St Audrey's fair in Ely.

Feast-day 23 June
Patron saint of Cambridge University

Ethelwold

c.912 Winchester — Beddington 984

'The Father of monks'

Pioneer of monastic reform together with his friend St Dunstan, whose unfailing energy he shared, he was known as 'son of thunder'.

The young Ethelwold served at the court of King Athelstan until his ordination by St Alphege the Bald, on the same day as that of his friend from the court, Dunstan. He decided after a few years to join Dunstan in his campaign to revive monasticism in England and was made prior of the Benedictine monastery in Glastonbury under Dunstan. Intrigued by what he had heard of Cluny's reforms in France, Ethelwold asked permission to visit the Continent but instead, in c.954, he was given the charge of re-establishing the derelict monastery of Abingdon in Berkshire. He took monks from Glastonbury to revive the community and set about building a new church there, contenting himself with sending his disciple Osgar to study at Fleury.

Revival and reform

During the exile of Dunstan in c.956, Ethelwold took his place as the key figure in the movement of monastic revival and upheld his friend's ideals in his role as tutor to the next king, Edgar. In 963 Ethelwold was consecrated bishop of Winchester and with the help of Edgar set about expelling all the secular clerics from the cathedral and Newminster, replacing them with Benedictine monks. The principle of a monastic cathedral, so characteristic of the English reforms, survived until the 16th century. Again with the support of the king he went on to revive other monasteries, refounding Etheldreda's monastery at Ely as an institution for monks only, and founding new ones at Peterborough and Thorney.

Capable leader

Ethelwold was a capable and practical leader who involved himself directly in the work of expansion; he worked up the scaffolding during the rebuilding of Abingdon until he fell off and broke his ribs and he also provided an aqueduct for the city. The monasteries which he revived became noted especially for the new and beautiful style of illumination produced there, and the vernacular work begun at Winchester provided reliable and responsible translations of Latin works such as the Rule of Benedict for non-monastic clerics. He was an austere and challenging prior and bishop, called 'Boanerges' (son of thunder) by one of his scribes, who demanded full commitment from his monks and was intractable in the face of opposition.

Death

He died on 1 August, four years after the consecration of his cathedral at Winchester, leaving a legacy of thriving monasteries that were to fill the bishoprics of England for the next century. It was probably he who compiled the *Regularis concordia* in c.970 to establish smooth practical running of the new monasteries which cemented the links between church and state.

Feast-day 1 August

Eusebius of Vercelli

c.283 Sardinia — Vercelli 371

Bishop of Vercelli

A staunch opponent with Athanasius of the Arian heresy, he suffered greatly for his intractable orthodoxy.

When Eusebius was still an infant his father was martyred for his Christian faith; the child's mother brought him from his native Sardinia to Rome to receive an education. After his ordination he worked in Piedmont as a lecturer and then in Vercelli, where he was made bishop in c.340. He radically reformed the church, becoming the first western bishop to live in a quasi-monastic community with his clergy in a way later adopted by Augustine and the canons regular. This has led some to regard him as co-founder with Augustine of the Austin canons.

Disgrace and exile

In 354 he was sent by Pope Liberius to request that Emperor Constantius call a council, the subject of which was to be an attempt to resolve the ongoing conflict between Catholics and Arians. The conference was convened in Milan the following year, and Eusebius caused an uproar by refusing to sign a condemnation of Athanasius and demanding that all those present signal their acceptance of the Nicene Creed before proceeding further to consider Athanasius's case. He remained staunch in the face of the emperor's threats of execution, avowing that secular power had no part in ecclesiastical affairs, and was finally exiled in disgrace to Palestine, in the custody of the Arian bishop Patrophilus.

It appears that Eusebius underwent great humiliation and maltreatment from his jailers, on one occasion staging a four-day hunger strike in protest at their treatment of him. He was moved to Cappadocia and Egypt, maintaining throughout his unshakeable opposition to the heresy, and finally returned to Vercelli after the death of Constantius in 361 when Julian the Apostate allowed all exiled bishops to return to their sees.

Further travels

From there he journeyed east yet again, first to Alexandria to a council attended by Athanasius and from there on to Antioch, where he tried unsuccessfully to heal a breach in the church between the followers of St Eustathius and those of Bishop Meletius over the contested bishopric. On his journey home he visited churches throughout Illyricum, encouraging and teaching, and arrived back at Vercelli in 363.

Final years and death

Even in his last years Eusebius remained energetically opposed to Arianism, and worked together with St Hilary of Poitiers to defeat the pronouncements of the Arian bishop of Milan, Auxentius. Eusebius is also reputed to be one of the authors of the firmly orthodox Athanasian Creed. He died peacefully in Vercelli on 1 August, but because he underwent such sufferings during his lifetime he is revered as a martyr in the Roman calendar. A manuscript of the Latin Gospels at Vercelli called the *Codex Vercellensis*, believed to be the oldest of its kind in existence, is attributed to his hand, and several of his letters survive to bear testimony to his character and scholarship.

Feast-day 2 August

Fiacre (Fiachrach)

d. Breuil c.670

The gardener saint

Originally more popular in France than in his native Ireland, his protection and patronage have been claimed by many different groups.

Originally a monk at Kilfiachra, Ireland, Fiacre chose voluntary exile on the Continent and travelled to France, where he was welcomed by the bishop of Meaux, St Faro. Faro granted him land for a hermitage at nearby Breuil where he built a hospice for travellers, now the site of the town of Saint-Fiacre-en-Brie.

Life at Breuil

Fiacre was renowned especially for his skill in horticulture, feeding his visitors with marvellous home-grown vegetables, and is regarded as the patron saint of gardeners. The legends of his life record that when he was given land by Faro, the bishop offered him as much land as he could turn in a day. Instead of using a conventional plough, Fiacre used only the tip of his staff to furrow the ground. On this land he then laboured to clear away the wild briars and bushes, and in addition to his cell and hospice, he cultivated a garden for himself. He was also something of a misogynist, refusing to allow women to enter his enclosure, and there are legends detailing the punishment visited on females who disobeyed this command even after his death. This may be the reason for his special patronage of those suffering from venereal diseases.

Death and cult

Some time after his death his relics were translated to a shrine in the cathedral at Meaux, which was a popular centre for pilgrimage in the 17th and 18th centuries in particular. Many miracles of healing were reported, including that of King Louis XIII, which Anne of Austria attributed to Fiacre's intercession. She visited his shrine on pilgrimage in 1641. He became known especially for his efficacy in the cure of haemorrhoids and fistula, which became known as 'St Fiacre's evil'. Outside the Hôtel Saint Fiacre in Paris, possibly so-named because of its position at the start of the pilgrim's route to Meaux, the first horse-drawn carriages to be offered for hire were situated in 1620. These carriages were hence known as *fiacres*, and since then the word, meaning 'taxi', has become a part of the French language.

It should be remembered that despite these somewhat quirky accretions to his legend, Fiacre was revered both during his life and after his death as an exceptionally holy, wise and above all charitable saint, whose popularity reached England and Ireland by the late medieval period. In art he is usually shown carrying a spade, sometimes with a basket of vegetables beside him, blessing the sick and surrounded by pilgrims.

> **Feast-day** 30 August
> Patron saint of gardeners, florists and taxi-drivers, invoked against fistula, haemorrhoids, venereal disease and sterility

Fillan

d. c.777

Abbot and hermit

The saint to whom Robert the Bruce attributed his victory at the battle of Bannockburn.

Fillan's father was Feriach, a Munster prince, and his uncle was Comgan, the Irish chieftain who was exiled to Scotland and settled with his sister St Kentigerna (Fillan's mother) in Lochalsh, where he founded a small monastery. He became a monk as a youth and spent some years as a hermit at Pittenweem, near St Andrews in Fife, before being elected abbot of a monastery on Holy Loch in Argyll. Although he held the post for several years, Fillan yearned to resume his solitary life, so he eventually resigned the abbacy and retired to Upper Glendochart (later known as Strathfillan) in Perthshire. Several place names in the district testify to his influence (although it should be noted that St Fillans on Loch Earn is named after another, earlier saint, Fillan the leper); he built a church near his hermitage and became renowned as a miracle-worker, a wise and mysterious holy man.

Picturesque legends grew up around his name, including one which reported that a wolf which killed the ox used by Fillan to transport building materials for a church was miraculously persuaded by the prayers of the saint to take the ox's place, allowing Fillan to continue with his construction.

Death and cult

Fillan died and was buried at Strathfillan. The popularity and early existence of his cult is attested by his inclusion in many Scottish and Irish martyrologies, and there is a famous story that Robert the Bruce attributed his victory at Bannockburn to the intercession of St Fillan, obtained by the relic of the saint's arm which he carried with him. In acknowledgement of the saint's part in his military success, Robert the Bruce restored the monastery at Strathfillan as an Augustinian priory.

One peculiar practice associated with the saint which continued until the beginning of the last century was that of attributing cures of the mentally ill to him: the sufferers were plunged into the pool of Strathfillan and then bound and left for the night among the ruins of Fillan's church. If in the morning they were found to be untied, they were believed to be cured. The square bronze bell and the bronze head of a pastoral staff (or Quigrich) believed to be his still survive, and can be seen in The National Museum of Scotland in Edinburgh.

Feast-day 9 January

Finbar (Barr)

c.560 Lisnacaheragh — Cloyne c.610 or 630

Founder of Cork

A mysterious and poetic Irish saint, whose widespread fame seems to have developed only after his death.

An illegitimate child of the clan of Ui Briuin Ratha, whose father was a metal worker and mother of royal extraction, Finbar was born in Co Cork, baptized at Lochan and educated by monks at Kilmacahil, Kilkenny. It was here that he received his nickname Fionnbharr, meaning 'white-head'. He is said to have journeyed to Rome on pilgrimage with several of the monks, visiting St David in South Wales on the way back home, and legend has it that when the Pope wanted to consecrate him as bishop on a subsequent trip to Rome he was divinely prevented, and Finbar instead received his consecration from heaven.

On returning to Ireland he lived for some years as a hermit by lake Gougane Barra, quickly attracting a number of followers and establishing the monastery of Etargabail which was to become a school renowned throughout Ireland. His more famous foundation however was that which began as a monastery on the river Lee, and which developed into the city of Cork. Finbar is traditionally believed to have been consecrated as the first bishop of Cork in c.600, and is thought to have died at Cloyne between 10 and 30 years later. His body was removed to Cork for burial.

Cult

Veneration for Finbar was at first only local, but a later Scottish cult developed, partly due to confusion with another Finbar (of Moville) and partly from the later missionary activity of monks from Cork. This latter is the most likely explanation for the naming and patronage of the island of Barra, off the west coast of Scotland.

Many fantastic miracles have been accredited to Finbar, perhaps the most poetic claim being that he crossed the Irish sea on horseback. It was said that for two weeks after his death the sun refused to set at Cloyne. Although he is venerated throughout Ireland and Scotland, and especially in Cork, the true centre of devotion to Finbar is his monastery at Gougane Barra.

Feast-day 25 September
Patron saint of Barra in Scotland and Cork, Ireland

Finnian

Leinster — Clonard c.549

The teacher of Irish saints

Founder of the renowned monastery and school at Clonard, which produced such influential spiritual leaders as St Columba of Iona.

Born and educated in Co Carlow, Ireland, Finnian spent much time in the monasteries of Wales studying under Saints Cadoc and Gildas, and it was in Wales that he took his vows as a monk. On returning to Ireland he founded several monasteries, including those at Aghowle in Co Wicklow and Mugna Sulcain, following the traditional monastic principles of his Welsh teachers. The most significant of these foundations was Clonard near Kinnegad in Co Meath, which with its central location drew thousands of followers to study there. The emphasis was on study of Scripture and the monastic form Welsh, that is originally Eastern: Finnian himself was known as the 'Master'.

Among the great saints and ecclesiasts to emerge from this hothouse of religious learning were St Columba of Iona and St Brendan the Voyager. It is traditionally believed that the 'Master' supervised the instruction of the Twelve Apostles of Ireland (of whom Columba, Brendan the Navigator and Canice are probably the most

famous) but the chronology of several of them, who are believed to antedate Finnian himself, makes this unlikely. It is certainly true however that Clonard proved the impetus for a wave of enthusiasm for monasticism throughout Ireland.

Death and cult

Finnian died on 12 December, a victim of the 'yellow plague' that was sweeping Ireland at the time and he was regarded by many, including the writer of his 10th-century *Life*, as a sort of sacrificial, redeeming figure. His relics remained in a shrine there until it was destroyed in 887. The monastery at Clonard declined as it fell under the power of the north of Ireland and the clan Ui Niall, and shared its abbacy with Kildare or Clonmacnoise. It later became a house of canons regular, although they retained the Office of St Finnian.

Although he is widely regarded as a bishop there is no clear evidence that Finnian was in fact ordained. He is probably the author of the penitential traditionally ascribed to him; written sometime after c.525 it is the oldest surviving manuscript of its kind, and draws inspiration from both Irish and Welsh traditions. It helped to further the principles of penitence, discipline and Bible study on which the foundation at Clonard was based.

Feast-day 12 December

Frances of Rome

1384 Rome — Rome 1440

The pious matron

Frances's vision was of a caring community operating within, not apart from, society.

Born of wealthy Christian parents in the Trastevere, Francesca Romera wanted to become a nun even as a child. Instead, at the age of 13, she complied with the wishes of her parents and married Lorenzo Ponziani. Once married she devoted herself to wifely duties and, together with Vanozza, the wife of her husband's brother, to charitable works within the city. Events in Rome gave ample scope for her compassionate nature; recurrent epidemics of plague and the outbreak of civil war meant that Frances and Vanozza were continually kept busy in the city's hospitals and among its poor.

When Ladislas of Naples captured Rome in 1408, the Ponzianos and their property were under threat, for they were known to be strong supporters of the Pope. Lorenzo was forced to flee and Frances took on the running of the entire household, in addition to her charitable work which she refused to neglect. Lorenzo returned in 1414, after the Ponziani property had sustained serious damage, his health destroyed, and Frances now devoted herself to nursing him as well as performing all her other duties. She remained cheerful in the face of other domestic tragedies; her son Evangelist had died in the plague of 1401 and his sister Agnes died 2 years later.

The foundation

By now Frances's example had attracted a number of Roman matrons to follow her example of leading a charitable life within society rather than removed from it in a religious community. In 1425, Frances organized her followers into a society which, while not taking vows, was based on the Rule of St Benedict. First called the Oblates of Mary, they later become known as the Oblates of Tor de Specchi, a more systematized community in association with the Benedictines of Mount Oliveto.

Lorenzo died in 1436; in their 40 years of marriage it was claimed that the couple had never quarrelled. Frances now entered the community she had established, was appointed superior, and lived in holiness and austerity there for the rest of her life. Her biographers attributed many mystical experiences and revelations to her, some more dubious than others. The most famous of all of these was her vision of her guardian angel, said to have guided her for 23 years, invisible to everybody else. She was a well-loved and well-respected figure by the time of her death, commanding the affection of the poorest in Rome as well as that of Pope Eugenius IV.

Cult

Frances was buried in what was at the time the church of Santa Maria Nuova; it has since become known as Santa Francesca Romana, and her relics remain there today. The Ponziani house in which Frances worked still survives as a centre for pilgrimage, now called Casa degli Esercizi Pii. She was canonized in 1608 by Paul V and named patroness of motorists by Pope Pius XI, presumably because of her guardian angel.

Frances Xavier Cabrini

1850 Sant' Angelo Lodigiono — Chicago 1917

The first American citizen to be canonized

The Italian immigrants in America were desperately in need of her vision and her compassion.

Francesca Maria (she later added the 'Xavier' in honour of Francis's missionary zeal) was born on 15 July, the thirteenth and last child of an Italian farmer. She was brought up strictly, much under the influence of her elder sister Rosa, and educated like her to become a schoolteacher, but in 1870 she was orphaned and turned instead to the religious life. After two years, during which time she qualified as a teacher, Frances applied to two convents, only to be rejected by both on the grounds of poor health.

Her potential was recognized however by the local parish priest of Codogno, who appointed her to teach in and reorganize a badly-managed orphanage there, the House of Providence. The foundress, Antonio Tondini, who was violently opposed to any interference, made life almost impossible for Frances and the pupils. In 1880 Antonio Tondini was excommunicated and the orphanage dissolved.

Frances left with seven of her pupils to found the Missionary Sisters of the Sacred Heart, which flourished eventually in an abandoned Franciscan friary at Codogno to become an order with houses throughout Northern Italy.

America

Frances visited Rome to obtain papal approval for her foundation, and she also tried to persuade the Pope to grant her strong desire to become a missionary to China. He persuaded her in a very different direction, however, towards the Italian immigrants in New York, demoralized and disillusioned in overcrowded squalor with few churches serving their needs. In 1889, conquering her childhood fear of water, Frances sailed for America with six sisters to found an orphanage there at the invitation of Archbishop Corrigan. Despite the setbacks and poor organization they encountered on landing, Frances succeeded in establishing the orphanage and moved it to West Park on the Hudson river, which became the central house of her American congregation. For over 25 years she travelled throughout the Americas and Europe; by the time of her death there were 67 houses devoted to nursing, care of orphans and education. The most famous is the Columbus hospital in New York, so named because its foundation in 1892 coincided with the fourth centenary of Columbus's discovery of the New World.

Death and cult

In 1907 the constitution of the order received final approval from the Holy See, and Mother Cabrini herself took American citizenship. She was a difficult character, intolerant of Protestants, so morally rigid that she refused to allow illegitimate children in her foundations, and she could be an inflexible businesswoman, but her scope of vision and accomplishment is outstanding. She died in the Columbus hospital in Chicago, alone and waiting for lunch, and was buried at Mother Cabrini High School in New York. In 1946 under Pius XII she became the first American citizen to be canonized; Pius also named her patroness of immigrants in 1950.

Feast-day 13 November
Patroness of immigrants

Francis Borgia

1510 Gandia — Rome 1572

Second founder of the Jesuits

An outstandingly holy member of an infamously evil family.

Francis's great-grandfather was the notorious Pope Alexander VI, his father was a duke in Valencia and his mother, Juana of Aragon, was the daughter of the illegitimate son of King Ferdinand V of Aragon. In his youth Francis was privately tutored to prepare him for entering into the emperor's court at the age of 18, where he became Marquis of Lombay. The following year, 1529, he married Eleanor de Castra, who was to bear his eight children, and was appointed viceroy of Catalonia by Charles V after 10 more years as advisor to the emperor.

After the death of his father in 1543, Francis succeeded him as duke of Gandia, but he faced opposition from leaders whose corruptions he had exposed and was obliged to withdraw to his private estate for some time. For the next few years he served as master of the household to Prince Philip.

A new Jesuit

After the death of his wife in 1546, Francis began to pursue the religious vocation which had attracted him all his life. He enrolled with the Jesuits in 1548 and set about providing for his children and handing his estates over to his heirs. This done, he was ordained as a priest. Francis had joined the society secretly and always attempted to conceal his influential connections, so that he rose on account of intrinsic merit. His sermons in Spain and Portugal attracted enormous crowds of listeners, and as commissary general in Spain (appointed by Ignatius Loyola himself) he founded many schools, seminaries and colleges, raising the profile of the order considerably. In keeping with his new vocation, Francis made strenuous attempts to reduce his corpulent girth by austerity; he had limited success and ruefully confessed that he found the attempt very difficult.

In 1564 he was summoned to Rome, and four years later was appointed father-general of the Jesuits. His rule was short but very effective and some have called him the second founder of the order. The Roman College (later the Gregorian University) was established with his support and direction, he expanded the society's number and the extent of its missionary work, drew up a revised set of rules, established the province in Poland and missions in America, and built St Andrews and the Gesù church in Rome. When plague swept Rome in 1566, Francis organized his priests for the work of caring for the sick and raised money to help the victims.

Death and cult

Francis died after returning from an exhilarating but exhausting preaching tour of Spain, France and Portugal in the company of the papal ambassador, Cardinal Bonelli. He is said to have spent his last moments blessing all his children and grandchildren by name. Canonization followed in 1671 and in iconography the saint's emblem is a skull crowned with the emperor's diadem.

Feast-day 10 October

Francis of Assisi

1181 Assisi — Assisi 1226

'Il Poverello'

Best-known today as an animal lover, the historical Francis was the impetuous and idealistic founder of one of the most influential monastic orders.

While Pietro di Bernadone, a wealthy silk trader from Assisi, was away from home on business in France his wife gave birth to a son whom she christened Giovanni. On his return, the boy's father insisted that he be renamed Francesco, 'the French one', struck by the coincidence that he had been in France at the time of the boy's birth and that his mother was from Provence.

Conversion

The young Francis followed his father into business, spending his spare time in hedonistic extravagance until his capture as a prisoner of war in 1202, when fighting against the Perugians. He was held for a year, and soon after his release underwent a long period of serious illness: the experience was a sobering one. In 1205 he returned to the wars, and on his return to Assisi the young man, already displaying a more serious and spiritual aspect, entered the run-down church of San Damiano. As he prayed, he saw a vision of Christ speaking to him, saying 'Repair my home, which is falling into disrepair'. Ever literally-minded, Francis began to raise the money to pay for the rebuilding of San Damiano by selling a bale of cloth from his father's warehouse. A fiery conflict ensued between father and son, which ended only when Francis dramatically renounced his inheritance, throwing down even the clothes he was wearing, and left empty-handed to espouse 'Lady Poverty'.

Begging around the town he raised enough money to complete the rebuilding of San Damiano, and lived otherwise as a homeless pilgrim, owning nothing, caring for the sick and always preaching. Within a few years he had attracted several followers; they settled at the Portincula chapel, near a leper colony in Assisi, forming a community dedicated to poverty and upholding Catholic orthodoxy. From there they preached throughout the area and gradually won favour. Their emphasis on the joy of poverty was refreshing and challenging, as was the sense of community life and interdependence. The brothers studied little as they did not even own books; simplicity rather than learning was the concern of the new community. They were known as the Friars Minor, an indication of their humility. The cathedral canon, Peter of Cattaneo, heard Francis's vows on 16 April 1209, and the community became officially known as the Franciscan order. Francis's simple Rule was unofficially approved by Pope Innocent III the next year.

Development of the order

By 1212, Francis felt that the time had come to extend his missionary activity. He founded the Poor Clares with St Clare, a community of women living by his Rule, and then he headed east. His aim was to convert the Saracens, but he was thwarted by shipwreck on his first attempt. He tried again the following year, but fell seriously ill in Spain and was forced to return to Italy. Finally, in 1219, he sailed east with a small group of friars to Palestine and Egypt, meeting with Sultan Malek al-Kamil in the besieged town of Damietta. The Sultan, although greatly impressed by Francis, remained unconverted; Francis returned after a time of pilgrimage in the Holy Land, disappointed by his failure and disillusioned by the Crusaders whom he had seen to be debauched adventurers rather than holy warriors.

By now the number of monks had grown to almost uncontrollable proportions, with foundations beyond Italy and movements to mitigate the harshness of the original, over-simple rule. In an attempt to organize his order more effectively Francis called the first General Chapter at the Portincula in 1219, which was attended by 5000 friars, with 500 more clamouring for admission. Recognizing his weakness as an administrator, Francis resigned as head of the order, having appointed Cardinal Ugolino to protect his ideals, and was succeeded by Brother Elias of Cortona. In order to formalize and contain the concessions which he disliked but for which he recognized the necessity, he drafted two new, more detailed and practical rules, both of which still survive. The second was submitted to Pope Honorius III and received his approval in 1223: it is still in use today. In addition he formulated guidelines for Tertiaries, lay men and women who wished to live by the principles of the order without entering the monastic life. In 1223 he preached before the Sultan in Egypt, who was so impressed that he promised to improve the conditions of his Christian prisoners and granted Francis and his followers the privilege of the Guardians of the Holy Sepulchre.

Later life and death

Many of Francis's most famous doings belong to the last period of his life, after his official leadership of the Franciscans. He built the first Christmas crib at Grecchia in 1223, beginning a custom still celebrated across the Christian world. Even more famous perhaps was his experience of the stigmata while praying on Mount La Verna in 1224, wounds on his body corresponding to those inflicted on Christ in his Passion; these were said to be visible until his death, although Francis usually kept them covered. His last years were marked by blindness and by intense pain, both from illness and from the attempts of doctors to cure him.

He died at the age of 45 at the Portincula, and was canonized only two years later by Pope Gregory IX, the former Cardinal Ugolino. Buried at San Giorgio in Assissi, Francis's relics were translated to the New Basilica specially built by Elias in 1230 which was later decorated with frescoes by Giotto. His remains now lie in a modest shrine, built in 1931, which is a centre for worldwide pilgrimage.

Cult and influence

The Franciscans became more organized and developed their intellectual influence under Bonaventure and other reformers, and became a unique force for reform and evangelism throughout Europe. The order was in some senses a victim of its own success; the developing movements of reform and scholarship within its ranks tended to compromise the original simplicity of Francis's ideals, especially his strictures on absolute poverty. Various factions developed over the next few centuries, for example the Observants, who were set apart from the Conventuals in 1517 by Leo X, held more strictly to the poverty ethic than their brothers. Francis's regret for the increasing complexity of his order is evident in the wistful tone of his *Testament.*

Francis himself has always been an enormously popular saint, loved for his austerely attractive poverty, his dramatic life story and his legendary affinity with nature. He is a favourite with artists, usually shown as a small Franciscan, bearded and bearing the stigmata, in any one of a number of scenes from his life: throwing off his clothes before his father and marrying Lady Poverty, surrounded by animals and birds, together with St Clare, St Dominic and the Virgin, or contemplating a skull. He has been popularly adopted as the patron of all animal lovers, which to some extent is a distortion of his concerns, and in 1980 was named patron saint of ecology.

> **Feast-day** 12 August
> Patron saint of merchants, animals, animal welfare societies and ecology

See illustrations on following page and p162.

St Francis *blesses the birds and commands them to be silent, by Giotto di Bondone. Upper Church of St Francis, Assisi.*

Francis of Paola

1416 Paola — Plessis 1507

Founder of the Minim Friars

Humility and austerity were the hallmarks of Francis's order.

Born of pious, poor parents in Calabria, the 13-year-old Francis spent a year living and studying at the Franciscan friary of San Marco at Paola before leaving on pilgrimage to Assisi and Rome. On his return at the age of 15, he became a hermit near Paola, living in a cave which overlooked the sea.

Minim Friars

In 1436, after five years of isolation, his reputation attracted two followers and the neighbourhood folk built three cells and a chapel for the small community. It was the beginning of the Minim Friars, so-called out of humility; soon others joined them and a monastery was built on the site. Francis drew up the Rule for his order, with its emphasis on penance, humility and works of charity, and a vow of abstinence from meat. It was an austere redirection of the Franciscan ideal, and it attracted many adherents. Learning was not generally considered important, and each community usually included no more than one priest. Francis also provided guidelines for nuns and tertiaries. His order received approval from the Holy See in 1474 and communities quickly developed throughout Europe, although none were founded

in Britain. They were originally known as the hermits of St Francis of Assisi, but in 1492 Francis directed that their name be changed as a sign of their humility.

Later life

Even in his lifetime, Francis was known for miracle-working and prophecy and was credited with the gift of supernatural insight. As Louis VI of France lay on his deathbed, he asked for Francis, convinced that his only hope of cure lay with this holy man. Francis arrived in France, summoned by Pope Sixtus II, and although he did not heal Louis he comforted him and prepared him for death in such a way that he won the lasting friendship of Louis's son, Charles VIII. He remained in France for the last 25 years of his life on friendly terms with the court: both Charles and Louis XII endowed monasteries for his order, and Francis lived and died at Plessis-les-Tours, a monastery built for him by Charles. He repaid his royal benefactors by working in the cause of peace, helping reconcile both Britain and Spain to France.

Cult

Many of the miracles attributed to Francis were connected with the sea, most famously the story that he once used his cloak as a boat. Needing to cross the Straits of Messina, Francis was unable to find a boat. Nothing daunted, he laid his cloak on the sea, tied one end to his staff to serve as a sail, and took his companions safely to Sicily. He was therefore named patron of seafarers in 1943. In art he is shown with the word 'charitas', sometimes levitated above a crowd or holding a skull and discipline, or scourge. He is also depicted sailing on his cloak.

> **Feast-day** 2 April
> Patron saint of sailors, invoked against plague and sterility

Francis of Sales

1567 Thorens — Lyons 1622

Jesuit and bishop

An intelligent and articulate proponent of reform and sound doctrine.

The eldest son of the Seigneur de Nouvelles, Francis was born in the family castle in Savoy on 21 August and christened Francis Bonaventure. He was privately educated in Annecy, then at Clermont, a Jesuit college in Paris. In 1588 he went on to study rhetoric, philosophy and theology at the University of Padua, where he became a doctor of law in 1591. The future seemed bright: he was faced with the prospect of a dazzling career, the offer of senatorship, a highly desirable marriage and the respect and envy of all Savoy. Francis however had decided to become a priest, and despite strong opposition from his family he was ordained in 1593 and became provost of Geneva. His education equipped him to be a memorable preacher, and he became known also for his works of charity to the poor.

His first mission as a priest was in the Chablais, attempting to convert the strongly Calvinistic people there back to Catholicism. He was frequently under attack and in physical danger, but by patient, compassionate preaching he succeeded in making many new converts and restoring many lapsed Catholics to their original faith.

Bishop of Geneva

In 1599 he was appointed coadjutor to the Bishop of Geneva, and, despite his initial reluctance, succeeded to the see in 1602. As bishop he was a leading figure in the Counter-Reformation movement, famed for his simple, straightforward preaching, his administrative prowess and his untiring intellect. Francis involved himself personally with the teaching of catechisms, and he also founded many excellent schools. It was during this time that he befriended Jane Frances de Chantal, a widow; he became her spiritual advisor and, guided by him, she founded the Order of the Visitation in 1610, usually known as the Visitandines.

Death and cult

It was in a Visitandine convent in Lyons that Francis died 12 years later on 28 December. His body was translated to Annecy the following month, and into a new shrine there in 1912. Canonized in 1665 by Pope Alexander VII and declared a Doctor of the Church in 1577, Francis was named patron saint of writers in 1923 for his example of persuasive and reasonable Christian writings. Two of his works are still very popular today: his *Treatise on the love of God* and *Introduction to the devout life*, the first guide to piety to be written for laymen. It grew out of advice and instruction which he had written privately to a cousin, Mme de Chamoisy, which he was later persuaded to publish. Many of his letters to Mme de Chantal also survive. He is immediately recognizable in art by his bald head and long beard; dressed in Franciscan robes and often holding a book he is also shown with a heart pierced by a crown of thorns, or occasionally with a picture of the Virgin.

Feast-day 24 January
Patron saint of writers, editors and journalists

Francis Xavier

1506 Navarre — San-chian 1552

Apostle to the Indies

After St Paul, Francis is probably the greatest single missionary in the Catholic Church's history.

Born of a wealthy Spanish Basque family, Francis left home to study at the University of Paris. While he was there he met and befriended Ignatius Loyola, and with five others they took monastic vows together at Montmartre in 1534, becoming the first Jesuits, and were ordained together as priests three years later in Venice.

Mission to Asia

Francis visited Rome in 1538 and two years later, in the year that the Pope granted official approval to the Society of Jesus, he was sent along with Fr Simon Rodriguez to the East Indies, the first of countless Jesuit missionaries. The voyage took 13 months; when Francis finally arrived he made his base at Goa and set about reforming the shabby morality of Portuguese Catholics there, who were notorious for cruelty and laxness. Having worked for several months to redeem the image of Christianity in the East, he spent the next seven years living alongside the peasants in India, Ceylon and Malaysia. He shared their lifestyle and was hugely successful in evangelizing the lower castes, but made little impact on the Brahmins. His most notable impact was among the Paravas of southern India, who clung tenaciously to their Christian faith for centuries.

In c.1548 he moved further east to Japan, where he formulated and translated a summary of the faith, travelling to Hirado then on to Yamaguchi and the capital, Miyako; in both places he met with little success. Re-turning to Yamaguchi, Francis decided to enlist royal support and, temporarily throwing off his rags, he exploited his Portuguese nationality to obtain the protection and financial backing of the ruler there. By the time he left his converts numbered 2000, and many were to suffer martyrdom in later persecutions for their faith.

Death

After returning briefly to Goa, Francis embarked on his final journey, a mission of which he had long dreamed, to China. He never reached the shore. On the island of San-chian, near the mouth of the river Canton, he fell ill waiting for the ship that was to drop him secretly on the mainland and died, accompanied only by a young Chinese Christian from Goa named Antony. His body was taken in quicklime to Goa, where it is still enshrined, and remained incorrupt there for a long time, a popular object of pilgrimage. His right arm is claimed by the church of the Gesù at Rome.

Cult and influence

In art Francis is usually represented as a young bearded Jesuit together with a torch, flame, cross and lily, and sometimes in company with Ignatius Loyola. He was canonized in 1622 and declared patron of all foreign missions by Pius XI in 1927. Missionary organizations and schools worldwide are dedicated to this great and tireless missionary, whose example of sensitivity, commitment and holiness has been an inspiration for missionaries ever since.

Feast-day 3 December
Patron saint of Roman Catholic foreign missions

Gall

c.550 Ireland — Arbon 645

The apostle of Switzerland

The most famous of the disciples of Columban.

Probably born in Leinster, Gall was educated at Bangor abbey under Saints Comgall and Columban and was ordained there. He accompanied Columban into voluntary exile on the Continent in c.585, along with 11 other companions, and helped to found the monasteries of Annegray and Luxeuil. The Irish monks were expelled from Gaul in 610 after controversy over the retention of Celtic observances over those of Rome. Gall followed Columban into the area around Tuggen, near Lake Zurich, and later to Bregenz.

Split from Columban

When Columban moved on to Italy in 612, however, Gall remained in Arbon, Switzerland. Various reasons have been suggested for the split: some legends claim that Columban accused Gall of malingering and in the subsequent disagreement they split up, with Columban imposing on his monk the penance of never celebrating Mass during his (Columban's) lifetime. Other sources cite Gall's ill health as his reason for staying behind. Certainly it was not the hope of self-aggrandizement away from the authority of his superior. After curing the fiancée of King Sigebert from supposed demon possession he was offered a bishopric, and the monks at Luxeuil begged him to become their abbot: he refused both of these honours. He lived instead as a hermit and wandering preacher based on the Steinach river near Lake Constance in modern-day Switzerland. The famous monastery of St Gall later grew up on the site, one of the most renowned centres of culture and learning of the Middle Ages. After the death of Columban, his fellow Irish monks sent their leader's pastoral staff to Gall as a sign of his forgiveness.

Cult

During his life he attracted many followers and undoubtedly ranks as one of the most important and pioneering Christian missionaries in Switzerland. It is difficult to be certain why Gall has traditionally been acknowledged as the patron saint of birds. According to one theory, this was due simply to linguistic confusion — the saint's name is very close to the Italian word for cock, *gallo*, and this apparent link may have begun the association. Another suggestion comes from the legend of his activities as an exorcist: it was thought that when he cast the demon out of King Sigebert's betrothed it flew out of her mouth in the form of a blackbird.

Feast-day 16 October
Patron saint of birds

Geneviève (Genovefa)

c.422 Nanterre — Paris c.500

Defender of Paris

Because of her work on behalf of Paris during her life, Geneviève has become its well-loved patron.

Journeying to Britain in 429, St Germanus of Auxerre met a young girl at Nanterre, near Paris, who earnestly expressed to him her desire to live for God. This was Geneviève, who at the age of 15 confirmed her childhood devotion by taking the veil. After the death of her parents she went to live in Paris with her godmother, where she spent her time in prayer, austerity and works of charity. She faced much misunderstanding and criticism for her self-imposed severity and for the many prophecies of danger to Paris which she made. At one stage an attempt was made on her life, but the continued support of Germanus finally convinced the Parisians of her authenticity, as did the fulfilment of many of her predictions. She correctly predicted in 451 that Attila and his Huns would bypass Paris, and the initial disbelief turned to respect when Attila did indeed change course and leave the city unmolested.

Her reputation was increased when she led an expedition to obtain food from Arcis and Troyes during the Frankish siege of Paris led by Childeric and brought back boat-loads of provisions to relieve the imprisoned inhabitants. Greatly impressed by her courage, Childeric and Clovis after him released prisoners at her request.

In 460 Geneviève built a church over the tomb of St Denis and she encouraged Clovis to build the church of St Peter and St Paul, where she was later buried. It was renamed St Geneviève and many miracles were reported there, but it became the Pantheon during the French Revolution, and her shrine was destroyed.

Cult

The Parisians of succeeding generations kept alive the memory of their protectress; during an epidemic in 1129, her relics were carried in solemn procession through the city's streets and the spread of the disease ended. The miracle is still celebrated annually in Parisian churches, and Geneviève is credited with many more miracles through her intercession for Paris. The *Life* on which much of our evidence is based is unreliable; it claims to be the account of an eyewitness but was in fact written much later, probably several centuries after her death. One very late tradition claims without foundation that she was a shepherdess in her early life.

In art Geneviève is shown with a candle, which a devil attempts to extinguish while an angel stands by to keep it alight. This is from an ancient legend that the Devil vainly tried to frighten the sturdy saint when she went to pray in the church at night by blowing out her candle. She is occasionally shown healing the eyesight of her mother, from another unreliable legend. Parisians resort to her in time of civic or national danger and this has ensured the continuing popularity of her cult.

Feast-day 3 January
Patron saint of Paris, disasters and fever

George

d. Nicomedia c.303 or Lydda c.250

The archetype of Christian chivalry

His popularity in England especially is astonishing, but his legend has little to do with his life.

Most of the details commonly associated with George are based on medieval fictions. All that is known for certain is that he was martyred either at Lydda in Palestine or Nicomedia, and that he was probably a soldier in the emperor's army. His cult is an ancient and popular one; he was called *megalomaryros* ('the great martyr') in the East and features in the western martyrology of Jerome. These antedate the sixth-century *Acts* of Pasicrates. From this point on much mythical material attached itself to the figure of this Palestinian soldier: the fullest and most popularized form of the legend is found in the 13th-century *Golden Legend* of Jacobus de Voragine, translated into English by Caxton.

The legend

According to Voragine's story, George was a warrior from Cappadocia. Passing through Sylene in Libya, he found the town terrorized by a dragon which demanded human flesh to satisfy its appetite. The victims were chosen by lot, and on the day George arrived it was the turn of the king's own daughter. She had been chained to a rock outside the city, dressed as a bride to await her death. George seized his lance and marched forth to meet the beast; he conquered it and led it tamely back to the town, drawn by the princess's girdle. He then told the townsfolk that he would kill the dragon

if they were to confess Christianity; naturally they were quick to comply and 15 000 men were baptized. The legend also includes more historically based material chronicling George's suffering and death in the persecutions of Diocletian and Maximinus.

Cult

Although known in England from about the seventh century, George's popularity increased dramatically during the Crusades. It was said that the victory over the Saracens at Antioch was due to a vision of Saints George and Demetrius which heartened the men. Edward III named George patron of his newly-founded Order of the Garter in c.1344, and Henry's famous invocation at Agincourt, immortalized in Shakespeare's play *Henry V*, made his name a rallying-call for nationalistic pride. He gradually overtook even Edward the Confessor as the favourite saint of the English.

George appears as a popular figure in several early mumming plays in England, some of which unashamedly proclaim English nationality for him, and countless ancient and modern churches have been dedicated to him. He was once regarded as patron of several European states, and as one of the Fourteen Holy Helpers in Germany, but it was in England that devotion to him remained the highest. The 'St George's Arms', a red cross on a white background, formed the basis of every British soldier's and sailor's uniform, and it is included as the sign of England in the Union Jack.

> **Feast-day** 23 April
> Patron saint of England, Portugal, soldiers, armourers and archers, invoked against plague, leprosy and syphilis

Gertrude of Helfta (Gertrude the Great)
1256 — Helfta c.1302

A life of spiritual experiences

One of the most influential of the medieval mystics, especially concerning the devotion to the Sacred Heart.

Although the details of her birthplace and infancy are unknown, it is clear that from the age of five Gertrude lived and studied in the convent of Helfta near Eisleben in Saxony cared for by the Benedictine nuns. Her welfare was entrusted especially to a nun named Mechtilde, with whom the young Gertrude became close friends.

Mystical experiences

She grew up to take her profession at the convent and at the age of 25 underwent a deep spiritual conversion. She was blessed with visions of Christ and other mystical experiences and revelations. The record of these experiences in her *Revelations of St Gertrude* or *The Herald of Loving-kindness* (it is now thought that only the second of the five volumes is actually her work, the others being written by others from her notes) demonstrates an emotive contemplation of the humanity of Christ, prefiguring the development of the devotion to the Sacred Heart. It is interesting that she ceased her studies in classical, secular areas after her conversion experience and concentrated all her intellectual energies on Scripture,

the Christian fathers (particularly Augustine, Gregory and Bernard) and the liturgy. Many of her visions were said to have taken place during the liturgy itself and despite their individuality and their emotive tone were certainly based on orthodox doctrine.

Mechtilde shared Gertrude's devout mysticism; the two supposedly collaborated on a series of prayers which gained widespread popularity, although some modern scholars have seriously questioned their authenticity. Gertrude recorded the visions of her mentor and friend in her *Book of Special Grace*; her work demonstrates an impressive intelligence as well as a visionary piety. Crippled by ill health in her later years, Gertrude died at Helfta on 17 November.

Cult

Although Gertrude is occasionally identified as an abbess this is through confusion with Gertrude of Hackeborn, sister of Mechtilde, who was abbess of the convent when Gertrude entered it as a child. She is correctly regarded however as one of the most significant of medieval mystics, whose influence spread through the publication of her books in Latin in 1536. Pope Innocent XI listed her in the Roman martyrology of 1677, and her feast was made universal in 1738, but she has in fact never been formally canonized.

> **Feast-day** 16 November
> Patron saint of the West Indies

Gertrude of Nivelles

626 Landen — Nivelles 659

The hospitable abbess

One of the best-known of all abbesses, Gertrude ruled her monastery with a wisdom that belied her youth.

Daughter of the pious Pepin of Landen and his wife Itta, Gertrude was raised in a very religious atmosphere; her sister Begga is also venerated as a saint. It is widely believed that in her youth she rejected an offer of marriage from the Merovingian king, Dagobert I.

On the advice of St Amand of Maastricht, Itta established a double monastery at Nivelles after her husband's death, which she entered as a nun. Gertrude was appointed superior and ruled her community wisely and responsibly, despite her youth, and was especially renowned for her hospitality towards Irish monks such as St Foillan, to whom she donated land and horses to enable him to found a monastery.

Death

In 656 Gertrude resigned as abbess and was succeeded by her niece; she wished to spend more time in prayer without the distractions of administration and she was in poor health after many years of austerity. She spent her final few years reading Scripture and performing penances, and is traditionally thought to have experienced many visions before her death at the age of 33.

Cult

Because of her renowned hospitality to pilgrims and monks Gertrude is known as the patron saint of travellers: pilgrims would traditionally drain a stirrup cup in her honour before beginning their journey. Since the souls of the dead were popularly thought to undergo a three-day long journey to the next world, Gertrude became known by extension as the saint in whose care these travelling souls spent their first night, before going on to spend the next night under the protection of St Michael.

Her feast-day in March is associated with the beginning of the new gardening season, fine weather on this day signalling the beginning of the year's work, and this is the source of her patronage of gardeners. Her iconography however cannot be explained so satisfactorily: she is usually associated with mice or rats, and is often shown in art holding a pastoral staff up which a mouse runs, and has traditionally been invoked against such pests. This may be due to conflation with earlier pagan folklore. As late as 1822, offerings of gold and silver mice were presented at her shrine in Cologne to secure her intercessory help in an infestation. One possible explanation for this odd association, which seems to bear no relevance to any events in her life, may be the fact that her feast-day tended to coincide with the time of year that field-mice awoke from hibernation and began to become a nuisance.

> **Feast-day** 17 March
> Patron saint of gardeners, travellers and the recently dead, invoked against mice and rats

Giles (Aegidius)

d. c.710

The protector-saint

Beloved for his reputation as a compassionate, protective patron.

The scanty facts known of Giles's life are that he was born during the seventh century, lived for some time as a hermit, and that he founded a monastery near Arles in Provence on land given by King Womba. The neighbourhood of the monastery was later known as Saint-Gilles.

This rough outline was coloured and elaborated by a famous early medieval legend, which claimed that Giles was born in Athens but performed a miracle there which brought him unwanted attention: he is said to have cured a sick beggar by giving him his own cloak. In addition to the acclamation which he received for the miracle, Giles dreaded the approval of his fellow men occasioned by his generosity, and he fled to the area around Marseilles. He studied with the celebrated St Caesarius of Arles and after two years became a hermit near Nîmes, at the mouth of the Rhône river.

Deeds

The most famous incident of Giles's life (according to his legend) occurred when King Womba was out hunting one day and he or one of his men shot into a thicket at a stag. They then discovered Giles, himself wounded by the arrow while he protected the hind in his arms. Some versions of the legend add that this hind was a pet who had supplied Giles with milk throughout his seclusion.

Another popular legend claims that Giles received confession from a king (identified by some as Charlemagne) who omitted to mention a particular sin, for which he nonetheless asked forgiveness. While Giles was speaking mass he received a vision of a heavenly tablet on which was detailed the sin. The writing faded as he prayed, and Giles chastised the astonished and repentant king. He is also said to have visited Rome where he received two beautiful wooden doors from the Pope; Giles threw them into the sea off the coast of Italy and they were miraculously washed up near his monastery on the south coast of France.

Cult

The cult which began in Provence after his death gained popularity as it spread with the Crusaders throughout Europe. He was popular as protector of the crippled and of nursing mothers, from the story of his protection of the hind, and for the belief that his intercession was effective even for sins not spoken aloud in confession. In art he is usually shown with a hind in his arms and the arrow in his hand. Many ancient churches and hospitals were dedicated to him, most notably the High Kirk on Edinburgh's Royal Mile and St Giles at Cripplegate in London. A fair still survives at Oxford on his feast day. He was also known as patron of blacksmiths and his churches can often be found at busy junctions where the smithies would also ply their trade, the one serving the spiritual needs and the other the practical needs of travellers.

Feast-day 1 September
Patron saint of beggars, cripples and blacksmiths

Gregory of Nazianzus

c.330 Nazianzus — Nazianzus c.389

The champion of Nicene orthodoxy

A contemplative, quiet man who desired only to be alone with God, he struggled to fulfil the various demands made upon him.

Son of two sainted parents, Bishop Gregory of Nazianzus and St Nanna, Gregory was born in Cappadocia and began his education there in Caesarea where he first met St Basil. He went on to the school of rhetoric in Caesarea, Palestine, and then to study law at the University of Athens in the company of Basil and Julian, later the apostate emperor.

His studies completed, Gregory abandoned his legal career to become a monk. He joined Basil at his retreat on the river Iris in Pontus, but in c.361 he returned to Nazianzus to help his father, now about 80, with the administration of his see. Despite his objections, he was ordained as a priest by the old bishop and in panic fled back to Basil. He quickly recognized the folly of his flight, and returned to face his new duties, writing an *apologia* which has become a classic statement on the responsibility of the clergy.

Friction with Basil

In 372 Basil appointed Gregory bishop of Sasima, a hostile and troubled see in Arian territory. The post had been created by Basil to strengthen his position against a neighbouring Arian bishop, and Gregory felt that he was being used for political purposes. He refused even to visit Sasima, and stayed in Nazianzus, administering the see after his father's death in 374 until the post was filled again. The disagreement was

to mar the friendship which had once been so close. The following year, Gregory suffered a breakdown and retired to Seleucia for the next five years to live in tranquillity as a hermit.

Bishop of Constantinople

In 380 he was called to the bishopric of Constantinople after the death of Emperor Valens. Persecution had left the church vulnerable to Arian heresy, but Gregory's articulate preaching in the church established in his own house soon restored sound doctrine. He brought upon himself slander and vitriol from the Arians, but was vindicated in 381 when Emperor Theodosius I at the Council of Constantinople confirmed the doctrine preached by Gregory, that of the Council of Nicaea, as the only authentic Christian doctrine. The Arians were called upon to concur or quit; most of them quitted. Gregory was made archbishop of Constantinople, but the hostility towards him resurfaced after his appointment and to preserve the peace Gregory resigned his post.

Death and cult

Back in Nazianzus, the see was again vacant and Gregory administered while a successor was chosen. He spent his final years in great austerity, writing his famous poems and an autobiography. He died there on 25 January and his relics were later translated to Constantinople and then to St Peter's in Rome. His impressive theological writings, promoting Nicene orthodoxy especially in teaching on the Trinity, won him the name 'the Theologian' during his life and a place among the four great Eastern Doctors after his death.

Feast-day 2 January

St Gregory of Nazianzus

Gregory Thaumaturgus

c.213 Neocaesarea — Neocaesarea c.270

'The wonder-worker'

Gregory's tireless preaching and miracle-working radically transformed his decadent see.

Given Gregory's central position in the affairs of his day and in the development of the church, it is frustrating that so little reliable evidence survives about him. Born of wealthy pagan parents in Pontus, he was originally named Theodore and studied for a career in law. He happened to meet Origen in Palestine and was so attracted by Origen's personal example and his teaching that he gave up all thoughts of a legal career, was converted and began studying theology under him.

Conversion of Neocaesarea

Gregory returned to Neocaesarea in about 238. There were only 17 Christians in the city, but they unanimously elected him their bishop and he took up the appointment with energy and vision. Much accumulated legend inevitably surrounds his episcopate, but it seems clear that he was gifted with the power to perform remarkable miracles, traditionally including the diverting of a river and the removal of a mountain. The decadent city of Neocaesarea quickly responded to his miracles and to his message and the small church grew daily. Gregory himself gained the respect of his followers and opponents for his demonstrable power, his humility and his absolute integrity. Equally attractive was his practice of celebrating the feasts of martyrs with games and feasting, involving the entire society in honouring the saints.

The nascent community faced persecution in 250 under Decius; Gregory advised his disciples to follow his example and flee the city. He left for the desert in the company of his deacon (an ex-pagan priest) but his hiding-place was betrayed. The soldiers sent to find him came back, reporting that they had seen only a couple of trees; their informer visited the spot himself to see Gregory and his deacon at prayer. Convinced of a miracle, he himself broke down and was converted. Even when persecution ended, Gregory's troubles were not over; plague struck soon afterwards and was succeeded by a Gothic invasion, described in his *Canonical letters*. He was forced to defend orthodoxy at the Synod of Antioch, 264–5, against the attacks of Samosata and others.

Death and cult

By the time Gregory died, it is said that Neocaesarea contained only 17 people who did not profess the Christian faith, remarkable testimony to his work of preaching and conversion. He had asked to be given no special burial place, but his body was later translated to Calabria, from where the cult spread through Sicily and Southern Italy. Because of the legend that he moved the mountain and another that he once stopped the flooding of the Lycus, he is frequently invoked at scenes of natural disasters such as floods and earthquakes, and his reputation for miracles naturally endeared him to those in desperate situations. According to Gregory of Nyssa he is the first to have experienced a vision of the Virgin Mary.

Feast-day 17 November
Patron saint of those in desperate situations, invoked against earthquake and flood

Gregory the Great

c.540 Rome — Rome 604

The apostle of the English from Rome

One of the most celebrated of Popes, he effectively founded and shaped both medieval papacy and popular religion in medieval times.

Son of the Senator Gordianus, Gregory was a model Roman citizen who became prefect of the city in his youth. In 573 however he sold his extensive assets of property to enable him to found a monastery in Rome and several others in Sicily, with enough remaining to make generous alms to the poor, and the following year he resigned from service of the state to enrol at St Andrew's, the monastery he had founded on Rome's Celian Hill. He lived a life of great austerity there, an enormous contrast with his previous experience, and suffered greatly with ill health throughout his life as a result. He spent several years in the monastery before being appointed one of Rome's seven deacons by Pope Benedict I, and the next Pope, Pelagius II, summoned him to the Byzantine court to act as papal nuncio. After six years, in which he impressed many by the quality of his service, he returned to St Andrew's in 586, becoming abbot there. He appears to have been much more comfortable with monastic Christian practice than with that of the declining empire of Byzantium.

Pope

From Rome Gregory intended to lead a monastic mission to evangelize the Anglo-Saxons; Bede claims that on seeing some fair-haired young slaves in the forum and being told their nationality he answered with the immortal words, 'non Angli, sed angeli' and immediately resolved to convert their country, but this is probably a fiction. His project had to be abandoned, however, when plague swept Rome and Gregory was recalled by Pelagius. Pelagius himself died of the plague in 590, and a reluctant Gregory was consecrated his successor on 3 September, the first monk ever to become a Pope.

His pontificate was to be a troubled but remarkable one. As well as the devastation wreaked in Rome by the plague, he had to face floods, famine, an invasion by the Lombards and massive corruption and incompetence within the church. He used his authority to battle against slavery, and he succeeded in reconciling to Rome the Gothic church of Spain, which had for a long time been under Arian influence. In addition he recognized the need for the Church to be independent from the interference and domination of the Byzantine court, which he mistrusted in ecclesiasical affairs. He passed over the head of the Byzantine exarch in Ravenna in negotiating a peace with the King of Lombardy, appointed govenors over Italian towns, and denounced the taxes levied on the Italians by the Byzantine authorities; for the first time the papacy was claiming for itself not only spiritual but also political authority. Yet Gregory's attitude to his position is revealed in the title which he chose and which has been retained by Popes ever since: 'Servant of the Servants of God'.

Mission to England

Gregory did not forget his thwarted intention to convert the Anglo-Saxons; in his place he sent Augustine and other monks from St Andrew's in Rome, and guided them closely by letter throughout the expedition. He wrote to King Ethelbert of Kent to congratulate him on his conversion in

131

601 and directed Augustine on the finer points of doctrine and ecclesiastical practice, and since the impulse behind the mission was originally his he has from the time of Bede and Aldhelm been acknowledged as the true apostle of the English, although their later devotion to Augustine and Aidan contested his title.

Works

In addition to his English letters, Gregory wrote widely and authoritatively on many other subjects. The fourth Latin Doctor of the Church, he committed himself to teaching the wisdom of the ancient fathers to new converts and to establishing sound doctrine and proper pastoral care among the clergy. His *Pastoral Care* was translated into Old English by King Alfred, and his two *Dialogues*, collections of miraculous occurrences, were hugely influential in the formation of popular medieval religious thought. While at court in Constantinople he wrote an exposition of Job, *Moralia.* His many letters reveal him to be a thoughtful and untiring leader, who concerned himself with every aspect of both Church and state. His authorship of the Gregorian Sacramentary is disputed, but it seems likely that he wrote at least some of its prayers, and he was influential too in the development of plainsong, developing several old forms and giving his name to Gregorian chant. The legend that he once freed the soul of a monk from Purgatory by saying 30 consecutive masses gave rise to the Gregorian trental, still in use today.

Death and cult

Although not a Benedictine, Gregory lived very much in that spirit, encouraged Benedictine monasticism and wrote the first *Life* of Benedict in Book II of his *Dialogues.* The Benedictines responded by promulgating his work worldwide, and he is often represented in the Benedictine habit. In his later years the gout and gastritis from which he had suffered for most of his life worsened, but he carried on with his enormous workload right until his death. He was quickly recognized as a saint, canonized by public acclamation, and his life and ideals have inspired generations of Christians ever since, from peasants to Popes. He is frequently shown with a dove at his ear or speaking into his mouth, recalling his belief that the Holy Spirit would often make theological points clear to him while he was actually speaking. Often shown alongside the other Doctors of the Church, Ambrose, Augustine and Jerome, he is differentiated from them by his papal tiara. Many churches, both ancient and modern, have been dedicated to him, and his feast-day has been celebrated universally from very early times.

> **Feast-day** 12 March
> Patron saint of masons, singers, musicians, students and teachers, invoked against gout and plague

St Gregory the Great. Ducal Palace, Urbino.

Helena

c.255 Drepanum — Holy Land c.330

Mother of the first Christian emperor

Revered both in connection with Constantine and as the finder of the True Cross, Helena's late conversion proved a formative influence in the spread of early Christianity.

Born in Bithynia (her birthplace later became known as Helenopolis), a strong tradition has her as the daughter of an innkeeper. An alternative legend, propagated by Geoffrey of Monmouth and widely accepted for some time in England, that she was born of an English prince, has been shown to be a romantic fiction. When she was about 20 she met the Roman general Constantius Chlorus who was captivated by her despite her humble position; they were soon married and she bore him a son named Constantine.

When Constantius was named Caesar by Emperor Maximian in 292 he divorced his low-born wife and made a more politically advantageous match with Theodora, stepdaughter of Maximian. Constantine was among six claimants to the imperial throne after the death of Maximian at York in 306; despite his popularity he was forced to fight for his claim and only became emperor after victory at the battle of Milvian bridge in 312. Helena's son conferred upon her the title of Augusta, demanded for her the respect due to the mother of the emperor and even had coins minted bearing her likeness.

Feast-day 18 August

Conversion

It was at about this time that Helena, now aged about 60, converted to Christianity. She and Constantine did much to promote the growth of the faith throughout the Empire, following the imperial edict of 313 proclaiming tolerance for Christians and the liberation of all religious captives. Helena was known as a quietly devout woman, who gave generously to endow churches and to help the poor, and spent her time giving aid to the needy. In 324 Constantine finally overcame Licinius to become emperor of the entire Roman Empire, both east and west, and he relocated his capital to Constantinople.

Death and cult

By now an elderly lady, Helena went on pilgrimage to the Holy Land where, near Mount Calvary, she is popularly supposed to have discovered Christ's Cross. This legend, which may be apocryphal, was strongly supported by Ambrose, and was immortalized in the ninth century by the famous poem of Cynewulf, *Elene*. Helena travelled throughout Palestine and the East, founding churches and befriending soldiers, prisoners and the needy before her death there, possibly at Nicomedia. Her body was returned to Rome for burial.

In England dedications to Helena seem to be concentrated in the north-east, perhaps because of Constantine's connection with York where he was first acclaimed emperor, but in various other locations such as Lancashire and the Isle of Wight the towns which grew up around the churches also bear her name. St Helena Island in the Atlantic was named after her because it was discovered by Spanish explorers on her feast-day. In art she is usually shown as one of the participants in the finding of the cross.

Hilarion

c.291 Tabatha — Cyprus 371

The first hermit of Palestine

Hilarion's example was followed by many subsequent Eastern holy men. Most characteristic of all these was the emphasis on withdrawal.

Our information about Hilarion comes largely from the *Life* of Jerome, who claimed to base his account on the writings of Hilarion's friend, Epiphanius, which are now lost. Several later versions of the saint's life are based on Jerome's account, but it appears that it is unreliable in some details. According to this source, Hilarion was born near Gaza of pagan parents. He converted to Christianity while studying at Alexandria, was baptized and journeyed to visit St Antony in his desert retreat, with whom he stayed for some time. On his return to Gaza he found that his parents had died; he gave away all that he owned to the poor and retired to become a hermit at Majuma in about 306.

Search for solitude

His lifestyle emulated that of St Antony, characterized by austerity and holiness, and he quickly attracted large numbers of disciples and sightseers, who had heard reports of his marvellous miracles. Soon he found himself in possession of land and goods, practically the leader of a community, and to regain the solitude he so desired he was forced to flee Palestine.

He lived first in Egypt but his fame had reached even there and he was soon obliged to move on to Sicily. After three years there his retreat was discovered by Hesychius, a faithful disciple who had pursued him westwards. Again the crowds began to arrive and again Hilarion fled before them to Epidaurus in Dalmatia on the Adriatic coast, and then on to Cyprus. He settled with Hesychius near Paphos but when the islanders discovered his identity he withdrew further inland to a remote spot about 12 miles away. There he was visited by Bishop Epiphanius of Salamis in about 403 and died in relative seclusion at the age of 80. His body was buried at Paphos, but later translated to Majuma.

Cult and influence

Hilarion's great appeal, which resulted in an enduring and universal cult, lay in his austere, holy monasticism, seen as an ideal, if exclusive, model for subsequent hermits and communities. His miracles were legendary even in his own day, and did much to popularize his cult.

Feast-day 21 October

Hilary of Poitiers

c.315 Poitiers — Poitiers c.368

The Athanasius of the West

One of the most formidable opponents of Arianism.

Coming from a background of wealthy, pagan parentage, Hilary's early career followed a non-spiritual bent. He trained as an orator and married as a young man, producing a daughter named Afra. In his studying however he found himself led irresistibly to acknowledge the existence and providence of God, and in 350 he converted to Christianity and was baptized. About three years later, while his wife was still alive, he was appointed bishop of Poitiers. He fearlessly championed Catholic orthodoxy against the prevalent heresy of Arianism, refusing to attend the council convened by Emperor Constantius in 355 at which those present were required to sign a condemnation of Athanasius. But Arian opposition was influential; Hilary was condemned at the largely Arian Synod of Béziers in 356 and exiled to Phrygia by Constantius in the same year.

Exile, however, did not silence the bishop. At the eastern Council of Seleucia in 359 Hilary's arguments against Arianism were so effective that the Arians appealed to the emperor to end his exile and allow this troublemaker to go back to Gaul. There was general rejoicing on his return to Poitiers in 360, which was accompanied by reform and renewed stability. Constantius's death in 361 ended the political ascendancy of the Arians and in 364 Hilary argued publicly and powerfully against the usurping Arian bishop of Milan, Auxentius, although since his opponent had the backing of Emperor Valentinian Hilary was unable to secure his deposition.

Works

Most of his writings are directed to the end of refuting Arianism by demonstrating the divine nature of Christ, especially *De Trinitate*. *De Synodis* deals with Eastern religious thought and practice, and he also wrote commentaries on the Psalms and Matthew's Gospel. He recognized the potential in the Arian method of propagating doctrine through public singing, but his attempts to introduce metrical hymns failed (apparently they were unsuitable for popular recitation) and the idea only really developed under Ambrose. Hilary's writing style, with its long and convoluted sentences, has been criticized by Jerome and others as being too obscure, but his three addresses to Constantius which survive show the power and fearlessness with which he defended orthodoxy. During his day he was regarded as one of the greatest theologians of the church.

Cult

He was named a Doctor of the Church in 1851, and his feast-day has traditionally been used to mark the beginning of Hilary term in Chancery and at some universities. In art he is often depicted with a child in a cradle at his feet, and he is known as the helper of backward children.

Feast-day 13 January
Patron saint of backward children, invoked against snakes

Hilda

614 Northumbria — Whitby 680

'Mother Hilda'

One of the outstanding English abbesses, she ruled capably and compassionately at Whitby for 22 years.

Related to the royal families of Northumbria and East Anglia, the young Hilda was baptized as a Christian along with her great-uncle King Edwin by Paulinus in 627. Until the age of 33 she lived much in the same way as any other, secular noblewoman, but then decided to become a nun, following her sister Herewitha to Chelles in France. She was recalled to Northumbria, however, by Aidan, who assigned her to a small nunnery on the north bank of the river Wear. Soon afterwards she moved to the double monastery at Hartlepool and was appointed abbess there after Heiu in 649; her rule was influenced mainly by Irish traditions, probably based on the Rule of Columban.

Whitby

In 657 she founded, or possibly refounded, an abbey at Streaneschalch, or Whitby, creating a double monastery along the lines of French institutions. The abbey established an excellent reputation for learning, building up an impressive library and producing at least five bishops, including Wilfrid of York and John of Beverley. As at Hartlepool, Hilda's monastery at Whitby strongly upheld the Celtic traditions of monasticism and Easter observance. In the growing confusion and unease as competing Roman practice became prevalent, she hosted the famous Synod of Whitby to resolve the issue, speaking for her part in favour of retaining Celtic observances. When the decision finally went in favour of adopting Roman practices, in line with the rest of Europe, Hilda and her community accepted the ruling without demur. Her example of compliance did much to promote unity and lessen ill-will in a divided church.

It was at Whitby that the cowherd Caedmon was welcomed as a monk and encouraged to compose his vernacular Christian poems, which were the source of sound doctrine for many illiterate folk. Hilda's reputation for wisdom and her accessibility were such that her help and advice were sought by people from every class, from peasants to rulers. She was known as 'Mother' for her all-embracing compassion, grace and charity.

Death and cult

For the last six years of her life Hilda suffered greatly from illness, although she refused to lighten her workload. She died at Whitby on 17 November, and her relics were supposedly translated to Glastonbury under King Edmund. However, since Whitby had been sacked in the Danish invasions a century earlier, the validity of these relics has been disputed, with Gloucester also claiming them. Several English churches, mainly in Yorkshire and Northumbria, were dedicated to her; and in art she is generally represented as an abbess, sometimes with a crown, often holding Whitby Abbey in her hand. One legend claims that wild birds stopped destroying a field of corn at her command, and this too was a popular subject for artists.

Feast-day 17 November

Hippolytus

c.170 — Sardinia 235

The sainted antipope

Although Hippolytus's zeal against heresy brought him into conflict with Rome, the Church has recognized and respected his uncompromising integrity.

Nothing is known of Hippolytus's early life. We first encounter him as a particularly learned priest in Rome, probably an old disciple of St Irenaeus, the opponent of Gnosticism in Gaul. His theological works, written in Greek, are among the most important of his day: Jerome called him 'a most holy and eloquent man'. But Hippolytus opposed the established church by denouncing Pope Zephyrinus for what he saw as his laxity in the matter of heresy. He accused him of not meeting the challenge of Sabellianism and Modalism with sufficient vigour and of showing too much leniency to sinners within the church.

Antipope

When Callistus I was elected Pope in about 217 Hippolytus's followers elected him antipope. The schism continued under Callistus's successors, Urban I and Pontian, and then Emperor Maximinus did not trouble himself with distinctions between Pope and antipope, and banished both Pontian and Hippolytus to the mines on the island of Sardinia. There Pontian succeeded in bringing Hippolytus back into communion with the church, and the two died reconciled

in exile, recognized as martyrs for their sufferings under persecution. Both bodies were returned to Rome under Pope Fabian and Hippolytus was reburied on the Via Tiburtina.

The other Hippolytus

This account of the historical Hippolytus has been greatly confused by mistaken identity. One such confusion is that of a martyred bishop of the same name who was killed by wild horses at the mouth of the Tiber. The second is named in the unreliable *Acts* of St Lawrence as the prison officer in charge of Lawrence who was converted by him and who helped to bury him; when the emperor discovered this he sentenced his recalcitrant officer to be scourged and torn apart by horses; he was tied by a long rope to two stampeding wild horses who dragged him to his death. His mangled body was reverently buried by the Christians in Rome. The story is suspiciously reminiscent of the classical legend of Hippolytus son of Theseus, and is probably no more than a Christianizing of ancient myth, prompted by the martyr's name. However it is this legend that has led to Hippolytus's traditional patronage of horses.

Works

In recent days, Hippolytus's reputation as a theologian has benefited from the discovery of several of his most important works, including his *Refutation of all Heresies*, found at Mount Athos in 1842, which systematically refutes Gnostic heresies by revealing their pagan sources (which is quite ironic in view of the confusion associated with his name). He also wrote the first known biblical commentary, on the book of Daniel, and probably his too is the *Apostolic Tradition* which is one of our most valuable sources of information about Church practices of the time.

Hubert

c.656 — Tervueren 727

First bishop of Liège

Whatever the truth of his conversion story, the work of Hubert during his episcopacy is testament to his saintliness.

Little of historical value is known of Hubert's early life. Thought to have been the son of the duke of Guienne, he is traditionally believed to have been a hedonistic courtier under Pepin of Heristal who went out hunting one Good Friday instead of attending church. It is said that the stag he was pursuing suddenly turned towards him, and Hubert clearly saw the emblem of a cross between its antlers, and heard a voice calling him to repentance. This conversion account is suspiciously similar to that of St Eustace and during the Middle Ages it was adapted to explain David I's founding of Holyrood Abbey near Edinburgh in 1128, but its popularity has given rise both to Hubert's patronage of hunters and to his emblem in art, a stag.

He became a priest under St Lambert, bishop of Maastricht, and on the bishop's assassination in about 708 Hubert was appointed his successor. During his episcopate he worked tirelessly to evangelize the pagan areas of his diocese, especially the forest of Ardenne, where he destroyed the pagan idols as he went around preaching the gospel, and was known as a great worker of miracles. In 716 he had Lambert's relics translated into a church he had built for the purpose in Liège, the place of his murder. He made this the new centre of his see, turning the church into his cathedral.

Death and cult

Hubert is said to have been warned of his death a year before it happened. He died on 30 May near Brussels after journeying to consecrate a new church at Brabant, and his body was returned to Liège and buried in the church of St Peter. It was later translated to Andain abbey in Ardenne, later known as Saint-Hubert. It was in Ardenne that he was first venerated as patron of hunters and trappers; this may have been the reason for the development of his conversion story. There is no official pronouncement to verify this popular patronage, but it is at least more readily understandable than his common association with rabies. This must presumably have arisen from the connection of dogs with hunting, since there is no specific instance in any version of his legend to suggest it. A common medieval remedy for those suffering from rabies was the application of a thread from the stole of St Hubert (said to have been given to him by the Virgin) to a small cut made on the forehead.

His conversion is frequently represented in art after the 14th century and the Wallace Collection in London houses a hunting horn claimed to be his. One legend tells how he suffered a near-fatal accident whilst fishing on the Meuse a year before his death, which is the basis for his reputation of protection again hydrophobia.

> **Feast-day** 3 November
> Patron saint of hunting and huntsmen, invoked against rabies and hydrophobia

Hugh of Cluny

1024 Semur — Cluny 1109

Abbot of Cluny

The long-serving abbot of Cluny, under whose direction the Cluniac reform swept Europe.

Although Dalmatius, count of Semur, was potent and respected throughout Burgundy and beyond, he was forced to capitulate when his eldest son Hugh decided against all expectations that he wanted to become a monk. Hugh entered the monastery at Cluny at the age of about 16, and four years later was ordained as a priest. By the age of 24 he had been appointed prior by abbot Odilo, and on Odilo's death in 1049 this promising and popular young monk was appointed abbot. He held the abbacy at Cluny for 60 years; when he took office the monastery was already a large and thriving one, with perhaps 60 daughter foundations, over which Hugh as abbot of Cluny took responsibility. Over the course of his abbacy, however, this number grew to about 2 000, located throughout Europe.

The Cluniac reform

The process of reform by which all this was achieved involved diplomacy and administrative brilliance on Hugh's part, a single-minded commitment to the propagation of the monasteries and their ideals, and a personal holiness that impressed the monks serving under him, his fellow abbots, and the rulers of the day. Odilo had tried to bring the Cluniac monasteries into a closer relationship with the mother house and Hugh continued this policy, uniting and strengthening the houses and building at Cluny the biggest abbey then known in Christendom, which was consecrated in 1095 by Pope Urban II.

Popes came and went over the course of Hugh's abbacy and he was advisor to most of them, participating energetically in the programs of reform initiated by Leo IX, Gregory VII and Paschal II. He served as papal legate in Hungary, Spain and Toulouse, and arbitrated between the Pope and the emperor at Canossa in 1077, and was influential in launching the first Crusade, speaking at the Council of Clermont in 1095. It seems that he had a gift, recognized by all these spiritual leaders, for psychological insight and sensitive diplomacy; he was valued for his impartial, ordered intelligence as much as for his spiritual qualities.

Cult and influence

The Cluniac reform movement spread to England with the foundation of St Pancras at Lewes, Sussex in 1078. During his abbacy the prestige and expansion of Cluny reached their height, and Hugh's enormous personal influence at the forefront of church and state affairs for 60 years was a shaping force in the 11th century, a time of great spiritual reform. He was canonized by Pope Callistus III in 1120.

Feast-day 29 April

Hugh of Lincoln (Hugh of Avalon)

c.1135 Avalon — London 1200

The first canonized Carthusian

Loved for his courage, his humour and his tireless work among the people, Hugh risked his life to secure justice for them.

Son of Lord William of Avalon in Burgundy, Hugh became motherless at the age of eight and was educated at the convent of Villardbenoît. He became a deacon of the Austin canons at 19, and was appointed prior of a monastery at Saint-Maxim.

Move to England

While on a visit to the Grande Chartreuse in 1160 he enrolled as a Carthusian there, was ordained and became procurator in c.1175. Henry II of England began to hear of Hugh's capability and holiness; he invited him to take the position of prior in his new Charterhouse at Witham in Somerset. This had been founded by Henry in 1178 as public penance for the murder of Thomas Becket, but with inadequate resources and the successive appointment of two unsuitable priors it had seemed unsalvageable. Under Hugh's quiet and efficient management however it quickly attracted a number of dedicated monks.

Hugh faced Henry with inflexibility, integrity and unshakeable good humour. He opposed his practice of keeping sees vacant to benefit from their resources, and in 1186 he was himself appointed bishop of Lincoln, a see vacant for 18 years. As bishop he opposed Henry's oppressive forestry laws and his habit of appointing seculars to ecclesiastical positions. Although he frequently awakened Henry's fiery anger,

Hugh remained unruffled; it is recorded that he once calmed his irate sovereign with a cheeky joke. He enjoyed the same playful and critical familiarity with Richard I, whom he incensed by refusing to pay the levy required by the king for his foreign war in 1197. He was equally fearless in the face of rioting mobs, repeatedly confronting those who persecuted and captured Jews during 1190-1.

The Lincoln schools gained a reputation for excellence under his scholarly influence, and he began the work of extending the magnificent cathedral, part of which survives today.

Death and cult

In 1199 he was sent to France on a diplomatic mission for King John, and took the opportunity to see Cluny and Cîteaux and to revisit the Grande Chartreuse. On his return to England he was overcome by sickness while attending a council in London. From his sick-bed he made arrangements for the completion of work on the cathedral, and for his own funeral, and died at the Old Temple on 16 November 1200.

He was canonized 20 years later, and the Carthusians spread his cult throughout western Europe. His relics were translated to a shrine in the Angel Choir in Lincoln in 1280, which became a popular destination for pilgrims. In art he is usually shown with his pet swan, or a chalice showing the Christ-child. He is regarded as the protector of sick children and has been widely recognized as one of the most attractive figures in church history.

Feast-day 17 November
Patron saint of sick children

Ignatius Loyola

1491 Loyola — Rome 1556

Founder of the Society of Jesus

The vision of Christian commitment put forward by Ignatius and his friends, one of spiritual discipline, education and missionary activity, inspired an army of Jesuit workers who literally changed the world.

Born in the family castle in the Basque province of Guipúzcoa (modern-day Spain), Iñigo de Recalde de Loyola was the youngest of the 13 children of his noble parents. As a youth he spent some time as page in the court of King Ferdinand the Catholic. He then trained to become a soldier, but his military career in the service of the Duke of Nagara was cut short when he received a shot to the leg during the siege of Pamplona, 1521. His right leg was broken and was incompetently set, which meant that it later had to be rebroken and set again. This traumatic experience left Ignatius with a pronounced limp for the rest of his life.

Conversion

It was while he was incapacitated, however, and convalescing slowly, that he began to read the lives of Christ and the saints which so impressed him that he converted to Christianity. As soon as he had recovered in 1522 he went on pilgrimage to Monserrat, where he dedicated his soldier's life to the service of God by symbolically hanging his sword over the altar, and lived for a year in prayer and penance at nearby Manresa, tending to the needs of the sick at the hospital there with devoted selflessness until

he attracted such attention that he withdrew to a solitary life of austerity. It was then that he began to write his famous *Spiritual Exercises*, not published until 1548. But he was still unclear about the direction his new religious life should take; he had formed a plan for converting the Muslims but was dissuaded by a community of Franciscans whom he met while on pilgrimage to Jerusalem. So on returning to Spain in 1524 Ignatius began to study, learning Latin and philosophy and going on to gain a Master of Arts from the university in Paris.

He engaged in much evangelical work during his student days, which puzzled the Spanish authorities as he was not ordained, and he was once imprisoned for a time on suspicion of being a heretic. Although he was declared clear of all faults when he was released, the authorities were cautious in these days of widespread unorthodoxy, and he was banned from teaching any religious message for the next three years.

The Society of Jesus

It was at Paris that Ignatius collected around him the group of students (one of whom was Francis Xavier) who practised his Spiritual Exercises and pledged themselves to the work of the Gospel, by mission to Palestine or in any other capacity dictated by the Pope. Three years later in 1537 the group met again in Venice, all ordained as priests by this time, and since war prevented them from going to Jerusalem they determined to found a new religious order in Rome, bound to loyalty under Pope Paul III. Their plan seemed to receive divine sanction when a vision of Christ appeared to Ignatius as he travelled to Rome with the rule of his new order and the terms of their vows to lay before Pope Paul III, which promised that all would go well. In an effort to commit themselves more effectively to charity, teaching and evangelism the group took a revolutionary step of abolishing the choral celebration of the Divine Office.

They received the official approval of Paul III in 1540, and in 1541 the group took their final vows as the Society of Jesus, with Ignatius as superior-general despite his initial reluctance. He spent the rest of his life supervising the new order in Rome. The hallmark of the Jesuits was total commitment, obedience and spiritual discipline (the order has been likened to a spiritual army) and from the beginning it was involved in missionary activity. Francis Xavier tirelessly evangelized the Far East, and subsequent Jesuit missionaries visited India, South America, Africa and other areas. They reached England in 1542, and were to prove an influential force in Catholic resistance to the Reformation there with men such as Edmund Campion and Robert Southwell.

The order also proved a potent force in the Catholic Counter-Reformation, providing high-quality Catholic education in their schools and colleges throughout Europe and arguing effectively against the creeds of Luther and Calvin, especially under Peter Canisius in Germany. Ignatius insisted that this counter-attack be pursued in a spirit of charity and prayerfulness, teaching by example rather than acrimonious diatribe. Back in Rome, where he lived from this time on, Ignatius founded a house for fallen women and a community for converted Jews, while always inspiring, advising and directing the members of his order in their various tasks. He was known as an uncompromising leader, yet his piety and his gift for friendship and loyalty made him loved rather than feared by his disciples.

Feast-day 31 July
Patron saint of retreats and spiritual exercises

Prayer of St Ignatius Loyola
Soul of Christ, sanctify me.
Body of Christ, save me.
Blood of Christ, inebriate me.
Water out of the side of Christ, wash me.
O good Jesus, hear me;
Hide me within Thy wounds;
Suffer me not to be separated from Thee;
Defend me from the malignant enemy;
Call me at the hour of my death,
And bid me come unto Thee,
That with Thy Saints I may praise Thee
For all eternity. Amen

This prayer is often used during Loyola's famous *Spiritual Exercises*.
Taken from *Manresa: or the Spiritual Exercises of St Ignatius* (The Catholic Publication Society, New York, 1975)

Death and cult

Ignatius died suddenly in Rome on 31 July, so unexpectedly that he did not even receive the last sacraments. He left behind a well-established order with over 1 000 members, operating in nine different areas of Europe and with additional missions throughout the world, to carry through his vision of reform, education and mission. He was canonized in 1622. Pope Pius XI declared him patron of retreats and spiritual exercises, and many churches and schools are also dedicated to him. His *Spiritual Exercises* have had a vast influence on succeeding generations, among Protestants as well as Catholics, and are still widely read today.

Isidore of Seville

c.560 Seville — Seville 636

'The schoolmaster of the Middle Ages'

His scholarship helped form the hearts and minds of all students of religion in the Middle Ages.

Isidore's noble Cartagenian family was blessed with an extraordinary number of saints: his siblings Leander, Fulgentius and Florentian are all venerated. It was under his elder brother Leander that the young Isidore mainly acquired his education, developing a monastic and learned turn of thought that would serve him well in later, clerical life.

Bishop of Seville

In c.600 Isidore succeeded Leander as bishop of Seville, and he ruled the see for the next 36 years. Among his priorities was the completion of his brother's work of converting the Arian Visigoths, and also the more effective organization of the Spanish church by means of synods and councils. The most famous of these, presided over by Isidore himself, were those of Seville in 619 and Toledo in 633, at which the canons which were to form the basis of Spain's constitutional law were laid down. One major result of these councils was the decree which ordered the foundation of a school in every diocese, connected to the cathedral. This pre-empted a similar decree of Charlemagne by several centuries. In these schools he expanded the horizons of learning, incorporating medicine, law and liberal arts in the curriculum. Isidore also encouraged the development of monasticism in Spain, and was renowned for his austerity and his charity to the poor. He died at Seville on 4 April.

Works

Isidore is perhaps best known for his writings, in particular the *Etymologiae*, an encyclopaedia of knowledge drawn from many fields which is perhaps more ambitious than strictly accurate. It was popular throughout the Middle Ages, but his more enduring contribution to scholarship, now regarded as the main source of information we possess, is his history of the Goths, Vandals and Sueri. He also wrote several biographies, treatises of theology and astronomy, monastic rules and a summary of orthodox doctrine. He performed an invaluable service to the church and to history by compiling a list of earlier church laws and decrees previously passed by ecclesiastical councils. Bede was in the process of translating passages from his *De natura rerum* ('On the Wonders of Nature') when he died. Isidore also completed the Mozarabic liturgy begun by his brother. His works were considered essential reading for any medieval cleric or monk, and Dante mentions both him and Bede in his *Paradiso*.

Cult

Surprisingly, Isidore was not officially canonized until 1598, and he was declared a Doctor of the Church by Pope Benedict XIV in 1722. In art he is generally shown as an aged bishop with a prince at his feet, often holding a pen and a book, or with his sainted brothers and sister.

Feast-day 4 April
Patron saint of farmers

James the Great

d. Jerusalem c.44

Friend of Christ

*One of the 'Sons of Thunder',
and also the first disciple to be
martyred for his faith.*

The Gospels agree that James was the son of Zebedee and brother of John, a fisherman who worked with them in his native Galilee. When he was called by Jesus, James was mending nets with his brother by Lake Genesareth.

After this calling, James and his brother stayed with Jesus throughout his years of teaching and miracles and appear to have been among his closest friends. James is specially mentioned in the Gospel accounts of the healing of Peter's mother-in-law and the raising of the daughter of Jairus, and was one of the three who witnessed the Transfiguration on the Mount of Olives and the agony of Jesus in Gethsemane. Jesus nicknamed the brothers 'Boanerges' (sons of thunder), traditionally because of their impetuous desire to strike the Samaritan village down with lightning because it refused Jesus hospitality. It was James and John (or, according to Matthew, their mother) who requested that Jesus reserve them seats in Heaven at his left and right hand.

In the subsequent history of the church, James was the first of the apostles to be martyred. His death by beheading at the

hands of Herod Agrippa I is recorded in Acts 12: 1–2. One legend claims that his accuser repented at the last minute and was beheaded alongside James.

Cult in Spain

Beyond the Biblical evidence little is known of his life, but a tradition beginning in the seventh century asserts that he preached in Spain; from the ninth century he was believed to have been buried there, his body brought from Jerusalem after his martyrdom. Modern scholarship largely rejects the tradition, and it is now widely believed that the shrine is built on the site of an early Christian cemetery in which a culted martyr was buried, but beyond their antiquity no more can be known about them. The influence of the tradition in Spain itself however was enormous. The shrine at Santiago de Compostela was one of the great centres of pilgrimage in the Middle Ages, and James became the rallying figure for Christian opposition to the Moors. Numerous stories of visions and miracles developed to support this view of James and the shrine remains popular in Spain even today. Along the route to Compostela a large number of Cluniac and Augustinian monasteries grew up to serve the many pilgrims making the journey through northern Spain.

The shrine was so significant that in art James is associated with a pilgrim's hat and staff and the cockle-shell representing Compostela, and occasionally at his martyrdom. He is regarded as the patron saint of Spain, and many churches are dedicated to him. Reading Abbey claims to possess the relic of James's hand, presented as a gift by Empress Matilda. He is known as the Great to distinguish him from the other apostle named James, called the Younger.

Feast-day 25 July
Patron saint of Spain, pilgrims, labourers and furriers

Jean-Baptiste Vianney

1786 Dardilly — Ars 1859

The beloved curé of Ars

His compassion, commitment and an all-embracing love were more effective means of service than learning or influence in state.

The son of a peasant farmer, Jean-Baptiste spent his youth as a shepherd on his father's farm but from an early age felt a calling to the priesthood. He had little by way of formal education, partly because of his situation and partly due to the outlawing of clerics in the French Revolution. At the age of 20 he commenced his studies for the priesthood, but although an ecclesiastical student he was mistakenly conscripted into the French army in 1809. He deserted and managed to return secretly to his studies, and was free to return home openly when Napoleon I granted an amnesty to all deserters in 1810. The next year he received the tonsure and in 1813 entered the seminary at Lyons. He encountered great difficulties in coping with the workload, and struggled hopelessly with Latin. His progress was slow, but he was finally ordained in 1815 as one of the most devout, if the most academically underqualified, graduate of the seminary. His ordination was supported by Abbé Balley, his vicar-general, who insisted that the Church had need of holy and devout men just as much as she needed learned ones.

Priest at Ars

Jean-Baptiste served as Balley's curate until the latter died in 1817; the following year he was appointed curé at the small village of Ars-en-Dombes. Here he proved himself an unexpectedly brilliant preacher and counsellor, and he violently attacked all manifestations of indifferent immorality. He campaigned against dancing, drinking and all immodest behaviour, gaining some enemies but winning the hearts of his villagers by his earnest and compassionate nature. He was particularly famed for his ability to read the hearts of those confessing to him (he regularly spent whole days hearing confession and weeping for men's sins), and was attributed with supernatural powers of divination, supposedly also subject to satanic attack by poltergeists.

Miracles were reported of him almost daily; word spread quickly and soon the road to Ars was crammed with visitors seeking out this obscure parish priest. Many contemporaries dismissed him, labelling his zeal insanity; Bishop Devie is reported as saying 'I wish, gentlemen, that all my clergy had a touch of the same madness.'

Death and cult

As Jean-Baptiste matured his severity mellowed and he developed a more sympathetic attitude to those seeking absolution, emphasizing in his teaching the enormity of the love of God. The continual demands on his time and energy left him exhausted, and he three times attempted to retreat to a Carthusian monastery but on each occasion felt bound to return home and meet the needs of his congregation. Weakened by his austere lifestyle he died at Ars on 4 August, aged 73. Having rejected all honours offered to him in life, he was canonized in 1925 by Pope Pius XI who in 1929 declared him patron of all parish priests.

Feast-day 4 August
Patron saint of Parish priests

Jerome

c.341 Strido — Bethlehem 420

The learned, irascible Doctor

Translator of the Vulgate Bible, he was unmatched for his learning, his scholarship and his fiery temper.

Eusebius Hieronymus Sophronius was born in Dalmatia, and in his early years was educated at home by his father and brought up as a Christian. Later he went on to study under the famous pagan grammarian Donatus in Rome, and became learned in rhetoric and classical literature. It was in Rome too that he was baptized, by Pope Liberius in c.360. By now Jerome was in the habit of making regular visits to the churches and catacombs of Rome, and after some travelling through Italy and Gaul, in 370 he decided to join a religious community at Aquileia, along with some friends. This was a scholarly group led by Bishop Valerian. A few years later there was a quarrel within the community: Jerome travelled east and in 374 arrived in Antioch, where two of his companions died. He lived for five years as a hermit in the Syrian desert, prompted to this new austerity by a vision in which he was judged by God as more Ciceronian than Christian. Accordingly he learned Hebrew rather than his beloved classics, and also wrote a life of Paul of Thebes, celebrating monasticism.

On his return to Antioch and against his wishes Jerome was ordained by Paulinus, but in fact he never said a Mass. Further study, under Gregory of Nazianzus, followed; he then translated Eusebius's *Chronicle* into Latin from the Greek and wrote a treatise on Isaiah's vision, his first Scriptural work.

The Vulgate Bible

In 382 Jerome went to Rome to serve as interpreter to Paulinus, who was aspiring to the see of Antioch. He remained there as secretary to Pope Damasus I and began the major task of revising the Latin version of the Bible to create a standard text. Beginning with the Gospels and Psalms, Jerome revised virtually the whole Bible to produce what became known by the 13th century as the Vulgate version. Using his knowledge of Hebrew and Greek to establish the meaning of the original text, Jerome drew on his rhetorical and grammatical training to produce a Latin translation of clarity and great readability based on the text of existing translations. In addition he wrote several important commentaries on Scripture, most notably that on Matthew's Gospel, and gathered around him a group of Christian women, mainly widows, whom he taught and encouraged, giving rise to much scandal which seems on the whole to have been unjustified.

A difficult sanctity

Despite his achievements Jerome found it easy to make enemies; he could be sarcastic, impatient and even, it seems, arrogant and aggressive. On the death of his protector Damasus, therefore, Jerome left Rome under something of a cloud to return east with several of his disciples, including Paula and Eustochium; in 386 they settled in Bethlehem. Paula began a community of nuns and Jerome founded a monastery where he lived for the rest of his life; they also founded a hospice to serve travellers and a free school for the local children in which Jerome taught Latin and Greek. The principle behind the community was that of prayerful study of both Scripture and Christian tradition. Jerome himself was especially concerned with the accuracy and accessibility of the Bible and in his translations and exegesis he drew on the original text and many different translations.

His devotion, learning and commitment to Christ are unquestionable, but his abrasive and sometimes egotistical dealings with other Christians, including the contempt he demonstrated in controversy with his childhood friend Rufinus, speak heavily against him. He even took issue with Augustine when that able theologian questioned Jerome's interpretation of a passage in Paul's letter to the Romans. It is said that Pope Sixtus V, contemplating a picture of Jerome in which the saint holds a stone with which to perform penance, commented that without this sign of voluntary penance Jerome would never have been numbered among the saints.

Death and cult

Jerome died in Bethlehem and his body was buried at the Church of the Nativity there, near the site traditionally believed to have been the birthplace of Christ. It was later translated to the basilica of Sta Maria Maggiore in Rome. He is regarded as one of the four Latin Doctors of the Church and his contribution to biblical scholarship is unequalled. Influential too were his works celebrating monasticism, his fascinating letters and his works against Jovinian which support chastity, and also against Origenism.

In art he is often represented as a cardinal, an anachronism prompted by his service to Pope Damasus. His emblem, appropriately enough, is a lion, which appears throughout the various representations of him as cardinal, scholar, Doctor and founder. This was because of a popular tradition that Jerome had once plucked out a thorn from a lion's foot, and that afterwards the grateful beast followed him everywhere as a tame pet.

Feast-day 30 September
Patron saint of librarians

St Jerome by Cosimo Tura. National Gallery.

Joan of Arc

1412 Domrémy — Rouen 1431

The Maid of Orléans

One of the most inspiring women in history and a powerful national symbol of France.

Youngest of the five children of Jacques d'Arc, a peasant farmer, from her earliest days Joan was exceptional for her piety. She was only 13 when she first heard her famous 'voices', accompanied by brilliant light, which instructed her to serve the Dauphin and save France. She identified them as messages from Saints Michael, Catherine of Alexandria and Margaret of Antioch, but despite her conviction her attempts to join the French army were met by scepticism and derision. She persisted, and after her prophecies of defeat were fulfilled at the Battle of Herrings in 1429, Robert de Baudricourt, commander at Vaucouleurs, sent her to the Dauphin, to whom she proved herself by seeing through his disguise. A group of theologians at Poitiers cross-examined her for three weeks and finally gave their approval to this remarkable girl and her mission.

Joan's first expedition was to relieve besieged Orléans; in April 1429, clad in a suit of white armour, she led her troops and saved the city, capturing several English forts, her men inspired by her visionary courage. In June of that year she secured another important victory over the English troops, capturing Troyes. When the Dauphin was crowned Charles VII at Rheims on 17 July 1429 Joan stood at his side, but even at the pinnacle of her achievement she suffered mockery and suspicion among courtiers, clergy and soldiers.

Trial and death

Still Joan continued to lead the army. A mission to recapture Paris in August failed and the winter months enforced idleness, but in the following spring she set out to relieve Compiègne, besieged by Burgundy, the ally of the English. She was captured there in May and handed over to the English, as Charles made no effort to save her. In Rouen Joan was charged with witchcraft and heresy; although she defended herself intelligently and steadfastly she was inevitably convicted. By some means of trickery or force she was persuaded to recant (the exact terms of this are a matter for debate) but when she defiantly resumed the male attire she had promised to abandon she was declared a heretic and burnt at the stake in the market-place of Rouen on 30 May. Her ashes were thrown into the Seine.

Cult

Twenty years later the case was reopened by a commission of Callistus III. They reached a verdict of innocent, but it was not until 1920 that Joan was canonized by Benedict XV. She is venerated as a virgin rather than a martyr. Joan has appealed to secular and literary minds as well as the pious, and many attempts have been made to explain her 'voices' and her significance as a patriot and as a woman in a male-dominated world. Her romantic life has inspired many artists, who usually portray her as a maiden in armour.

> **Feast-day** 30 May
> Second patron saint of France, soldiers

John Chrysostom

c.347 Antioch — Pontus 407

The golden-mouthed saint

An outspoken and persuasive preacher of absolute integrity.

Fatherless as a baby, John was brought up as a Christian by his mother. He studied oratory under the famous pagan rhetorician Libanius and theology under Diodorus of Tarsus, was baptized as a young man and then abandoned a promising legal career in c.373 to live as an ascetic in a mountain community near Antioch. The austere life ruined his health, and in 381 he returned to Antioch to be made deacon. Five years later he was ordained as a priest by Bishop Flavian of Antioch, whom he served for the next 12 years. His powerful sermons soon gained him the nickname Chrysostom, 'the golden-mouthed'. His method was that of the Antiochene school: he interpreted Scripture literally and sought to show how it applied practically to contemporary life. In 398 he was appointed patriarch of Constantinople, despite his objections, and began wholeheartedly to reform the church of his day.

Powerful enemies

John's primary concern was the misuse of wealth by the rich: in his reforms he made huge personal donations to the poor, cutting back on clerical pomp and extravagance, and funding missions to the East. He was outspoken too in his condemnation of secular extravagance, and although beloved by many he made many influential enemies. Among them was Empress Eudoxia, condemned by John for her vanity and lack of charity, and many prominent churchmen, including his thwarted rival for the title of patriarch, Theophilus of Alexandria.

Under Theophilus's leadership, the Synod of the Oak in 403 condemned John on 29 charges. Most were spurious; they included an unsupported accusation of Origenism and a charge of having personally attacked the empress in a sermon. John was banished but it was an unpopular move; Eudoxia finally repented when an earthquake shook the dissatisfied city and John was recalled, only to recommence his outspoken preaching, denouncing the frivolity and immorality of the public games celebrating the erection of a silver statue of Eudoxia in the city. Within months Theophilus had secured his banishment anew at a largely Arian council in Antioch, and in 404 John was exiled by Emperor Arcadius despite the support of the Pope, many western bishops and the people of his own see.

Death and cult

He travelled to Armenia, where he wrote many extant letters describing his sufferings, and was then moved on to Pontus where he died of exhaustion, treated harshly by his captors. His body was returned to Constantinople 31 years later, to be buried in the Church of the Apostles there.

John's sermons are remarkable for their ageless, practical tone. He is venerated as one of the Greek Doctors of the Church in the West, and in the East as one of the three Holy Hierarchs and Universal Teachers, and gave his name to the revision of the Greek liturgy accomplished by the influence of Constantinople. In art his emblem is a beehive, symbol of eloquence.

Feast-day 13 September
Patron saint of preachers, invoked against epilepsy

John Fisher

1469 Beverley, Yorkshire — London 1535

Bishop and martyr

John Fisher's unshakeable tenet was allegiance to God and Rome before his king.

Son of a textile merchant in Beverley, John was educated at the Minster School until the age of 14 when he entered Cambridge University. Distinguishing himself in both his Bachelors and Masters degrees, he was then elected a Fellow of Michaelhouse (later absorbed into Trinity College). In 1491 he was ordained, and in 1501 was appointed Vice-Chancellor of the University. He resigned this post in 1502, together with his mastership of Michaelhouse, to become chaplain to Lady Margaret Beaumont, the mother of Henry VIII. Lady Margaret and Fisher worked together to reform and endow the university, founding St John's and Christ's Colleges, providing endowments for chairs in divinity at both Oxford and Cambridge and for student scholarships, and generally to improve the standard of scholarship. They arranged for the inclusion of Greek and Hebrew in the curriculum, and appointed the great humanist Erasmus professor of divinity and Greek.

Fisher was appointed Chancellor of the University in 1504, and elected bishop of Rochester in the same year, caring for both his small see and his colleges with the same informed commitment. He wrote widely and was widely read; his sermons especially were famous throughout the continent and he received much acclaim for his work against Luther and his defence of orthodox Catholic doctrine on the Sacrament. Renowned and respected for his holiness and learning, it was no surprise that he was appointed confessor to Catherine of Aragon, the first wife of Henry VIII, in 1527.

When Henry began his moves toward divorce in 1529, Fisher, who had already declared this marriage to a brother's widow to be legal, defended its validity stolidly at the Legatine court. He led the outcry against the king's supremacy in the Church and defended the authority of Rome in convocation, qualifying Henry's new title 'Head of the Church of England' with the phrase unacceptable to Henry: 'so far as the law of Christ allows'.

Death and cult

This determined and articulate opposition could not be tolerated: in 1534, after conviction on a charge of encouraging Elizabeth Barton, a nun whose visions denounced Henry's second marriage, Fisher was sent to the Tower along with Thomas More. He had refused to take the Oath of Succession, which would effectively mean acknowledging the supremacy of the king. While in the Tower, he wrote the treatises *Spiritual Consolation* and *Ways to Perfect Religion* for his sister, a Dominican nun. He refused to reconsider his refusal, and although he was nominated a Cardinal by the new Pope Paul III he was convicted of high treason and sentenced to death in June 1535. Fisher was courteous even on the scaffold, pardoning his executioner. His body was buried without rites, and his head displayed for two weeks on London bridge, then cast into the river. He was canonized on 19 May 1935, and his feast is celebrated along with that of his fellow martyr, Thomas More.

John of the Cross

1542 Fontiveros — Ubeda 1591

Poet, mystic and theologian

Disgrace and misunderstanding haunted him in his attempt to lead the Carmelite movement into reform.

Juan de Yepes y Alvarez was born on 24 June in Spanish Old Castile into an impoverished noble family. His father died while he was a child, and his mother moved with John to Medina del Campo, where he attended the catechism school. John was early apprenticed to the silk-making trade, but soon abandoned it to study at the Jesuit college in 1563, he enrolled with the Carmelite order in the town and went on to study theology in Salamanca before being ordained as priest in 1567.

Discalced monks

By now John was considering a move to the Carthusian order, seeking more complete and prayerful solitude. On a visit back to Medina he met Teresa of Ávila, who persuaded him instead to join her reform movement within the Carmelite order. Teresa had already founded the Discalced Reform for nuns, and in 1586 John and four other friars founded the first men's community at Duruelo. It was then that he took the name 'John of the Cross'. In 1571 he was appointed rector of the new house of studies at Alcala, and in 1572 began a five-year service as confessor and spiritual director of the nuns at Ávila, the mother house of Teresa's movement.

His work of spreading the reform brought him to the attention of the Carmelite leaders, and dissension between Calced and Discalced groups of the order reached such a height that in 1577 John was arrested and imprisoned at Toledo. The conditions in prison were harsh, yet he wrote some of his finest poems here, including 'Noche obscura del Alma' (Dark Night of the Soul). After nine months he escaped, and soon afterwards the Discalceds were formally recognized as distinct from the Calceds and were granted a separate province; John founded and ran a college at Baeza from 1579 to 1581. In 1582, the year of Teresa's death, he became prior at Granada and three years later was appointed provincial of Andalusia, then prior at Segovia.

Death and cult

Throughout this time John was occupied with the foundation of new houses, but the new Order was suffering from serious internal dissention between extremists and moderates. The extremists gained the ascendancy and John, who had always been a staunchly moderate voice, was exiled to suffer humiliation and maltreatment as a monk in remote La Peñuela. He fell sick there and died at Ubeda on 14 December.

His mystical works, such as the *Spiritual canticle*, are among the most renowned in Christian literature, combining a profound poetic sensitivity and vision with a searching intellect and a well-developed theology. His cult quickly became popular beyond the Carmelite Order; he was canonized in 1726 and named a Doctor of the Church in 1926. He is usually shown in art writing before a crucifix, often illuminated by heavenly light, and sometimes with an eagle holding a pen in its mouth.

Feast-day 14 December

151

John the Baptist

d. c.30

Herald of Christ

The voice in the desert who proclaimed the coming of Jesus.

John's father was Zechariah, a priest in Jerusalem, and his mother Elizabeth was a kinswoman of the Virgin Mary. They were both elderly at the time of John's birth, which was foretold by an angel to a disbelieving Zechariah in the Temple (Luke 1: 5–23).

No more is known of John until he appears in c.27 as a wandering preacher in the desert beside the Jordan, the river in which he baptized those who came out from the towns to listen to him (this is the reason for his association with spas). He lived like an Old Testament prophet, in austerity, denouncing sin and demanding repentance. Because his message was 'Make straight the way of the Lord!' he has recently been adopted as the patron of motorways.

Coming of Jesus

Jesus came to be baptized by John, who recognized him instantly and saw the Holy Spirit descending on Christ like a dove. As Jesus's ministry began, John's work decreased. He was an outspoken and fearless speaker however, denouncing the hypocrisy of the religious leaders and attacking Herod Antipas, who had married his niece Herodias. He was imprisoned, and followed news of Jesus's ministry from jail, on one occasion sending messengers to ask Jesus to confirm whether he was indeed the Messiah.

Death and cult

Herodias now sought revenge, and her opportunity came when her daughter Salome pleased Herod so much by her dancing that she was offered any gift she named. At her mother's prompting she requested the head of John the Baptist on a dish. Herod regretted his rashness but was too proud to break his oath; John was beheaded.

He is believed to have been buried at Sebaste in Samaria, where there is evidence of a fourth-century cult, but the tomb was destroyed by Julian the Apostate. Although various relics are claimed by Rome and elsewhere, it is unlikely that many are authentic. John has always been one of the most popular of saints, beloved of monks for his solitary and austere desert life, and regarded as particularly effective in preparing the heart to receive Christ. Countless churches have been dedicated to him, and he is regarded as a patron of the Knights Hospitallers, who are protectors of the Holy Sepulchre in Jerusalem and of pilgrims to the Holy Land.

Since he proclaimed the 'Lamb of God', John's emblem is a lamb, and he often carries a long cross signifying his mission and Christ's sacrificial death. He is frequently shown playing alongside the Christ-child. As an adult he is shown in animal furs, preaching or proclaiming Christ, and his execution is a favourite scene. Unusually, John's principal feast celebrates his birth rather than his death, calculated to be six months before that of Christ. It is believed that he was sanctified from Original Sin in the womb.

Feast-day 24 June
Patron saint of motorways, farriers, tailors and the Knights Hospitallers

John the Evangelist

d. Ephesus c.100

The one that Jesus loved

Youngest of the disciples and the only one to die a natural death, his theological and pastoral writings are among the best-loved passages of Scripture.

A Galilean fisherman who worked with his father Zebedee and his older brother James the Great, John was called from Lake Genesareth along with James by Jesus. He seems to have shared with his brother the fiery temperament that earned them the nickname 'Sons of Thunder', but there is no reason to reject the tradition that John himself was the disciple he writes about as 'the one Jesus loved'.

Along with James and Peter, John was present at the healing of Peter's mother-in-law, the raising of Jairus's daughter, the Transfiguration and the agony of Jesus in the Garden of Gethsemane. He was sent along with Peter to prepare for the Last Supper, and when the women reported the angel's appearance to them at Christ's tomb it was Peter and John who ran to the garden; the younger and fitter John reached the tomb first but hesitated to enter. John is the only disciple named as being present at the Crucifixion, when Jesus handed his mother into his care.

Paul refers to Peter, James and John as the pillars of the church in Jerusalem. John was with Peter at the healing of the lame man in the Temple, was imprisoned with him and journeyed with him to Samaria to visit the converts there. He seems to have fulfilled a strongly supportive role to the more outspoken Peter.

Works

His most enduring legacy is his biblical writing; the Gospel of John, now widely accepted as his, was written towards the end of his life some time after the three Synoptic Gospels, and its tone is very different from theirs. John assumes familiarity with the life of Christ and is more concerned with contemplation and exploration of theological truths, always emphasizing Jesus's divinity. His three epistles too are thought to be authentic, but the style of *Revelation*, supposedly written after a vision on Patmos, is so widely different from his other works that his authorship, at least in the usual concrete sense, has been seriously doubted.

Death and cult

After the events documented in Acts, John is traditionally believed to have settled in Ephesus, from where he visited Rome during the persecutions of Domitian and miraculously emerged unhurt after being thrown into boiling oil. After this he is thought to have been exiled to Patmos (where he is supposed to have written Revelation) before returning to Ephesus on the death of Domitian in 96, where he wrote his Gospel and epistles before dying peacefully a few years later.

John's emblem as an evangelist is an eagle, and he is often shown with a cup containing a viper, symbol of the poisoned drink which he was challenged to swallow by a priest of Diana in Ephesus. Many churches have been dedicated to him, and he is claimed as patron by writers, theologians and all trades involved in the production of books.

Feast-day 27 December
Patron saint of theologians, writers and all aspects of the book trade

See illustrations on following page and p177.

153

St John the Evangelist, *from the* Lindisfarne Gospel-book(AD *720*). *British Museum*

Joseph

First century BC — First century AD

The foster-father of Christ

After accounts of the nativity, the life of Mary's husband is difficult to trace.

Although descended from King David, Joseph was a poor man who earned his living as a carpenter: 'an upright man' as he is called in the Gospels. The tradition that he was elderly at Jesus's birth, originating with the apocryphal *Protevangelium* of James, is unfounded; he was probably no more than a few years older than the Virgin Mary.

When he learned that his fiancée was pregnant Joseph was understandably concerned, knowing that the child was not his, but he resolved to spare Mary public humiliation and even death by breaking off the engagement quietly. He was reassured of her virtue by an angel in a dream, and the marriage went ahead. He witnessed the visit of the Magi in Bethlehem. According to Matthew, it was to Joseph that the angel appeared with first a warning to flee to Egypt and then the command to return when the massacre of the Innocents took place. Matthew's Gospel largely presents the nativity story from the point of view of Joseph, while Luke concentrates more on the experiences of the Virgin Mary.

Suspicious of Herod's successor in Israel, Joseph took his wife and the Christ-child back to Nazareth where he presumably recommenced his trade. He and Mary took Jesus to be circumcised and presented to God in the temple at Jerusalem and he was present and concerned, as Mary was, when the 12-year-old Jesus was left behind in the

temple at Jerusalem after Passover. This is the last mention of him in the Gospels. It seems likely that he died before Jesus's ministry began; Mark records that Jesus was told that his mother and brothers wished to see him and at the crucifixion Jesus entrusted his mother to the care of John the Evangelist.

Cult

His cult began in the East with the popular apocryphal *History of Joseph* in the fifth century and only gained widespread popularity in the West in the 15th century: his name was added to the Roman calendar in 1479. In medieval mystery plays, Joseph is portrayed as a human character who provides light relief from the more venerable and sacred figures of Christ and the Virgin. Figures who were influential in propagating his cult include Bridget of Sweden, Teresa of Ávila (who dedicated her reformed Carmelite house at Ávila to him) and Ignatius Loyola. As a human father-figure and tradesman he is widely loved and respected, with many churches and hospitals being dedicated to him. In art he nearly always appears in groups of the Holy Family, usually as an old man carrying a flowering rod and sometimes surrounded by his carpentry tools. He was declared patron of the universal Church by Pius IX in 1870, and Pope Leo XIII proclaimed him as a model for fathers in 1889.

Feast-day 19 March
Patron saint of carpenters, fathers, workers, social justice and travellers, invoked in doubt and when house-hunting

---

Jude

First century

'Judas, not Iscariot'

Best known as the patron saint of hopeless causes because of superstition associated with his unfortunate name.

In Luke's Gospel and the Book of Acts, thought to have been written by Luke, the list of apostles includes the name of Jude but in Matthew and Mark it is replaced by the name Thaddeus; it is widely accepted that the two names refer to the same apostle, believed to be the brother of James the Younger and author of the epistle of Jude. This letter is similar in content to that of Peter's second letter and neither is overtly addressed to any one person or church. Some scholars claim that it was written in the second century to the Gnostics, and this is supported by the caution of the early church: the epistle was named among the *Antilegomena*, the disputed books. The case against its authenticity is strengthened by the fact that the epistle refers to the apostles in the past tense.

Although he is consistently listed among the Twelve in the Gospels, there is no mention of Jude's calling by Jesus, nor any hint as to his occupation before his discipleship. The only incident of note connected specifically with his name took place at the Last Supper, when Jude asked Jesus why it was that he revealed himself to the disciples and not to the world, to which Jesus replied that he and his father would visit all those who loved and obeyed him.

Legend

After Pentecost little is known of Jude's activities. Following the apocryphal *Passion of Simon and Jude* he is traditionally believed to have preached with Simon in Persia, where they were both martyred. Confusion of Thaddeus with Addai has given rise to a tradition that he preached in Mesopotamia. The relics of Simon and Jude were supposedly translated to St Peter's in Rome around the eighth century, with Rheims and Toulouse also laying claim to some relics.

Cult

Jude is best known in modern days as the patron saint of hopeless cases, a familiar name in the personal columns of *The Times* for appeals for help or expressions of gratitude. This is said to have originated from the uncomfortable similarity of Jude's name to that of Jesus's betrayer, Judas Iscariot: the faithful avoided seeking his help for fear of confusion and hence he was only resorted to in desperate situations, when prayer to all other saints had failed.

There are a few ancient churches dedicated to Saints Simon and Jude, but none for either alone. In art he is generally represented with the club of his martyrdom, occasionally holding his book, and sometimes holding a ship while Simon carries a fish, founded on an assumption that, as cousins of Zebedee, they too were fishermen.

Feast-day 28 October
Patron saint of hopeless causes

Julian the Hospitaller

Date unknown

Saved by hospitality

Although most probably the hero of a pious, romantic fiction rather than a historical figure, Julian's protection has been claimed by generations.

The facts about Julian are few; he has no shrine, no date and no known country of origin. His popularity stems from the story first found in the 13th century, written by Vincent de Beauvais, and immortalized in Jacobus de Voragine's *Golden Legend* and more recently by Flaubert in his *Trois Contes*.

Legend

According to this tradition Julian was a nobleman who, while hunting a stag in his youth, was reproached by his prey and warned that he would one day kill his own parents. In an attempt to avoid such a terrible destiny, Oedipus-like, Julian fled the country and arrived at a foreign court where he performed such outstanding service that he was knighted by the king, and married a rich widow with whom he received a magnificent castle as dowry. Ever since he had run away from home, however, his mother and father had sought him unceasingly and one day, while Julian was absent from his castle, they finally arrived at their son's door and his wife gave them her own room to sleep in. When Julian returned his wife was out at church; he however, on entering her room and discovering the body of a man and woman in the

bed, instantly assumed that she had taken a lover and killed the couple in fury. As he left the castle he met his wife returning from church and discovered his dreadful mistake.

Driven by anguished remorse, Julian left his castle vowing to perform a suitable penance. He and his wife eventually came to a ford across a wide river, and there they built a hospice for travellers and the poor. Julian would also, like Christopher, guide travellers across the river. One night, responding to cries for help, he found a traveller sick and almost dead from cold outside. He brought the man, a leper, into his house and gave him his own bed to sleep in but could not save his life. As the man died, Julian saw a vision of his departing soul which reassured him that God had accepted his penance, and soon afterwards he and his wife died.

Cult

The story caught the imagination and devotion of many: numerous hospitals have been dedicated to Julian, particularly in the Netherlands, and he is considered to be the protector of ferrymen, innkeepers and travellers. This patronage was extended in an interesting direction to include wandering musicians and circus folk. Various scenes from the legend are depicted in art, most commonly the killing of his parents in bed. Two famous cycles of his life from the 13th century survive in the stained glass at Chartres and Rouen.

Feast-day 12 February
Patron saint of ferrymen, innkeepers, travellers, wandering musicians and circus people

Kentigern (Mungo)

c.518 Lothian — Glasgow c.603

The apostle of Cumbria

The first bishop of Strathclyde, who is known affectionately by his petname throughout Scotland and especially in Glasgow.

Although few facts are known of Kentigern's life, in Scottish folklore he is a potent figure around whom many legends have grown up. The earliest extant sources are from the 11th and 12th centuries, such as Jocelin of Furness's *Vita Kentigerni*, but they contain elements which are considerably older.

According to these legends, Kentigern was the illegitimate grandson of a British prince, possibly Urien. His pregnant mother, a princess named Thenew (or Theneva) was thrown from a cliff when her shame was discovered, and being found alive at the bottom was placed in a coracle and left to drift on the Firth of Forth. She ran aground at Culross and was taken in by St Serf, who gave her child the pet name Mungo ('dear friend') in addition to his more formal name Kentigern, 'chief lord', when it was born.

Life

Serf raised Mungo, who grew up to become a hermit in Glasghu (modern Glasgow) in the traditions of Irish monasticism, known for his holiness. He founded a monastery there at Cathures and was consecrated first bishop of Strathclyde in c.543. His see was torn apart by fighting and political unrest; one legend claims that Kentigern fled to Wales in 553 where he met St David at

Menevia and founded a monastery at Llanelwy and a bishopric before returning to Scotland. However, since this legend is unsupported by dedications or evidence of a cult there it seems very unlikely. More probably he fled or was exiled to Cumbria before returning to Hoddam (modern Dumfries) and then to Glasgow at the invitation of the new king, Rederech Hael, in 573. Another legend claims that he exchanged pastoral staffs with the elderly St Columba, who was believed to have paid him a visit in c.584. He died an old man in Glasgow, and his relics are claimed by the cathedral of St Mungo there.

One of the most famous anecdotes associated with Kentigern tells how he came to the aid of an unfaithful queen, who had given the king's ring to a lover. The outraged king had thrown the ring into the sea and challenged her to find it within three days or face dire consequences. Kentigern comforted her, and one of his monks miraculously caught a salmon, inside which the ring was found unharmed.

Cult

Many Scottish and some English churches have been dedicated to Kentigern under his petname Mungo. Along with his mother Thenew he is regarded as the patron saint of Glasgow. The legend of the ring and the salmon forms the basis of the heraldic arms of Glasgow, and it is the most popular artistic depiction of the saint. He is also shown meeting St Columba in the presence of a column of fire.

Feast-day 14 January
Patron saint of Glasgow

Leo the Great

c.390 Rome — Rome 461

Inheritor of the authority of Peter

Pope at a time of crisis for Rome, Leo is one of the greatest of the Latin Fathers.

Nothing is known of Leo's early years, although it is thought that he was born in Tuscany or of Tuscan parents in Rome. We first hear of him as a deacon under Popes Celestine I and Sixtus III, obviously a figure who commanded respect within the church since he corresponded with Cyril of Alexandria and had a treatise by John Cassian dedicated to him. He was called to act as peacemaker between Aetius and Albinus, quarreling generals whose emnity was laying Gaul open to barbarian attacks, and it was while he was still in Gaul that Leo learnt that he had been appointed Pope. After his consecration on 29 September 440, he began his pontificate by giving a series of 76 sermons which still survive, dealing with faith and charity and opposing various prevalent heresies.

At the Council of Chalcedon in 451, convened to settle a doctrinal issue on the nature of Christ, Leo produced his *Tome*, a concise statement of the Incarnation which was well received at the time and which has served to clarify the doctrine for the Church ever since. However the council also ruled that the see of Constantinople be elevated above those of Alexandria and Antioch, a move which threatened the supremacy of Rome, and one which Leo strongly opposed.

Fall of Rome

The next year Italy was attacked by the Huns under Attila, and it seemed that defenceless Rome would inevitably fall, but Leo secured a personal interview with Attila and persuaded him to accept tribute rather than plunder the city. He had less luck three years later with Genseric, leader of the Vandals: despite Leo's intercession Rome was sacked and looted for a fortnight. Leo did obtain a promise that the city would not be burnt, and after its devastation he was able patiently to set about rebuilding the city and its churches and restoring the stricken population. To those citizens held prisoner in Africa he sent priests and money. He possessed throughout everything a quiet and unshakeable belief in the doctrinal and spiritual supremacy of Rome, and his example brought new respect and influence to the papacy. In a time of political upheaval, with as many failures as successes, Leo's insistence on the centrality of Rome, combined with an exemplary personal holiness and fortitude, provided a model for the papacy throughout the coming centuries.

Death and cult

Leo died in Rome on 10 November, and was buried at St Peter's where his relics were enshrined on 28 June 688. The Leonine Sacramentary contains collects that may be his, and were at least inspired by his teaching, and on the strength of the *Tome*, his sermons and his letters he was declared a Doctor of the Church by Benedict XIV in 1754. In art he is usually represented with a dragon, often in the company of St Peter, whose authority as first bishop of Rome Leo believed to be located and transmitted in the papacy.

Feast-day 10 November

Louis IX

1215 Poissy — Tunis 1270

The model medieval ruler

His rule was a golden age for Gothic architecture, Christian kingship and France.

Twelve-year-old Louis succeeded to the throne of France after the death of his father, Louis VIII, in 1226. During his minority his mother, the part-English Blanche of Castile, acted as regent, defending the throne ably in the face of rebellion. In 1234 Louis married Margaret of Provence, sister-in-law to King Henry III of England, by whom he had 11 children; the next year he reached his majority and took upon himself the kingship, retaining his capable mother as advisor.

Victory at home

Louis appears to have ruled as an ideal Christian king, administering justice impartially, fighting capably and courageously to defend his country and demonstrating his piety on every occasion. At home he was obliged to defend himself against rebellions in southern France in 1242–3, and in 1242 he defeated Henry III of England in battle at Taillebourg, conquered Poitou, and the following year defeated Raymond VII of Toulouse. Later, by two judicious treaties with ambitious England and Aragon, he established peace in his kingdom.

Disaster in the East

Louis's ventures eastwards, although greatly daring, were less successful. After an illness in 1244 Louis had determined to go on Crusade, so in 1248, leaving Blanche as regent in his stead, he sailed for the Holy Land. He captured Damietta in 1249 but was defeated by the Saracens at Mansura

the following year, and he and his men were held to ransom. Once freed he visited the Holy Land where he remained in Acre, accomplishing little, until the death of Blanche in 1254 obliged him to return to France. He travelled East again in 1270 but this expedition was to prove even more disastrous than the last: he contracted typhoid on landing in Tunis and died on 25 August.

The pious king

He left behind an enduring legacy in France: in addition to the many religious and educational establishments founded by him, he had built the famous church of Sainte Chapelle in Paris to house a relic believed to be Christ's crown of thorns, presented by Emperor Baldwin of Constantinople in 1239. His spiritual legacy is summarized in his *Testament*, advice to his son in which he sets out clearly his ideals and practical guidelines for living. The *Life* by John of Joinville, a friend and fellow soldier, affectionately details the saint's failings as well as his virtues and presents a man characterized by integrity, generosity of spirit, courage, good sense and a piety manifest in his aversion to swearing as much as his devotion to the cause of the Crusades.

Iconography and cult

In art Louis is often shown carrying a model of the Sainte Chapelle, which has led to his patronage of stonemasons and sculptors. As he personified the ideal virtues of the medieval monarch so impressively, he was proclaimed the model and patron of the French monarchy and, by extension, of the French military.

> **Feast-day** 25 August
> Patron saint of French monarchs and soldiers, and of stonemasons and sculptors

Luke

First century

The learned doctor

Luke's vivid accounts are our most direct link with the life, doctrine and doings of the early church.

Practically all the information we have about Luke comes from the New Testament. A doctor (Colossians 4: 14), believed by Eusebius and Jerome to be of Greek origin, he accompanied Paul on his second missionary journey and stayed on in Philippi to lead the church there until c.57, when he rejoined Paul on his third missionary journey. He was with Paul during the shipwreck on Malta and under house arrest in Rome, and after Paul's death is traditionally believed to have gone to Antioch in Greece to lead the Christian community there until his death as an old man: unsubstantiated tradition holds that he remained unmarried throughout his life. Some traditions claim that he was martyred, but this seems unlikely. His relics have been claimed by Constantinople and Padua.

Works

Luke is widely recognized as the author of the Gospel that bears his name (although there is no record of his authorship before the second century) and the Book of Acts, our main source of information about the early church, and in both he proves to be a careful and observant historian. He frequently anchors his narrative in secular history by reference to events external to the biblical events, and recent archaeology has tended to confirm the historicity of his account.

His Gospel is notable for its emphasis on Jesus's compassion, especially as it was manifest towards those on the fringe of New Testament Jewish society: women, the poor, lepers, Samaritans, Gentiles. Being a Greek himself he is careful to emphasize the universality of Christ's sacrifice, whereas Matthew the Jew is more concerned with portraying Jesus as the promised Jewish Messiah.

It is possible that Luke visited Mary in Jerusalem before writing his Gospel (dated between 70 and 90); certainly his version of the nativity story is told sensitively and with much detail from the point of view of Mary. He is traditionally accredited with making several icons of the Blessed Virgin, which has led to his patronage of artists, but this is unsubstantiated. The Book of Acts was written in Rome, either during Paul's imprisonment or shortly after his death, and tells with vivid detail of the growth of the early church under the Holy Spirit from the Resurrection to c.63. Some legends claim that he was himself one of Jesus's 70 disciples, but he is more likely to have been a disciple of Paul.

Cult

In art Luke's evangelistic emblem is an ox, perhaps because he mentions Zechariah's sacrifice in the temple at the beginning of his Gospel, and this has led to his patronage of butchers. He is often shown painting the Virgin or holding his book, dressed in his doctor's robes and cap.

> **Feast-day** 18 October
> Patron saint of butchers, bookbinders, doctors, painters, sculptors, glassworkers and surgeons

See illustrations on following page and p177.

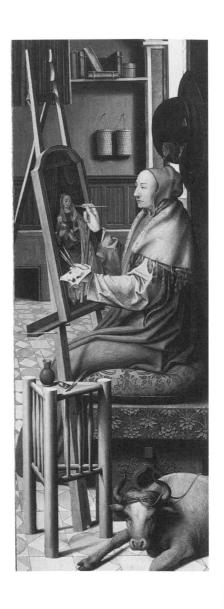

St Luke painting the Virgin and Child.
Altarpiece panel after Quinten Massys.
National Gallery.

Madeleine Sophie Barat

1779 Joigny — Paris 1865

Foundress of the Society of the Sacred Heart

Despite her tractable disposition, Madeleine possessed great ability and strength of character.

Jacques Barat, a cooper and the owner of a small vineyard in Burgundy, produced two children with strong religious leanings. Louis, his son, was a promising student for the priesthood while his daughter Madeleine, 11 years younger, performed without complaint the strict penances and disciplines imposed upon her by her brother, who took charge of her education. Louis was arrested in 1793 in Paris for rejecting the civil constitution of the clergy, and on his release he brought his sister to Paris to continue to supervise her education, which was by now almost exclusively religious.

Society of the Sacred Heart

At this stage Madeleine hoped to enter a Carmelite convent, but in 1800 she was guided by the advice of her brother and one Abbé Varin, a priest greatly concerned with women's education, to join a new community founded by the latter. The aim of the new institution, the Society of the Sacred Heart of Jesus (the female counterpart of the Society of Jesus) was to promote educational work among all classes. At the first foundation, in Amiens, Madeleine was appointed superior in 1802, although at 23 she was the youngest member of the group. During her rule of 63 years the convent was to make further foundations in France and

beyond, and even in America, under Sister Philippine Duchesne.

The order received papal approval from Leo XII in 1826, and its reputation for academic excellence soon established it as one of the most popular educational orders in Europe. Much of its success was due to the intelligent way in which the curriculum and methods of teaching were arranged: a general plan for all the houses was drawn up in Paris to ensure a consistently high standard, but provision was made for incorporating new educational ideas and adapting to particular situations. By the end of her lifetime there were more than 100 houses in 12 countries. Madeleine travelled to many of them, founding new schools and visiting existing ones to encourage and improve them. During the early days of the community one superior took advantage of Madeleine's absence to discredit her leadership, but her position was secure by 1815 and the work of expansion continued apace.

Death and cult

Madeleine was known for her wisdom and astuteness; it seemed that she could sense when the time was right to begin a new venture and when to hold back. She was considered so vital to the work of the school that when she expressed a desire to retire at the age of 85 a helper was appointed for her instead, and she carried on as superior for another year before dying on 25 May. Her body, believed to be incorrupt, lies at Jette in Belgium. Madeleine was canonized in 1925, and the influence of her foundations is still acknowledged throughout Europe.

Feast-day 25 May

Malachy (Mael Maedoc)

c.1094 Armagh — Clairvaux 1148

The pioneer of Gregorian reform in Ireland

His systematic attempts at reform revolutionized the monastic traditions of Ireland.

The son of a schoolteacher, Malachy became a monk under abbot Imar and was ordained a priest by St Celsus in 1119. For some time he continued studying, now under St Malchus of Lismore, and when Cellach of Armagh was away in Dublin Malachy ran his diocese as vicar. In this difficult area, scarred by pagan traditions and repeated Viking attacks, he tried to reform both clergy and society. Malachy's system crystallized under the tuition of Malchus, archbishop of Rome, who taught him the Gregorian reform programme and its application to monastery, church and society.

Monastic reform

In 1123 Malachy was entrusted with the revival of the deserted abbey at Bangor in Co Down, and the following year he was made Bishop of Connor and Down. With a handful of monks he built a wooden church and set about reviving the spiritual life of his see, where few priests were available, little money was forthcoming in tithes and the authority of tradition was preferred over that of the church. His commitment and ability were producing results when he was forced from his diocese by war. He fled to Lismore where he founded the monastery at Inveragh.

Named the next metropolitan of Armagh by the dying Cellach in 1129, he was unable to take up the post for several years; the archbishopric had traditionally been hereditary and his rival Muirchertach had the support of Cellach's clan. Malachy was reluctant to cause trouble, and it was not until the papal legate Gilbert of Limerick intervened that he finally took jurisdiction at least in part of the diocese. This uneasy settlement lasted until Muirchertach's death; Malachy reclaimed Armagh from his successor Niall, who still retained much of his influence in the north. Finally Malachy resigned in 1137 and a compromise accepted by all parties was elected, Gilla the abbot of Derry.

On returning to Connor Malachy formally divided it into two sees, Connor and Down, becoming bishop of Down himself. In 1139 he journeyed to Rome, seeking papal approval for the reforms made and pallia for the archbishops of Cashel and Armagh. He visited Bernard of Clairvaux on the way and left a few monks with him for training. His quest for the pallia was unsuccessful, but Pope Innocent II made him papal legate for Ireland. On his return Malachy founded the monastery of Mellifont in 1142 with his Cistercian-trained monks.

Death and cult

After the Synod of Innishpatrick in 1148 Malachy was again sent to seek papal approval for the pallia but he died on the way, in the arms of Bernard at Clairvaux who wrote his *Life*. He was buried at Clairvaux and his cult was approved in 1190. The *Prophecies of St Malachy*, which purport to detail the attributes of future popes, are a 16th-century fake. In art Malachy is represented giving an apple to the king to restore his sight.

Feast-day 3 November

Margaret Clitherow

1556 York — York 1586

The pearl of York

One of those who risked their lives to defend their faith and help their fellow Catholics in the dangerous days after the Reformation.

Thomas Middleton, a candle-maker in York who later became sheriff there, brought up his daughter Margaret as a Protestant. She was married to a wealthy butcher named John Clitherow in 1571 and three years later she converted to Catholicism. Her husband remained staunchly Protestant, but the marriage seems to have continued on good terms, despite the fines which John was repeatedly obliged to pay because of his wife's absence from the Protestant services. As Margaret became more outspoken and active in her faith she was imprisoned for two years, and profited from the confinement by learning to read. On her release she set about establishing a small school in her house for the benefit of her own children and those of the neighbourhood. Her husband allowed her to carry on these dangerous activities in their home, even acquiescing when Margaret gave shelter to fugitive priests in a secret room built specially for the purpose.

Discovery

Suspicion grew however, and in 1586 John Clitherow was brought before a court to explain his son's absence; the boy was in fact studying at a Catholic college on the Continent. The house was searched. No incriminating evidence of Catholic activities was found but in subsequent questioning one of the children of the school, terrified by the threats of his interrogators, revealed the location of the secret room, in which were found the vestments and vessels for Mass, and Margaret was brought to trial.

Death and cult

Wanting to spare her friends and children the ordeal of testifying against her, Margaret stolidly refused to plead, insisting that 'Having made no offence, I need no trial'. She held to her refusal, and was therefore sentenced to the penalty, death by pressing (the *peine forte et dure*). On 25 March in the Tolbooth at York she was crushed to death under a 800-pound weight, killed within 15 minutes.

Because of her charming and compassionate nature, and also the terrible death which she suffered, Margaret Clitherow has always been a popular martyr. She was canonized by Pope Paul VI in 1970, one of the Forty Martyrs of England and Wales, and she is especially venerated in York, where the place of her trial and imprisonment still survives. A relic of her hand has been preserved at the Bar Convent there.

Feast-day 25 October

Margaret Mary Alacoque

1647 L'Hautecour — Paray-le-Monial 1690

Saint of the Sacred Heart

Founder of the devotion to the Sacred Heart, who faced misunderstanding and hostility throughout her life as a nun.

Born in Burgundy on 22 July, Margaret Mary was the fifth of the seven children of Claude Alacoque, a royal notary, and Philiberte. Her father died when Margaret was only eight and she was sent to school at the Poor Clares in Charolles, where she made her first communion. But after only two years at the school she was forced to leave through ill-health and between the ages of 10 and 15 was bedridden with rheumatic fever. Even after partial recovery, she remained weak and heavily dependant on her mother and relatives. It was during these years that her devotion to the Blessed Sacrament, her contemplative nature and her sense of the spiritual value of suffering were nurtured, and from the age of 20 she began to experience visions of Christ.

A troubled visionary

Margaret rejected the possibility of marriage and in 1671 enrolled in the Visitation Order at Paray-le-Monial, where after a year as a somewhat clumsy but likeable novice she made her profession as a nun. Over the next three years she experienced her most famous series of visions: in them Christ is said to have instructed her to spread devotion to the Sacred Heart and to nominate a feast-day in its honour, and to have given her the devotion known as 'Holy Hour'.

But Margaret's efforts to obey were met initially by disbelief and rejection by her superior, Mother de Saumaise, and although she was eventually won over, Margaret faced much opposition from theologians and members of her community. Their lack of sympathy is perhaps understandable: many must have found it difficult to acquiesce gracefully when Margaret informed the community that she had twice been asked by Christ to serve as victim for all their shortcomings. One source of unfailing support was the Jesuit confessor to the convent, Claude la Colombière, who made her visions more widely known and insisted on their genuineness.

Final years and cult

The full support of her community was only obtained in 1683, when Mother Melin became superior and elevated Margaret to be her assistant and later novice-mistress. In 1686 the convent began to keep the feast of the Sacred Heart; two years later a chapel was built in its honour in Paray-le-Monial, and the feast quickly spread to be kept by other houses of the Visitation order.

Margaret died in the convent on 17 October, and in 1765 Pope Clement XIII officially approved the devotion to the Sacred Heart. She was beatified in 1864 by Pius IX, and canonized by Benedict XV in 1920. Her title as 'Saint of the Sacred Heart' is shared with St John Eudes and Claude la Colombière.

Feast-day 17 October

Margaret of Antioch (Marina)

Third or fourth century

'The very great martyr, Marina'

Margaret's colourful tortures have always fascinated the pious, defying the reservations of the established church itself.

Despite her popularity and influence, Margaret is almost certainly a fictitious character and her legend was declared apocryphal by Pope Gelasius as early as 494. The *Acts* were written by one Theotimus, an attendant who claimed to be an eye-witness to his mistress's death, but they are patently forged. No reference to her occurs in ancient liturgy, but her cult spread from the East and gained popularity in the Middle Ages and particularly during the Crusades.

According to legend, Margaret's father was a pagan priest in Antioch, Pisidia, named Aedisius. When his daughter became a Christian he threw her out of the house, and she was forced to become a shepherdess. Her charms soon won her the unwanted attentions of the prefect of Antioch Olybrius, but when his amorous advances were spurned he revenged himself by denouncing her to the authorities as a Christian and Margaret was then put through a catalogue of horrific and fantastic tortures. One of the most famous of her ordeals was being swallowed by Satan in the form of a dragon, but the cross which she carried so irritated his throat that he was forced to spew her out, unharmed.

The attempts of the authorities to execute her by means of fire and drowning failed, and the members of the crowd which had gathered to watch her execution were converted by the miracles they saw and

executed in their turn. Finally, Margaret was beheaded with most of her converts in the persecutions of Diocletian. She was buried at Antioch, but it was claimed that her relics were stolen and taken to San Pietro della Valle and translated from there to Montefiascone in 1145. A further, partial translation is claimed for Venice in 1213.

Cult

Many benefits are traditionally associated with her invocation, including a promise that all those who read or spread her legend would receive a heavenly crown. The legend that she emerged unharmed from the dragon's belly is obviously the reason for her patronage of safe childbirth, although some versions of her legend claim that she herself promised her special protection to all pregnant women who called upon her. She is also said to have promised to intercede for anyone who invoked her upon the deathbed, to save them from the clutches of the Devil.

Obviously, these incentives did much to further the popularity of her cult. Countless churches were dedicated to her, especially in Norfolk, many *Lives* were written, and she is a popular figure in art, usually shown emerging from the belly of the dragon or transfixing it with a long cross. Joan of Arc claimed that Margaret's voice was one of those telling her of her mission to save France, and she was one of the Fourteen Holy Helpers. Her cult was suppressed in 1969.

Feast-day 20 July
Patron saint of women, nurses and peasants, invoked in childbirth and against barrenness or loss of milk

---

Margaret of Cortona

1247 Laviano — Cortona 1297

Patroness of penitent women

Converted to a holy life after a youth of luxury and immorality, Margaret of Cortona's penitence and charity were legendary.

Margaret of Cortona was born into a Tuscan peasant family; her mother died when Margaret was only seven, and when her father remarried two years later his wife was unsympathetic towards her young stepdaughter. At the age of 18, Margaret, now renowned for her beauty, ran away from home to become the mistress of a young nobleman from Montepulciano, whose name she does not mention in her *Confessions*. She lived with her lover for nine years in ostentation and luxury, and bore him a son, before his death at the hands of an unknown murderer in 1273. According to legend his hound returned alone to lead Margaret to his master's body, hence she is frequently represented with a dog pulling at her robe and a skull beneath her feet.

A new way of life

The death of her lover shocked Margaret into penitence; she made a public confession of her sins in a church near Cortona in Tuscany and appealed to her father but he refused to allow her back in his house. She and her son were finally taken in by two ladies of the church, Marinana and Raneria. From now on Margaret's life was as self-denying as it had previously been self-indulgent. She enrolled as a Franciscan tertiary and underwent a reclusive probation of three years, during which time her spiritual advisors were Friars John da Castiglione and Giunta Bevegnati. They frequently urged her to moderate the more extreme forms of self-chastisement to which she subjected herself, including self-mutilation, sleep deprivation and the wearing of haircloth. Margaret devoted herself to works of charity and to prayer and counsel which converted many, but she faced slanderous gossip concerning her relationship with the friars. The rumours, later proved to be unfounded, were so serious that in c.1289 Friar Giunta was transferred to Siena.

Margaret is renowned for her supernatural experiences, including visions of Christ as a peacemaker, frequently admonishing rulers. Friar Giunta records many of these visions in his *Legend of St Margaret*, supposedly dictated by the saint herself. In response to one vision, in 1286 Margaret set up a community of women to care for the poor and sick, to extend the charity she had hitherto practised from her own home, which she named *Le Poverelle*. She established a hospital for the work of the order in Cortona, and she also founded the Confraternity of Our Lady of Mercy, whose members were pledged to support it.

Death and cult

Margaret died at the age of 50, after 29 years of penitence, and her allegedly incorrupt body lies in the church at Cortona with a statue by Giovanni Pisano showing her with the dog that led her to her lover's body. Although acclaimed as a saint immediately after her death, she was not formally canonized until 1728.

Feast-day 22 February
Patron saint of female penitents

Margaret of Scotland

c.1045 Hungary — Edinburgh 1093

A civilizing influence

She crusaded tirelessly for a Scottish church and government more in line with the standards of Europe.

During the rule of the Danes in England, the ousted Anglo-Saxon royal family lived in exile in the court of St Stephen of Hungary and it was here that Margaret was born and educated, grand-daughter of Edmund Ironside and daughter of Prince Edward d'Outremer and Agatha, a German princess. In 1057 she was brought back to England, to the court of Edward the Confessor, but her family found themselves in danger yet again after the Norman Conquest of 1066 and fled England a second time, arriving under the protection of Malcolm III (Malcolm Canmore) at his court in Scotland.

Malcolm married the beautiful, pious Margaret at Dunfermline castle in 1070, and their marriage seems to have been an exceptionally happy and fruitful one. The new queen was well-loved, renowned for her devotion and charity, and she was industrious in her care for her adopted country. It was largely due to Margaret's influence on her husband that the reputation of the Scottish court was improved in Europe; she insisted on the adoption of Anglo-Norman standards of civilization in a culture which had previously cared very little for such niceties, and nurtured in the illiterate Malcolm an appreciation of books, learning and art.

Margaret pressed too for a reforming movement in the lacklustre church of Scotland, and founded many monasteries, hostels and churches, including in 1072

Dunfermline Abbey, which became the Scottish equivalent of Westminster Abbey, burial ground for a line of Scottish monarchs. She also revived the famous monastery at Iona, founded by Columba. Margaret's influence in the social, political and religious spheres was decidedly English: her reforms have been regarded as unwanted interference almost as frequently as saintly endeavour.

Death and cult

Eight children were born of the marriage of Malcolm and Margaret; David became one of the best-loved of Scottish kings and was canonized like his mother, Alexander also became king, and Matilda, who married Henry I of England, is the link in the English royal family between the ancient Anglo-Saxon and the Norman lines. Another son was killed along with his father in a rebel attack on Alnwick Castle in 1093. Four days later, broken-hearted and worn out by a life of austerity and childbearing, Margaret herself died at Edinburgh Castle and was buried beside her husband in Dunfermline Abbey. After a papal investigation into her life and various alleged miracles her relics were translated on 19 June 1250. They were further translated (along with those of her husband) during the Reformation, when they were taken to Madrid for safety, and it was at this time that the Jesuits at Douai secured her head. The only Scottish saint to be universally venerated in the Roman calendar, Margaret was named a patron of Scotland in 1673. She is usually represented in art carrying a black cross as she goes about her charitable work visiting the sick.

Feast-day 16 November
Patron saint of Scotland

Mark

d. c.74

The first Gospel-writer

A key figure in the early church, Mark worked closely with both Paul and Peter.

The identification of Mark the evangelist has long been an area of interest and debate for scholars; it is now widely accepted that the author of Mark's Gospel is the same John Mark whose mother welcomed the apostles into her house in Jerusalem, the cousin of Barnabas and probably a Levite, and possibly the young man who followed Jesus after his arrest and avoided capture by slipping free from his robe when he was caught (this incident is recounted only in Mark's Gospel).

Mark accompanied Paul and Barnabas on their first missionary journey but at Perga in Pamphylia he left them to return to Jerusalem. The reason for this is unclear, but Paul was obviously so disappointed in him that he refused Barnabas's request that Mark accompany them on the next missionary journey. This was the reason for the split between Paul and Barnabas; Paul left for Asia Minor while Barnabas and Mark went on to evangelize Cyprus. The breach appears to have been healed however: when Paul was imprisoned in Rome for the first time we find Mark with him as a helper (Colossians 4: 10).

The interpreter of Peter

In Rome Mark was a disciple of Peter, who refers to him warmly as 'my son'. It is thought that Mark based much of his Gospel on the eye-witness accounts and the teaching of Peter, and in 130 Papias, bishop of Hierapolis, called him 'the Interpreter of Peter', a title supported by Clement of Alexandria. It was in Rome that he probably wrote his account of Jesus's life and teaching sometime between 60 and 70, the first of the Gospel-writers whose work was almost certainly used as a source by both Matthew and Luke. His style is vivid, observant and somewhat rushed, which seems to support the hypothesis that it is based on the memories of Peter.

Death and cult

A strong tradition has Mark as first bishop of Alexandria; this is supported by Eusebius but no other ancient authority. He is said to have been martyred there in the reign of Nero, and in 829 his supposed relics were translated from Alexandria to Venice to be enshrined there in the original church of San Marco. This church was burnt in the following century, but the relics were translated into the new church on the site and commemorated by a magnificent series of mosaics in the 12th and 13th centuries. For this reason he is regarded as the patron saint of Venice. Mark's emblem in art is a winged lion, and he is usually shown holding his Gospel as a book or scroll, and occasionally as a bishop on a throne decorated with carved lions.

Feast-day 25 April
Patron saint of Venice, glaziers and notaries, invoked by captives

---

See illustration opposite and on p177.

*St Francis and **St Mark**. Altarpiece panel by Antonio Vivarini. National Gallery.*

Martin of Tours

c.316 Sabaria — Candes c.400

Symbol of charity

An act of simple generosity transformed Martin's life into a selfless quest for holiness and compassion.

Born in Pannonia (modern Hungary), the son of a pagan Roman army officer, Martin was brought up in Pavia. He joined the army, probably as a conscript, but his life changed in c.337, when he tore his cloak in two and gave half to a freezing beggar. That night Christ appeared to him in a dream, wearing the half of the cloak he had given away. Martin was converted to Christianity, refused to continue fighting, was imprisoned and eventually discharged. It is said that when accused of cowardice, Martin offered to stand unarmed between the warring lines.

First Frankish monastery

Returning to Pannonia Martin converted his mother and others, then preached against Arianism in Illyricum to such effect that he was banished from the country. On returning to Italy he angered the Arian bishop of Milan, Auxentius, and was exiled from that country also. He lived for some time as a recluse on a small island off the coast of Liguria. When Hilary of Poitiers returned to his see from banishment under Emperor Constantius in 360 Martin joined him there and was given land at Ligugé on which to establish a hermitage. He was soon joined by disciples, and the group developed into a semi-eremitical community, the first monastery ever founded in Gaul.

After 10 years at Ligugé Martin was popularly acclaimed bishop of Tours in 372,

despite his objections. Even as bishop he lived in a cell close to his cathedral at Tours and then at Marmoutier, where a community of 80 monks soon grew up. He founded several other monasteries and set about destroying pagan temples and sacred trees in the hitherto unreached areas beyond the towns, protected miraculously from harm despite heathen opposition. Various miracles were attributed to him during his episcopate of 25 years, including the raising of a dead man.

Martin was also involved in doctrinal disputes, most famously with the Gnostic Priscillianists. But while rejecting their doctrine, Martin held that their leader should have been tried by the Church rather than the Imperial court and appealed on these grounds against the death sentence served upon him, risking accusations of complicity with heresy.

Death and cult

After Martin's death near Tours on 8 November his cult spread quickly. Hundreds of villages and churches in France are dedicated to him and his shrine at Tours became the major centre for French pilgrimage. He is most frequently represented in art dividing his cloak with a beggar, a symbol of charity and hospitality which has associated him with innkeepers. His emblem is a ball of fire over his head. The popularity of his feast is demonstrated by a second, later emblem, a goose: his feast-day often coincides with the migration of geese. Similarly, the phrase 'St Martin's Summer' refers to the spell of good weather which frequently occurs around this time.

Feast-day 11 November
Patron saint of France, soldiers, beggars and innkeepers

Mary Magdalene

First century

Loyal follower of Christ

Revered throughout the Church's history as a penitent whose changed life testifies to the love and power of Christ.

Mary probably came from Magdala, a town on the west coast of the Sea of Galilee, and when Jesus began his ministry in Galilee she was one of the women who followed and supported him. The Gospels record that Jesus cast seven demons out of her, and throughout the church's history she has stood as the archetypal repentant sinner. Mary was one of the group of women who stood at the foot of Jesus's Cross and it was she, together with Joanna and Mary the mother of James and Salome, who discovered the empty tomb and heard the angel proclaim Christ's resurrection. Most memorably of all, however, she was the first to see the risen Lord who appeared to her in the garden of his burial later that day; blinded by her tears, she at first supposed him to be the gardener.

Legends

Western tradition has identified Mary Magdalene with Mary the sister of Martha in Bethany and, more enduringly, with the woman 'who was a sinner' mentioned by Luke, who annointed Jesus's feet with expensive ointment, washed them with her tears and dried them with her hair (Luke 7: 37–8). This identification was strongly propounded by Gregory the Great, and has greatly influenced the iconography and popular cult of Mary Magdalene in the West, but it is now widely accepted that these are three separate women.

Tradition has also supplied details of her life beyond the Gospel accounts; she was believed to have accompanied her supposed siblings Martha and Lazarus (raised from the dead by Jesus) to Provence where she preached and lived as a hermit until her death at Saint Maximin, but this is now largely discredited. Another legend has her travelling to Ephesus with the Blessed Virgin Mary and John the Apostle, where she is believed to have died and been enshrined. A later addition to this legend claims that she was originally betrothed to John but that he broke the engagement off when he was called by Jesus.

Cult

The enormous popularity of Mary is attested by the many ancient and modern dedications of churches, and of colleges at both Oxford and Cambridge. She appears universally in medieval calendars, and was widely regarded as a patron saint of repentant sinners and contemplatives. This tradition of repentance, together with her obvious closeness to Jesus, made her especially well loved among the pious. In art she is usually shown with long hair and holding a jar of ointment (because of her probably mistaken but enduring identification with the penitent at Simon's house), often weeping in penitence, and she is often included in scenes of the Passion and Resurrection. The idea of the penitent, weeping woman has given rise to the now rather perjorative term 'maudlin', meaning excessively sentimental or mawkish, which derives from her name.

Feast-day 22 July
Patron saint of repentant sinners and the contemplative life

173

Mary, Blessed Virgin

First century

The mother of God

The most revered and beloved of all the saints, Mary has attracted numerous improbable legends, but her obedience, compassion and her unique closeness to Jesus have assured her centrality in the Church's devotion.

All the factual information which we have of Mary's life is found in the New Testament, particularly in the nativity accounts in the Gospels of Matthew and Luke in which the divinity of Jesus, the virginity of Mary, and her obedience to God are all emphasized. Luke's account in particular is written from Mary's point of view. Nothing is known of her parentage or place of birth, although tradition has her as the daughter of Anne and Joachim. Although Jesus's ancestry is traced in the Gospel accounts through Joseph, it is assumed that Mary was of the same family.

The birth of Jesus

Mary was living in Nazareth when she was visited by the archangel Gabriel, who announced the incredible news of the Incarnation and Mary's part in God's plan, which she acccepted simply and obediently. Her fiancé Joseph, who had planned to dissolve the engagement quietly on hearing of Mary's pregnancy, was also visited and reassured by an angel and the marriage went ahead. Soon afterwards Mary visited Elizabeth, then pregnant with John the Baptist, and on hearing Elizabeth greet her as the mother of God Mary expressed her thanks by singing the *Magnificat.*

She and Joseph were visiting Bethlehem for the census when Jesus was born; afterwards they were forced to flee to Egypt to avoid the jealous anger of King Herod, who had been told of the recent birth of a king of the Jews. After their enemy's death they settled in Nazareth, and little more is known of Jesus's early life beyond a journey to Jerusalem for Passover, when he was left behind only to be found by his distraught parents in learned discussion with the Jewish teachers in the temple.

The Gospels and beyond

According to John's Gospel it was Mary who prompted Jesus to perform his first miracle, the changing of water into wine at the wedding of Cana. After this she is mentioned as the mother of Jesus several times but does not feature in the gospel accounts until the crucifixion, when Jesus entrusts her into the care of John the Evangelist as they stand at the foot of his cross. Presumably Mary lived in John's household after this. She was with the apostles at Pentecost but, as during Jesus's lifetime, her role in the early church was so much one of quiet support that it is difficult to know exactly where or how she lived, or when she died. Jerusalem and Ephesus both claim to have been the place of her death; in the eastern tradition the claim of Jerusalem is generally favoured.

Church doctrine

The doctrine of Mary's bodily assumption into heaven (declared dogma by Pope Pius XII in 1950) is ancient, widely accepted at least from the sixth century, and from this time her role as intercessor in heaven has been increasingly emphasized. She is believed to have been the only human free from Original Sin from her conception (the doctrine of the Immaculate

Conception was declared dogma in 1854 by Pope Pius IX), although this belief, unlike that of the Assumption, was challenged by various members of the medieval church including the Dominicans and Thomas Aquinas.

She is traditionally believed by Catholics to have remained a virgin after the birth of Jesus, and so is unique in her role as model of both virgin and mother. In one popular analogy she is seen as the second Eve, whose purity and obedience to God enabled the second Adam, Christ, to sacrifice himself and redeem mankind. Mary was a figure with whom the suffering could readily identify, whose humanity they could love, and her unique position as fully human yet closer to God than any other saint or angel made her an obvious choice for intercessary prayer. The second Vatican Council provided a doctrinal statement on Mary which insists on her dependence upon and subordination to her Son, and shows her as a model for the Church.

Representation in art

Byzantine art characteristically presents Mary formally, as a crowned and sceptred queen, but in the Renaissance much emphasis was placed upon her humanity and compassion. The stylised medieval portraits gave way to more tender, realistic depictions of the Virgin with her child or, most poignantly, with her crucified Son. The most famous examples of these are the *Pietàs* of Michelangelo. The iconography of Mary is complex and laden with significance, embracing almost the entire history of the Christian church.

Feast-days and cult

Many feast-days are devoted to Mary, several of which have recently been reduced: 1 January is the celebration of Mary's part in the Incarnation and Redemption, 31 May is devoted to the Visitation, and the Annunciation is celebrated on 25 March.

The Purification of Christ in the Temple, commonly known as Candlemas, is on 2 February, Our Lady of Sorrows on 15 September, and devotion to the Immaculate Heart of Mary falls on the Saturday following the second Sunday of Pentecost. It was under this title that Pope Pius XII dedicated the entire human race to her in 1944. She has been claimed as patron in various capacities by countless organizations, countries and groups. There have been several reported visions of Mary, most notably at Lourdes, Fatima, Medjugorje and La Salette. Some genuine and many less reliable mystics have claimed inspiration or direction from Mary, but those who appear to have been genuinely guided tend to exhibit a tranquil strength of purpose rather than a religious hysteria.

Patron saint of the entire human race

The Blessed Virgin Mary, *from* The Annunciation *by Poussin. National Gallery.*

Matthew

First century

Author of the first Gospel

Matthew's Gospel is a lucid and authoritative account to the Jews of their promised Messiah.

Our information about Matthew comes almost exclusively from the Gospel accounts, beyond which little is known except his highly probable authorship of the Gospel that bears his name, written between the years 60 and 90. He was probably born in Galilee, the son of one Alpheus, and worked as a tax-collector until he was called by Jesus. He is traditionally thought to have been called Levi before his conversion but this may well have been a tribal designation, Matthew the Levite, rather than an alternative name. His profession would have made him a man despised by other Jews: tax-collectors (or publicans) served the oppressing Romans and it was widely recognized that they supplemented their pay by extortion. They were banned from religious communion in the temple and avoided in the social and business spheres. When he heard Jesus's summons Matthew abandoned his despised yet lucrative lifestyle, but in the list of disciples in his own gospel he uniquely places Thomas (the Doubter) above himself and adds to his own name 'the publican'.

The Gospel

Matthew's Gospel is characterized by an emphasis on Jesus as the fulfilment of Jewish messianic hopes, and by a special interest in his human genealogy. He, like Luke, appears to draw heavily from Mark's account but includes much of his own material. In 130 Papias noted that Matthew originally wrote in Aramaic, which accords with the impression of a Jew writing for Jewish readers, however the earliest extant fragments are in Greek. The style is concise and quite formal, especially well-suited to public reading and teaching. Among the four evangelists, the other three of whom are linked with symbolic beasts, Matthew is represented by the figure of a winged man in recognition of the human concerns expressed in his Gospel, especially the family of Christ.

Death and cult

The later life and death of Matthew are unknown, although one strong tradition claims that he preached in Judaea, Ethiopia and Persia where he is said to have been martyred. Some authorities place his martyrdom in Ethiopia or Persia, others in Tarsuana, beyond the Persian Gulf. His relics were believed by some to have been transported from Ethiopia to Finistère in Brittany, from where they were translated to Salerno by Robert Guiscard. His head has been claimed by four different churches in France.

Matthew is a popular figure in art, shown as an evangelist writing his Gospel at his desk aided by an angel or as an apostle carrying either an instrument of martyrdom (usually a spear or sword) or a money-box, recalling his earlier profession. In later representations he sometimes wears glasses, presumably the distinguishing mark of an accountant or financial clerk. He was declared patron saint of Italian accountants by Pope Pius XII in 1954, and of tax-collectors and customs officials by decree of the Sacred Congregation of Rites in 1957, and this was later extended to include security guards.

Feast-day 21 September
Patron saint of accountants, bookkeepers, tax-collectors, customs officers and security guards

---

*The four evangelists with their traditional symbols: a man for **St Matthew**, a lion for St Mark, an ox for St Luke, and an eagle for St John. The* Hautvillers Miniatures *in the* Gospels of Hebron *(ninth century). Municipal Library, Epernay.*

Michael the Archangel

No date

Captain of the heavenly host

A Christian cult which is closely linked with Jewish heritage.

One of only three angels to be venerated by the Western church (the other two are Gabriel and Raphael whose feast began only in this century), Michael's cult is ancient and extremely popular. He appears in Judaeo-Christian traditions as the deputy of God himself, carrying out the Almighty's commands in relation to mankind.

He is mentioned twice in the Old Testament by Daniel (10: 13 and 12: 1) as the protector of the chosen people Israel and a chief prince of the heavenly host, and in the New Testament he features in Revelation, as the conqueror of the satanic dragon and is mentioned by Jude (v9) arguing with the Devil for possession of Moses's body. He is referred to frequently in apocryphal writings in both Jewish and Christian traditions. One such work, the second-century *Testament of Abraham* in which Michael attempts to reconcile Abraham to the fact of death, credits Michael with intercessary powers so strong that he can even rescue souls from Hell.

Cult

His cult proper began in the East, maybe in Phrygia, where he was regarded as a special protector of the sick. A famous vision of Michael on Monte Gargano in south-east Italy, which probably inspired St Aubert to build the shrine of Mont-Saint-Michel in France, promoted veneration in the West and a well known basilica on Rome's Salerian

Way was built in his honour. Michaelmas day (29 September) was the feast commemorating this dedication, but it is no longer observed.

Michael was thought to have appeared during a plague in Rome and in some tradition is regarded, Charon-like, as the receiver of the souls of the dead. This may be the origin of the popular spiritual 'Michael row the boat ashore' and is probably the reason for his frequent patronage of cemeteries, of death or of those in danger of dying. In the West he is best known as a warrior saint, whose care was the protection of soldiers and victory over the forces of evil. Unsurprisingly, he was often invoked by military leaders as a sign of the right on their side.

In art he is most frequently shown with a sword, either battling with or standing in triumph over a dragon or the prostrate Satan. One famous modern sculpture of this type is that outside Coventry Cathedral. Many British churches were dedicated to him, often commemorating visions, for example that of St Michael's Mount in Cornwall. He is also depicted, especially in medieval art, weighing the souls of the dead, a reference to the widely-held belief that he was entrusted with the power of judgement over them. The former feast-day, which commemorated the dedication of the basilica in Rome, has recently been altered to include devotion to Raphael and Gabriel, and is now often called 'St Michael and all Angels'.

Feast-day 29 September
Patron saint of Brussels, the sick and battle, invoked when tempted, or when storm-tossed at sea

St Michael by *Piero della Francesca. National Gallery.*

Nicholas

Fourth century

The children's saint

Nicholas is associated with mysterious, generous giving and the protection of the defenceless.

Despite his enormous and enduring popularity which has led to his being invoked as patron and protector by countless different groups, to say nothing of his prominence in European folklore, the facts about Nicholas extend no further than that he was bishop of Myra in Lycia (south-western Turkey) at some point in the fourth century.

He is thought by some to have been born at Patara in Lycia into a wealthy family, and on becoming bishop of his decadent see, transformed it with his piety, energy and miracles. Several attempts have been made to include him among the fathers present at the Council of Nicaea in 325 who had suffered under the persecution of Diocletian, but there is insufficient evidence to establish this. There is evidence of a cult in the East as early as the sixth century, which gained popularity in the West during the 10th century, but his fame was secured after his relics were translated to Bari in 1087, after a Muslim invasion of Myra, and a new church inaugurated by Pope Urban II was built over them. The reputation of his shrine was increased by the emission of some perfumed substance called 'mana' or 'myrrh' which attracted countless pilgrims.

Legends

More influential than the biographical facts however have been the legends that have grown up surrounding his name. Perhaps the most famous is that of his intervention to save the honour of three poverty-stricken sisters; their father could not afford their dowries and in desperation was about to give them over to prostitution. Hearing of this, Nicholas secretly came by the house at night and threw a bag of gold, sufficient for one sister's dowry, through the window on three different occasions. This is the source of the traditional sign for pawnbrokers, three golden balls.

Frequent representation of the story, with the three rounded money bags, may have led to a different version of the legend in which the three balls became the severed heads of three murdered children, whom Nicholas found and restored to life. The mystical number three recurs in Nicholas's legends; he is also said to have saved three prisoners who had been falsely condemned from execution by warning Emperor Constantine of their innocence in a dream, and to have miraculously rescued three sailors off the coast of Turkey.

Cult

As patron of children, Nicholas's feast-day became associated in the Low countries with the giving and receiving of presents. Dutch settlers in North America created the modern figure of Santa Claus by linking Saint Klaes with the Scandinavian god Thor, figure of reward and punishment whose chariot was driven by goats.

Nicholas is usually shown in art with the three balls of gold, or else worshipping God as a baby, from the legend that he abstained from his mother's milk on Wednesdays and Fridays. His feast has recently been reduced by the Catholic church.

Feast-day 6 December
Patron saint of Russia, children, pawnbrokers, unmarried girls, perfumiers and sailors

Ninian (Nynia, Ringan)
c.360 — c.432

Traditionally known as the apostle of the Picts

The earliest known Christian leader in Scotland, the exact extent of Ninian's influence on Celtic Christianity is a matter of dispute.

Much discussion exists as to the reliability of Bede's account of Ninian concerning the authenticity of his source material and the accuracy of his traditional title, apostle of the Picts. According to Bede's sources, Ninian was a British bishop who had studied at Rome and been ordained and consecrated bishop there before returning home to preach the Christian gospel among the Southern Picts.

He is said to have established his centre for evangelism at Whithorn in Galloway, where a stone church which he built may have given rise to the name by which Bede knows it, *Candida Casa* ('white house'). Recent archeological evidence suggests that there was indeed an early church with white-painted masonry on the site, and several inscribed Christian stones nearby suggest the existence of a monastery. Some believe that Ninian built his church using masons from St Martin's monastery in Tours, others explain the dedication to St Martin, noted by Bede, by the type of monasticism practised by Ninian or the possibility that he brought a relic of Martin to his chapel in Whithorn. It was originally thought that Ninian visited Martin on his journey to Britain from Rome, but this seems unlikely given the chronology that subsequent scholarship has established.

The prevalence of place names dedicated to Ninian in Scotland and northern England seems to suggest an improbably wide apostolate, and there has been much debate over the true extent of his evangelism. It seems certain that his personal influence was directed at least to the area around Whithorn, and that his inspiration was behind many of the missionaries who later evangelized southern Scotland. Whatever the facts of Ninian's own apostolate, the subsequent influence of Whithorn among the Celtic Christians must be acknowledged.

Cult

Several biographers have chosen Ninian as their subject, although their accounts are generally more useful for ascertaining the extent of his cult in the biographer's day than for the historical facts of Ninian's own life. This is especially true of the most famous, the 12th-century *Life* by St Ailred. According to this account, Ninian was born near the Solway Firth, the son of a Christian king, and after being instructed in Rome was sent to evangelize Britain by the Pope. These *Lives* emphasize his miracles, especially his curing of a chieftain's blindness, and the subsequent large numbers of conversions. His shrine survived as a popular centre for pilgrimage until the 16th century and by then his cult had spread to southern England and Denmark.

Feast-day 26 August

Odilia (Ottilia)

d. c.720

Abbess of Odilienberg and Niedermünster

Born blind and given her vision during baptism, Odilia's incredible legend has inspired popular devotion in Alsace and beyond.

According to legend, which is our only source of information for this enigmatic but popular saint, Odilia was born at Obernheim, in the Vosges Mountains, the daughter of the Alsatian Lord Adalric. The legendary details of her life are largely fantastic: her father wished to put her to death, despising her as a family disgrace since she had been born blind, but her mother Bereswindis persuaded him to allow her to give the child to a peasant woman who would know nothing of her background. So Odilia was sent to Baume-les-Dames near Besançon, and at the age of 12 entered the convent there. She was baptized by Bishop St Erhard of Regensburg and during the ceremony, as the bishop touched her eyes with the consecrated oil, she was miraculously able to see. Her brother Hugh arranged for her to return home to be reconciled to her father, but Adalric was so incensed on first hearing of her return that he struck his son and killed him.

Adalric soon changed his mind however and welcomed his daughter back, replacing his former indifference with extravagant affection, and attempting to arrange for her a suitable and advantageous marriage with a German duke. Odilia fled to avoid the match, wishing to remain a virgin, and her father pursued her with murderous intent. On catching her however Adalric was so impressed by her miraculous protection from his anger that he agreed to let her convert his Alsatian castle at Hohenburg (now Odilienburg) into a convent, the abbess of which Odilia naturally became.

Death and cult

Odilia went on to found a second convent at Niedermünster, where she lived until her death on 13 December. She was renowned for her piety, visions and miracles, and her shrine became a popular centre for pilgrimage in Alsace and neighbouring European countries, frequented especially by those suffering from blindness or diseases of the eye. It still attracts visitors today. As late as World War II there was a prophecy attributed to St Odilia in popular circulation in France.

Feast-day 13 December
Patron saint of Alsace and the blind

Odilo

c.962 Auvergne — Sauvigny 1041

Institutor of the feast of All Souls

Although of unprepossessing appearance, Odilo carried on the work of reform from Cluny with energy and great ability.

Born of a noble family, Odilo joined the monastery at Cluny as a young man and rapidly gained responsibility. He was made coadjutor to abbot Mayeul in 991 and three years later succeeded him as fifth abbot of Cluny. He ruled the monastery for 55 years, during which period the abbey became arguably the most important in western Europe. He set about increasing the number of Cluniac foundations and strengthening their relationship with and dependency upon the mother house at Cluny. The Cluniac reform movement developed throughout Europe, involving an increasing number of monasteries in France and many others linked associatively in Italy and Spain. His building programme of expansion at Cluny was imitated by many daughter houses, and became a hallmark of the reform movement, but more importantly he sought to rebuild the spiritual life of his monasteries, recalling the monks to the original spirit of Benedict's Rule and the true purposes of monasticism.

When famine devastated the area during his abbacy Odilo sold off many of the monastery's treasures to help feed the sufferers, famously quoted as saying that he would rather be damned for an excess of mercy than of severity. He was also a prominent figure in promoting the *treuga Dei* ('truce of God'), which enforced a suspension of hostilities over weekends and major religious feasts, and the *pactum Dei* ('treaty of God'), which guaranteed sanctuary for refugees in churches and secured protection for church property and clerics from attack in war. These measures were significant in the political and economic as well as the ecclesiastical world.

All Souls Day

Perhaps his most enduring achievement was the introduction of All Souls Day, the day following the celebration of All Saints, to be observed by monks in all Cluniac monasteries in memory and prayer for the dead. Odilo originally intended the commemoration to be for departed monks, but the feast was extended to include all the dead and was celebrated in monasteries and churches throughout the western Church. He was famous too for his teaching on the Incarnation and the role of Mary in Catholic doctrine, and later writers such as Bernard owed much to him.

Death and cult

Odilo died at the monastery of Sauvigny on one of his regular tours of inspection at the age of 87, and was canonized in 1063. Because of his association with All Souls Day he is usually represented with a skull at his feet, his prayers releasing souls from the fires of purgatory.

Feast-day 1 January
Invoked for souls in Purgatory and against jaundice

Odo of Cluny

c.879 Tours — Tours 942

Second abbot of Cluny

In the early days of Cluniac influence, Odo's direction led the monastery into its famous programme of reform.

The son of Abbo of Maine, a knight of Tours, Odo spent his childhood in the households of Count Fulk II of Anjou and Duke William of Aquitaine, who would later go on to found Cluny. He enrolled as a canon of St Martin's in Tours and studied music and other disciplines for several years in Paris and it was here that he first read the Rule of St Benedict; he was so impressed by it that he resigned his canonry and became a monk at Baume-les-Messieurs in 909 under the abbecy of Berno, who was soon appointed first abbot of Cluny. Odo became director of the monastery school there and in 924 became abbot of Baume. Three years later he succeeded Berno as second abbot of Cluny and developed his predecessor's programme of reform. In 931 he received authorization from Pope John XI to take control of the monastic reforms throughout northern France and Italy. Berno had recognized the importance of protecting the monastery from secular interference by seeking charters of immunity from Popes and kings, and Odo followed this wise course. This greatly aided the scope and efficacy of the reform movement launched from Cluny, which was to spread throughout Europe over the coming centuries under such great leaders as St Odilo and St Hugh of Cluny.

Odo also insisted on strict spiritual disci-pline among his monks, including chastity, poverty, silence and austerity. These measures contrasted strongly with the lax practices of many contemporary clerics, and helped the growing reputation of Cluny as a centre of spiritual life and a model for monasticism. He ruled a growing number of monasteries directly, but his influence extended over countless more.

Influence beyond Cluny

Secular authorities were quick to recognize his spiritual integrity and impartiality; he was called upon to act as mediator for various leaders including Alberic of Rome and Hugh of Provence in 936 at the instructions of Pope Leo VII. He achieved a temporary peace by arranging a marriage between Alberic and a daughter of Hugh, but was forced to return to Rome to patch up the agreement twice in the next six years. When he died at the monastery of St Julian in Tours soon after celebrating the feast of his patron, St Martin, he was a respected and influential figure in both monastic and popular opinion. His mercy and charity were legendary, and he left several writings, including a life of St Gerald of Aurillac and an epic poem on the redemption of mankind. In art he is recognizable by the inscription on the book which he holds, 'Statuta Cluniacens'.

A later Odo, St Odo the Good, was a monk from the abbey of Fleury in France, one of those reformed by Odo of Cluny, who went on to become Archbishop of Canterbury.

Feast-day 18 November

Olaf

995 — Stiklestad 1030

The Pirate King of Norway

A warlike king who met a violent death, Olaf is nevertheless regarded as a martyr for his attempts to Christianize Norway.

Son of the Norwegian Lord Harold Grenske, Olaf Haraldsson (also called Olaf the Fat) spent the early part of his career as a warring pirate in a Viking band. He became a Christian and was baptized in Rouen, and in 1013 he journeyed to England to fight with King Æthelred II against the invading Danes. On his return to Norway he recaptured much of the country from Danish and Swedish possession, decisively defeating Earl Swein at Nesje in 1016, and proclaimed himself king of Norway.

A brief rule

Olaf's reign was just but harsh: he attempted to unify the factious country under his control. Some early attempts to impose Christianity had achieved little success, and when Olaf tried to impose his faith on the inhabitants he inevitably met with much opposition. A revolution was led against him by the nobility in 1029, supported by King Cnut of England and the Danes, and Olaf was sent into exile. He attempted to muster forces from Sweden to regain his kingdom the following year, but was defeated and killed at the Battle of Stiklestad on 29 July 1030.

Nationalistic cult

After his death, Olaf became a martyr, a symbol of nationalist independence and sanctity although he had commanded little love in his country during his life. Cnut's son Swein, who ruled in his place, was an unpopular alien, and after Cnut's death in 1035 many Danes fled Norway and Swein was succeeded by Olaf's son Magnus. With his son on the throne, Olaf's cult developed quickly into a national observance. It was said that healing springs of water flowed from his grave by the shores of the river Nid, and many miracles were reported. One of Olaf's friends and helpers in establishing the Norwegian church, the English bishop Grimkell, declared Olaf a saint and built a chapel over his grave. The body was enshrined there, supposedly incorrupt, and the church later became the cathedral of Nidaros (modern Trondheim), a centre for pilgrimage throughout Scandinavia and beyond.

With the Viking invasions the cult spread to Britain; there were over 40 ancient church dedications, and Olaf was a popular Christian name in pre-Conquest England. His translation in Gaelic, *Amlaibh* or *Aulag*, gave rise to the common Hebridean surname Macauley, and in English it produced variants such as Tooley Street, from a collapsed form of 'saint Olaf'. In art he is shown as a king brandishing a lance or halberd, after trampling a crowned demon underfoot.

Feast-day 29 July
Patron saint of Norway

Oswald of Northumbria

c.605 Northumbria — Maserfelth 642

Martyr-king of Northumbria

A figure in whom were combined the ideals of Anglo-Saxon folk-hero and saintly Christian king.

The son of Æthelfrith, King of Northumbria, Oswald was forced to flee to Scotland when his father was killed in battle by Redwold of East Anglia and Edwin of Deira became King of Northumbria. Oswald was converted to Christianity at Iona, and on Edwin's death in 633 he and other exiled royals returned to Northumbria. The kingdom was now in the hands of the Christian king of Gwynedd, Cadwallon, against whom Oswald successfully led his greatly inferior army at Hevenfelt near Hexham in 634. He slew Cadwallon and succeeded to the throne, attributing his victory to a vision of St Columba and a wooden cross around which he had led his army in prayer before the battle.

One of his first actions as king was to send for help from Iona, missionaries to aid in the task of evangelism among his new subjects. First he received a harsh bishop, whose inflexible rule met with little sympathy or success among the Northumbrians and who soon returned to Iona declaring that the English were unteachable. The next missionary sent from Iona was a close personal friend of Oswald's, the more kindly and charismatic Aidan who spoke little English. According to Bede, the king himself interpreted Aidan's sermons to the people and he gave him the island of Lindisfarne on which to establish an episcopal seat and monastery close to the castle at Bamburgh. The work of conversion continued apace, with thousands of Northumbrians being baptized.

Under Oswald's rule the divided halves of Northumbria, Bernicia and Deira, were united; his authority as overlord was acknowledged by other Anglo-Saxon kings and his holiness and justice by his subjects, and he made a good marriage with Cyneburga, daughter of the first Christian king of Wessex, Cynegils.

Death and cult

However his reign was to be a short one: Penda, the pagan king of Mercia, led a large army against him at the battle of Maserfelth (Old Oswestry) and he was defeated and killed there on 5 August, aged only 38. It is said that his dying words were a prayer for all the loyal followers who fell with him. Penda gave orders for his body to be ritually mutilated as an offering to Woden. The various limbs were recovered and venerated in diverse places, contributing to the spread of his cult. The head, buried at Lindisfarne, was later placed with the remains of Cuthbert for safe-keeping and was discovered at the opening of the tomb in Durham in 1827.

Oswald was a popular king who was quickly regarded as a saint after his death; there is evidence for his feast-day as early as the late seventh century. In art he is usually shown with a raven and a jar of sacred oil denoting kingship, and there are also depictions of his death and of St Cuthbert holding his disembodied head.

Feast-day 5 August

Oswald of Worcester

c.925 — Worcester 992

Bishop, archbishop and abbot

Proponent of monasticism along with Dunstan and Ethelwold, and close friend of the king.

Born in England of Danish extraction, Oswald was educated by his uncle Odo, archbishop of Canterbury. He was ordained and became a canon at Winchester for several years before going on to become a Benedictine monk at Fleury-sur-Loire, a Cluniac monastery which boasted a claim to the relics of St Benedict and an enviable tradition of intellectual and monastic discipline. After this monastic training Oswald returned to Britain in about 958 as a priest under another ecclesiastical uncle, Archbishop Oskitall of York.

Monastic revival

His first appointment of real importance came when St Dunstan recommended him to King Edgar for the post of bishop of Worcester in 962. As bishop he worked closely with Saints Dunstan and Ethelwold in their attempts to revive monasticism and the spiritual life in England. He founded a monastery at Westbury-on-Trym near Bristol in his first year in office, but his most famous foundation was that of Ramsey in Huntingdonshire, which was to produce the houses of Pershore and Evesham among others. He brought Abbo of Fleury to Ramsey for some years, whose scholarly influence greatly benefitted both the monastery and the wider English monastic tradition.

In 972 Oswald was appointed archbishop of York, but he retained his see of Worcester and it was there that he directed his interest and energies. Four attempts to revive Ripon monastery in Yorkshire were a failure, and his vision of revival remained within the confines of Wessex and Mercia. As a bishop and archbishop, Oswald's biographers are at pains to emphasize the affection which he commanded among the common folk of his diocese, his charisma and his concern for social justice. However it also seems to be the case that he was somewhat acquisitive, working closely with King Edgar to secure large tracts of lands for his monasteries. His retention of Worcester and residence at Ramsey have also been questioned, given that at the time he was archbishop of York.

Death and cult

Oswald retained his dioceses even after 975 and the death of Edgar with whom he had been closely linked in working to acquire land for his monasteries and churches, during the anti-monastic reaction which followed. Some of his monasteries were dispersed but he retained Ramsey, although it was in neither of his dioceses, and in 991 he reopened the church there after damage caused by a falling tower. He is said to have realized that it was his final visit; the next Lent he died at Worcester on 28 February just after completing his usual Lenten practice of washing the feet of twelve poor men and waiting on them as they ate. He was reciting psalms as he died, and his *Life* written shortly afterwards remarks on his contentment in the face of death. His cult was quickly established and enduringly popular; he is shown in art driving off the Devil with a stone, or washing the feet of the poor.

Feast-day 28 February

Pancras

d.c.304

The child martyr

Best-known now for the railway station named after him in London, Pancras's legend is somewhat unreliable.

Beyond the fact that he was martyred and buried on Rome's Aurelian Way, very little is known about Pancras. Unreliable authorities claim that he was born in Phrygia, the son of a pagan noble, but was orphaned early in life and came to Rome in the company of his uncle. Both were converted to Christianity there, and at the age of only 14 Pancras is believed to have been beheaded in the persecutions of Diocletian. The details are uncertain, but his martyr-

> **Feast-day** 12 May
> Patron saint of children, invoked against cramp, headaches and perjury

dom began an important cult which centred around the shrine containing his body in the magnificent church on the Via Aurelia.

Cult

He was revered by many notable figures, including Gregory the Great who dedicated a monastery to him in Rome, and Augustine, who dedicated a church to him in Canterbury. He appears too in the martyrology of Bede and other early English calendars, partly because Pope Vitalian sent some relics to King Oswiu of Northumbria in the mid seventh century.

About six ancient English churches were dedicated to Pancras, one of which, in North London, gave its name to the famous railway station and cemetery. In art Pancras is represented as a boy knight, carrying the palm of the martyr and a lance with a pennant showing a cross. He is sometimes shown as a martyr without armour, and occasionally trampling a Saracen. Because of his tender age, he is often invoked as one of the patron saints of children.

St Pancras Station, London.

Patrick

c.389 — Saul, Co Down c.461

The apostle of Ireland

Patrick has become a potent figure of myth and legend in Irish folklore.

Patrick's exact birthplace is unclear; it is thought to have been somewhere between the mouths of the Severn and the Clyde, but some claim that he was born in Boulogne-sur-Mer or at Kilpatrick, near Dumbarton. His father Calpurnius was a Romano-British official and deacon and his grandfather was a Christian priest. Patrick was carried off to slavery in Ireland by a raiding party when only 16. Sold to a chief of Antrim named Milchu, Patrick served his master by looking after his beasts for six years, during which time he became a man of prayer and sincere religion. At the end of this time he escaped, after being informed in a dream that he would soon go to his own country, and persuaded the crew of a ship to take him with them to the Continent. He soon returned to Britain, having faced danger and near-starvation during his adventures abroad, and began his clerical training. He went back to France, perhaps to study at the monasteries of Tours and Lérins, before becoming a disciple of St Germanus at Auxerre. He was consecrated as a bishop, and in 432 (the date is disputed) was appointed successor to Palladius as missionary bishop of Ireland by Pope Celestine I.

Mission in Ireland

On his return to Ireland Patrick travelled throughout the island, evangelizing tirelessly and organizing the churches and monasteries. Palladius's evangelism had been largely ineffective, and concentrated mainly in the south-east, so Patrick faced an enormous task. He had much success in converting Irish chiefs, including his old master Milchu, and secured the attention of the Irish king Laoghaire at Tara, Co Meath, by miraculously overcoming the Druids. In about 454 he established his espiscopal seat at Armagh, which became the centre for Christianity in Ireland, and began organizing the nascent Irish church along the traditional lines of territorial dioceses. Although he encouraged monasticism, it is likely that the characteristically monastic Irish church was a later development. Despite his own basic education, he encouraged scholarship and the study of Latin.

Works and cult

His surviving authentic writings, his *Confession* and a letter to Coroticus, reveal him as an ill-educated but passionately sincere man, convinced of his divine mission and angered by the opposition of those he believed should have helped him. He was fearless in pursuit of his aim, to destroy paganism, and always retained a sense of dependency on God born of his early days as a slave and exile.

Later legends had Patrick expelling snakes from Ireland, and explaining the doctrine of the Trinity by reference to a shamrock, and these have become his emblems. He is often credited with single-handedly converting Ireland, but while his contribution was outstanding, this work took many more years than these legends allow. Irish immigration to America propagated his cult there and New York's main cathedral is dedicated to him.

Feast-day 17 March
Patron saint of Ireland

Paul

c.3 Tarsus — Rome c.66

The apostle to the Gentiles

Probably the most influential figure after Jesus in the history of Christian thought, doctrine and mission.

Born of a Jewish family in the Roman province of Cilicia (modern-day Turkey), Saul of Tarsus was a fervent follower of the Jewish law. At the age of 14 he studied as a Pharisee under the famous rabbi Gamaliel in Jerusalem and, following the rabbinic tradition of studying a trade as well as the law, learnt tent-making also. Although Aramaic was his mother tongue and he had a strong Hebrew education, Saul's birth in Tarsus automatically gave him the status of a Roman citizen and he spoke Greek fluently; he was eminently qualified for his later role as apostle to the Gentiles. The changing of his name from Saul to the Hellenic form Paul, traditionally associated with his conversion, may have been a Romanization present from childhood.

Conversion

As a Pharisee, Paul persecuted the early Christian church relentlessly. His concern was for strict application of the Jewish law which this new sect appeared to be flouting; he was present as a passive but complicit spectator at the stoning of the first Christian martyr, Stephen. His conversion took place as he travelled from Jerusalem to Damascus intent on further persecution of the nascent church when he experienced a mystical vision of the risen Christ speaking the famous words, 'Saul, Saul, why do you persecute me?'. The revelation seems also to be linked to his conviction that his mission was to take the news of Jesus to the Gentiles.

After his conversion, Paul spent three years in prayer and solitude in Arabia and then preaching back in Damascus, where opposition against him became so violent that he was forced to flee to Jerusalem, escaping in a basket let down over the city walls. In Jerusalem he met Peter, James and the other apostles who were understandably nervous until convinced by Barnabas of Paul's sincerity. Preaching in Jerusalem, Paul again faced much opposition; he finally returned to Tarsus for some years until introduced by Barnabas to the church at Antioch.

Man with a mission

From Antioch, Paul was to make his three celebrated missionary journeys which effectively began the spread of Christianity throughout the world. On his first journey (c.45–9) to Cyprus and various cities throughout Galatia (now central Turkey), Paul developed the formula that was to characterize his missionary work: preaching in centres of commerce and culture, he first addressed the Jews and when rejected by them took his message to the Gentiles, thereby establishing the first Gentile churches throughout Asia Minor and later in Europe.

After this journey, Paul was embroiled in conflict with the Christian Jews in Jerusalem, most notably Peter, over the conditions required of Gentile converts. Paul held that the law had been superseded by the sacrificial death of Christ, and hence it was unreasonable to impose the conditions of Jewish law, especially the old covenant sign of circumcision, on the new, non-Jewish converts. The disagreement culminated in the first Apostles' council, held in Jerusalem in c.50. Paul won the Jews over but as a kind of compromise he agreed to acknowledge the centrality of the church at Jerusalem and pledged to support it by raising money from the new Gentile congregations.

On Paul's second missionary journey in c.51–4 he was led on from Asia Minor by a dream, and in the commercial and military centre of Philippi the gospel was preached in Europe for the first time. Paul and Silas were imprisoned by the authorities there but miraculously released; they faced further persecution in Thessalonica and Berea and were forced on to Athens, where Paul delivered his famous sermon on 'The Unknown God'. He then spent a year and a half in the Roman provincial capital of Corinth, a busy cosmopolitan city notorious for its licentiousness. He stayed and worked with the tent-makers Aquila and Priscilla, and built up a strong community of believers despite much persecution from the Jews there. He finally returned to Antioch, after visiting Ephesus again and delivering money to the church in Jerusalem.

His third journey, a tour of inspection of the churches established in Asia Minor, began in 53 with a two-year stay in Ephesus. After a riot of the city's silversmiths, enraged because Paul's teaching was jeopardizing their lucrative trade in statuettes of Diana, Paul went on through Achaea, Macedonia and Miletus to Jerusalem. Here Jewish antipathy towards him reached such a pitch that he was gaoled for his own protection by the Romans and secretly despatched to the govenor Felix at Caesarea in 58. He awaited trial for two years, until Felix was succeeded by Festus, and then, faced with the unwelcome prospect of trial before a Jewish court, Paul utilised his rights as a Roman citizen to appeal for trial before the emperor.

Journey to Rome

The book of Acts records Paul's voyage in c.61 as fraught with danger. Adverse winds delayed the ship beyond the safe sailing season, and it was caught in a storm and finally wrecked just off the coast of Malta. Paul was bitten by a viper on the island but to the amazement of the inhabitants he shook the snake off and suffered no ill effects. (This episode seems somewhat sensational, and most scholars suspect a hand other than Luke's.)

On reaching Rome Paul was placed under house arrest, apparently in relative comfort and able to receive visitors and to write letters freely. Acts ends here and there is some confusion over subsequent events. Paul may have been convicted and executed soon afterwards, but it seems possible that after two years in captivity he was acquitted and went on to Ephesus and even Spain (according to Clement of Rome writing only 30 years after Paul's death), before recapture and death in the Neronian persecutions.

Death

In any event, there is a strong and plausible tradition that Paul was beheaded on the Ostian way at Tre Fontane, just outside Rome (hence he is often represented in literature by a sword as well as the book symbolising his writings). His body is now in the Basilica of San Paolo fuori le Mura there. Although it is claimed that he was martyred on the same date as Peter, this probably originates in the fact that the two share a feast day, 29 June, on which they are revered as co-founders of the Catholic church.

Influence

The epistles of Paul, many of them written in captivity to encourage young congregations and to ensure the doctrinal unity of the church, are the oldest surviving Christian documents, and the majority of the New Testament apart from the Gospels and Revelation is dominated by his life or voice. Scholars dispute the Pauline authorship of some epistles, especially Hebrews, but Galatians, Romans and the first and second to the Corinthians at least are widely acknowledged to be his.

Paul's evangelistic energy and the conviction of his preaching helped to establish the church in Asia Minor and Europe, but the full extent of his impact reaches well beyond his lifetime. The doctrine and vision expressed in his epistles have influenced every generation of Christian thinkers, and his fortitude and faithfulness in the face of suffering have been an example to later oppressed Christians. His dramatic conversion has inspired such artists as Michelangelo, Caravaggio and Brueghel the Elder, and the most striking musical commemoration is the oratorio by Mendelssohn.

Feast-day 29 June
Patron saint of tent-makers and saddlers, invoked against poisonous snakes

The Fall of St Paul by Michelangelo da Caravaggio. Balbi di Piovera Gallery, Genoa.

Paul of the Cross

1694 Ovada — Rome 1775

Priest of the Passion

Founder of the Barefoot Clerks of the Holy Cross and Passion, renowned for his austere holiness.

The eldest son of a father whose ancestry was noble but whose circumstances were reduced to that of a businessman, Paul Francis Danei was born near Genoa in Piedmont, Italy on 3 January. His family were devout, and from an early age Paul committed himself to a life of austerity and religion, renouncing the chance of both a sizeable inheritance and an advantageous marriage. At the age of 20 he volunteered to fight with the Venetian army against the Turks but within a year found that he was not suited to the soldier's life. He was discharged from the army, and spent the next few years living as a hermit in prayer and penance at Castellazzo, searching for a direction for his religious zeal.

The Passionists

Finally, in 1720, he received the enlightenment he had sought: he experienced a vision in which the Blessed Virgin, wearing a black habit with a cross and the name of Jesus in white, instructed him to found a congregation whose mission should be centred on the cross and passion of Christ.

He secured approval from the bishop of Alexandria for his visions, and proceeded to Rome with the Rule for his proposed foundation to seek papal approval. He was disappointed on his first journey, but when he returned in 1725 Pope Benedict XIII granted his permission. Paul began his new order at Monte Argentaro, Tuscany in 1727, with his brother John and a few companions, after being ordained as a priest in Rome. The congregation was characterized by an austere and penitential regime, preaching which focused fervently and almost exclusively on the Passion of Christ, and a commitment to active ministry in the service of the sick, the lapsed and the dying.

Many of those who enrolled with the congregation left, claiming that its regime was excessively harsh, but nevertheless the order expanded, with the founding of a convent for Passionist nuns and a few other houses by the time of Paul's death in 1771. Papal intervention however meant that its more extreme severities were mitigated. Much of its success was due to the compelling preaching and personality of its founder, who was also credited with miraculous powers of healing and divination. His letters reveal an intense interest in mystical theology, but he himself apears to have distrusted some of the mystical experiences to which he was subject.

Death and cult

Paul died in Rome on 18 October and was buried in the church of St John and St Paul. He was canonized in 1867. One of his major concerns was the restoration of England to the fold of Catholicism, and his disciples in the 19th century worked tirelessly in this aim in England; one, Dominic Barberi, was to receive Cardinal Newman into the Catholic church.

Feast-day 19 October

Peter

d. Rome c.64

Leader of the Apostles

The impetuous, charismatic disciple who went on to become head of the Christians in Jerusalem and the first Pope of the Catholic Church.

Peter was born Simon, son of John, in Bethsaida, and he worked with his brother Andrew as a fisherman by Lake Genesareth. From the account of Jesus healing his mother-in-law we know that he was, or had been, married, but nothing is known of his wife. According to John's Gospel it was Andrew who introduced his brother to Christ, who then gave Simon the name *Cephas* (Peter), meaning 'the rock', saying that Peter was the rock on which his church on earth would be built, and later that Peter would be given 'the keys of the kingdom of heaven'. It is upon this foundation that the Catholic church's teaching on the supremacy of the papacy, the line following from Peter as first bishop of Rome, is based.

In lists of the apostles, Peter is always named first and he is mentioned more frequently than any other disciple in the gospels. He was one of the three present at Jesus's transfiguration, the raising of Jairus's daughter and the agony in Gethsemane and witnessed most of Jesus's miracles, yet he deserted him in the Garden and betrayed him in the courtyard of Pontius Pilate. Christ had predicted this betrayal, as he had predicted Peter's subsequent repentance. After the resurrection and ascension Peter was acknowledged as the head of the Christian community in Jerusalem. It was he who first preached to the Gentiles, leading many to conversion at Pentecost, and who performed the first of the apostles' miracles

recorded in Acts, healing the lame beggar at Jerusalem's Beautiful Gate.

Later life

Imprisoned by Herod Agrippa in c.43, Peter was miraculously freed by an angel but the New Testament gives little further information on his movements. He appears to have preached in Samaria, Antioch and elsewhere, and to have been rebuked by Paul at Antioch for his unwillingness to be seen eating with Gentile believers. According to a very early tradition he went on to become the first bishop of Rome and was martyred there under Nero; although not conclusively proven this seems to have been supported by modern scholarship and archaeological investigations. The tradition that he asked to be crucified upside-down is more dubious.

Works and cult

He is widely regarded as the author of 1 Peter but scholars have argued over the authenticity of the second epistle; it apears to have been written much later, referrring to the first epistle as 'Scripture' and appearing to be derivative of Jude. His influence is acknowledged in the Gospel of Mark, but other documents such as the *Gospel of Peter* and the *Acts of St Peter* all date from the second century or later.

Peter has been venerated from the earliest days of the church, regarded as its powerful patron and as the doorkeeper of heaven (he is usually shown in art holding a set of keys).

Feast-day 29 June
Patron saint of fisherman and many other trades, invoked for a long life

---

194

Peter Claver

1580 Verdu — Cartagena 1654

'The Slave of the Negroes'

The colonization of the New World brought with it the inhumanity of the slave trade, against which Peter battled.

A native of Catalonia in Spain, Peter studied at the University of Barcelona and enrolled with the Jesuits at the age of 20 at Tarragona. He continued his studies in Majorca, at the Montesione College in Palma, and it was here that he met St Alphonsus Rodriguez who encouraged his desire for missionary work in the New World. He left Spain as a missionary to New Granada, landing at Cartagena (modern Columbia) in 1610. Five years later he was ordained as a priest there.

The New World

The city was a centre for the ubiquitous slave trade: blacks from West Africa were shipped to the port in apalling conditions and kept in enclosures there like animals before being distributed to traders or their new masters. Peter worked alongside the Jesuit Father Alfonso de Sandovel, who had already spent 40 years trying to relieve the sufferings of the slaves both practically and spiritually. When the slaves were herded into their enclosures Peter would visit them bringing food, medical care and comforts such as brandy and tobacco, preaching the message of the gospel all the time by means of a team of interpreters. He aimed to bring a sense of dignity and worth to these men, who had been treated so inhumanly by their captors, by teaching of the redemption available through Christ.

When the slaves were sold to mines and plantations Peter followed up his care by paying regular visits to check on their conditions, ensuring at least that the basic laws for their protection were fully observed. He made himself unpopular with many of the masters and slave-traders, but his influence among the slave community was enormous. He baptized hundreds of thousands in his 40-year ministry, and won the admiration of many for his unselfish commitment, gaining some support at least among the Spanish of the city.

In addition to his work among the slaves, Peter spent much of his time visiting the inmates of the city jail and patients in the local hospitals. His spiritual encouragement was extended to all classes, and he also ministered to the many visitors to the city, making an annual visit to the port to preach among the sailors and traders there. He was known for his disciplined and austere life, and was attributed with miracles, prophecies and divination.

Death and cult

When plague struck Cartagena in 1650 Peter was one of those infected, and he never fully recovered. He carried on with his work as best he could, but spent much time alone in his cell, apparently neglected and mistreated by the black slave appointed to look after him, and died alone.

His friends and enemies united in extolling this extraordinary man; the Spanish gave him a civic funeral and the slaves arranged their own Mass. He was canonized in 1888 and in 1896 was named patron of 'all missionary activities among negroes' by Pope Leo XIII.

Feast-day 9 September

Peter of Alcantara

1499 Alcantara — Arenas 1562

A celebrated Spanish mystic

Peter's asceticism rivalled that of the Desert Fathers. He is famous for his reformed Franciscan congregation.

The son of the governor of Alcantara, in Estremadura, Spain, Peter Garavito was educated locally and then followed in the footsteps of his father by going on to study law at the University of Salamanca. At the age of 16 he became an observant Franciscan at Manjaretes, following the ascetic regime there and performing extreme penances and austerities. He won such respect that in 1521 he was sent to found a new monastery at Badajoz, although he was not ordained for another three years. He preached extensively throughout Estremadura and was appointed superior of various houses but his real desire was for solitude and a yet more disciplined monastic life. Finally he was allowed to take up the post of guardian at Lapa, a remote house of contemplation, and here he wrote his famous *Treatise on prayer and meditation*, before serving as chaplain with the court of King John III of Portugal.

The Alcantarines

In 1538 he became minister provincial of the Observants' province of Estremadura; it was already renowned for its severity, and Peter's attempts to reform it even further were a failure. He resigned in 1540 and left for Arabida near Lisbon, where he lived as a hermit and then as superior of a community of monks attracted to this eremetical life. He secured approval from Pope Julius III to establish a new order, based on a rule drawn up by Peter himself, which closely followed that of St Francis with additional disciplines and austerities. The new congregation, known as the Alcantarines, was based in a friary at Pedrosa, a Franciscan reform movement whose influence spread far beyond its original confines.

Much of Peter's activities and character are known from the autobiography of Teresa of Ávila, to whom he described his outstanding personal austerities. She recorded that he slept and ate with almost unbelievable economy, and that although he spoke little, his words were well worth hearing. He encouraged her greatly in her founding of the first congregation of reformed Carmelite nuns, acting as her confessor and helping her practically in her own spiritual and mystical life.

Death and cult

Peter died shortly after the opening of Teresa's first convent at Ávila, kneeling in his monastery at Arenas on 18 October. He was canonized in 1669 and named patron saint of Brazil in 1669 and of Estremadura in 1962. In art his extraordinary penances and his mysticism are recalled in the visual representation of a radiant Franciscan levitated before a cross, with nearby angels carrying instruments of mortification such as a girdle of nails and a chain. He is also shown walking on water with a friend, a star shining above his head, or with an inspirational dove at his ear.

Feast-day 11 October
Patron saint of Brazil and Estremadura

Philip

First century

Follower of Christ

A disciple of unquestioned devotion, he appears to have lacked the confidence of some of his fellows.

As with many of the apostles, most of our information about Philip comes from the New Testament. He was born in Bethsaida in Galilee and was probably an early follower of John the Baptist. John's Gospel records how Jesus called Philip, who then brought Nathanael (otherwise known as Bartholomew) to his new master. John also records that Philip was present at the feeding of the five thousand (John 6: 1–15); he was asked by Jesus how much money would be required to feed the crowd and replied (quite rightly in human terms) that it would cost over 200 silver coins for everyone to have even a little. He was approached by Greek Jews wishing to speak to Jesus (John 12: 20–2) and sought advice from Andrew. He was the apostle who asked Jesus 'Lord, show us the Father' (John 14: 8) and he was present with the other disciples at Pentecost when the Holy Spirit came down upon them and Peter delivered his famous sermon; beyond these instances, all in John's Gospel, he is not mentioned by name in the New Testament except in lists of the apostles.

Philip is sometimes assumed to be identical with Philip the Deacon, mentioned several times in the Acts of the Apostles; there is no basis for this identification, but it has given rise to some traditions which emphasize the importance of Philip's daughters in the early church.

Death and cult

The most convincing tradition of Philip's later life is that he preached in Greece and Phrygia and died in Hierapolis, traditionally martyred by crucifixion under Domitian. He is believed to have been buried there, and his relics to have been translated to Rome and enshrined in the Basilica of the Twelve Apostles. Along with James the Great, Philip is venerated as a secondary patron saint of Uruguay.

In art he is usually shown with the long cross of his martyrdom, and often with loaves and fishes recalling his part in Jesus's miracle. He often appears in company with his brother, St Andrew. Because of confusion with Philip the Deacon he is often also shown with the Ethiopian eunuch who was converted by the other Philip on the road to Gaza (Acts 8: 26–39).

Feast-day 1 May
Patron saint of Uruguay

Richard of Chichester (Richard De Wych)

1197 Droitwich — Dover 1253

Bishop of Chichester

A likeable and humble man, who remained as down-to-earth and accessible as a bishop as he had been on his father's farm.

The young Richard, son of a yeoman farmer, was a boy given to study rather than the farming life, but when he was orphaned he helped restore the fortunes of the family by working for several years on the badly-run estate he inherited. After a time he gave responsibility of the estate over to his younger brother Robert and, refusing the offer of an advantageous marriage, went to study at Oxford, Paris and Bologna. At Oxford he established a life-long friendship with his tutor Edmund Rich, and went on to gain a doctorate in canon law at Bologna. After seven years in Italy he returned to Oxford and was appointed Chancellor of the University in 1235 and then chancellor to the archbishop of Canterbury, St Edmund of Abingdon.

When Edmund was exiled to Pontigny Richard accompanied him and was with him at his death in 1240. He then spent two years in Orléans studying theology with the Dominicans there.

A contested appointment

On his return to England Richard served as a parish priest at Charing and Deal and was then reappointed chancellor to the new archbishop of Canterbury, Boniface of Savoy. In 1244 he was elected bishop of Chichester, a post contested by the rival claim of Ralph Neville, supported by King Henry III. Eventually the case was brought before the papal court, and in 1245 Pope Innocent IV decided in Richard's favour and consecrated him bishop, despite the defiance of Henry, who confiscated the episcopal properties and revenue. It was not until two years later and a threat of excommunication that these were restored to the see, and Richard was finally admitted to the bishop's palace. For the next eight years he administered and reformed his see, living simply at Tarring and growing figs in his spare moments. He was accessible to his flock and inflexible in opposing abuses, insisting upon celibacy and orthodoxy among his clergy and giving unstintingly to the needy especially in times of famine.

Death and cult

Richard strongly supported the Crusades; he had a vision of the Holy Land opened again to pilgrims, and spent much time near the end of his life preaching to recruit new Crusaders. While he was at Dover urging this cause he died on 3 April at the Maison Dieu, a house for poor priests. After canonization in 1262 his body was translated to a shrine in Chichester cathedral in 1276, a popular centre for pilgrimage until the Reformation when the shrine was destroyed and the body reburied secretly.

Because of a legend that he once dropped the cup at Mass without spilling the Host, his emblem in art is a chalice. His humility and his farming background have endeared him to generations of labourers.

Feast-day 3 April
Patron saint of the guild of coachmen of Milan

Rita of Cascia

c.1380 Roccaporena — Cascia c.1457

The reluctant wife

Much of her popularity stems from her unhappy marriage from which she was released by her husband's death. She is traditionally invoked by women in similar situations.

Rita was born near Spoleto in Italy. As a young girl living in Umbria she wished to became a nun, but bowing to the will of her elderly parents she was married at the age of 12. Her husband, much given to drunkenness, violence and infidelity, treated her appallingly, but Rita lived with him for 18 years patiently enduring the insults and ill treatment, and she bore him two sons. One day he was brought home dead, having been repeatedly and savagely stabbed in a violent brawl. His two sons swore revenge, but they both died soon afterwards with this vengeance unfulfilled and Rita was left alone.

The widowed nun

She now sought admission to the Augustinian convent Santa Maria Maddalena at Cascia but was refused three times, as the foundation's rule was to admit only virgins. She persisted, and finally the superior relented; her enrolment was accepted in 1413. As a nun Rita became famous for her penance and prayerfulness, and in 1441, after

meditating so intensely on Christ's Passion that she received a wound in her forehead like that from a thorny crown, she was hailed as a mystic. This wound remained with her for 15 years and could not be healed. She was also much involved in practical care for the needy and in prayer for sinners, many of whom she converted.

Death and cult

On 22 May Rita died at Cascia of tuberculosis; several further miracles were attributed to her after her death and her supposedly incorrupt body was translated into an elaborate tomb along with the approbation of her cult by the bishop. Rita was beatified in 1626 and canonized in 1900 and her cult is enormously popular today, especially in Italy. She is frequently hailed, like Jude, as a patron of desperate cases, and especially by women suffering in unhappy marriages. Because of the advanced age of her parents when Rita was born, she is often invoked by women who long for children and by the infertile.

Despite the popularity of her cult, however, the first biography of Rita was not written until 150 years after her death, by which time many inaccuracies must have been mixed with the facts. In art she is usually shown being wounded by a thorn from Christ's crown as she prays before a crucifix, or receiving a crown of roses from the Virgin and one of thorns from the saints.

> **Feast-day** 22 May
> Patron saint of desperate cases, invoked by childless women and the infertile

Robert Bellarmine

1542 Montepulciano — Rome 1621

A great Catholic apologist

A short man with an astonishing intellect whose doctrinal attacks were furious but never personal.

Born near Siena on 4 October, Roberto Francis Romulus Bellarmine, known for his prowess in literature, music and rhetoric as a youth, enrolled with the Jesuit order at 18, against the wishes of his father. He spent some years teaching classics in Piedmont and Florence and studying theology in Padua and Louvain. In 1570 he was ordained at Ghent, and elected to the chair of theology at Louvain, where he promoted the study of Hebrew, paving the way for a full revision of the Vulgate, and lectured on the *Summa theologica* of Aquinas, attacking the teachings of Baius. He gained a reputation as a brilliant theologian and preacher, and in 1576 was appointed professor of controversial theology at the new Roman College.

Over the next 11 years, Bellarmine drafted his great work *Disputations on the Controversies of the Christian faith*. It was an answer to the Protestant *Centuries of Magdeburg*, so well argued and displaying such a command of Scripture and Protestant theology that it was often assumed to be the work of a committee.

In 1592 he became rector of the Roman College and two years later was appointed provincial of Naples. In 1597 he became theologian to Pope Clement VIII, and produced two catechisms which remained in use until quite recently. When he was appointed cardinal in 1599, against his own wishes, he refused to give up the life of austerity to which he was accustomed, and continued to live almost exclusively on bread, water and garlic.

Promotion continued when he was made archbishop of Capua in 1602, but three years later he was recalled to Rome by the new Pope Paul V to act as chief spokesman of the Catholic church against the attacks of the Protestant reformers. He filled the role admirably, relying on reasoned debate rather than dogma or rhetoric for his effect. He countered the two-volume attempt of King James I of England to justify his supremacy in the Church of England and produced a controversial work, *De potestate papae*, which denied the concept of divine right in kingship. However his views on the supremacy of the papacy were too moderate for many Catholics, incurring the displeasure of Pope Sixtus V in particular. He was on friendly terms with Galileo, to whom he advised caution whilst remaining sympathetic.

Death and cult

There was some talk of Bellarmine succeeding Clement to the papacy; he himself avoided the issue, but he was persuaded to hold a prominent position in the Vatican from 1605 onwards. In his final years he turned to devotional rather than controversial work, producing a famous treatise on *The Art of Dying Well* and a commentary on the Psalms and Christ's words from the Cross. He died at the age of 79 and, surprisingly, was not canonized until 1930. He was named a Doctor of the Church the following year.

Feast-day 17 September

Rose of Lima

1586 Lima — Lima 1617

The flower of Lima

The first canonized saint of the New World.

Born to Spanish parents of moderate means, Rose was christened Isabel de Santa Maria de Flores but at her confirmation by St Toribie, archbishop of Lima, she took the name by which she had been popularly known since childhood.

Renowned for her beauty, Rose took pains to disfigure her good looks in an attempt both to repel possible suitors and to guard against any sensual pride of her own. It is said that she rubbed pepper into her face to make the skin blotchy, and that she once covered her hands with lime, disabling herself for a month, because she had been complimented on their smoothness. Despite the frequent objections of her parents, the ridicule of acquaintances and the concern of her friends, Rose refused to mitigate the austerities she practised upon herself.

Mystic recluse

Her parents' financial situation worsened after an unsuccessful mining venture, and Rose worked to help support the family, labouring in the garden and plying her needle late into the night to produce works of embroidery and other stitching. The harshness of this life suited Rose well, but her parents soon began to insist that she take a husband. Rose resisted the idea, taking a vow of virginity to confirm her resolution, and instead, against their wishes, she joined the Dominican tertiaries at the age of 20 and took St Catherine of Siena as her model. She lived as a recluse in a hut at the bottom of the garden in which she worked so hard, and her reputation for mystical experiences, visions and suffering spread throughout the city. An ecclesiastical enquiry vindicated her spiritual gifts.

Although she lived a reclusive life, Rose was greatly concerned with the care of others in need and she is regarded as the founder of Peru's social service. When earthquakes hit Lima many in the city attributed its survival to the intercession of its beautiful recluse. But Rose suffered from personal temptation and spiritual aridity as well as from the persecution of others, and many psychologists have questioned the extremity of her lifestyle. Theologians have countered by arguing that her example was an attempt to redress the corruption of the time in which she lived.

Death and cult

For the last three years of her life, plagued by illness, Rose lived in the house of the government official Don Gonzalo de Massa and his wife. She died after one last painful illness, aged only 31, and was given a funeral of honour in Lima. Canonization followed in 1671, a year after Pope Clement X had declared her patron saint of Peru. Her patronage was later extended to include the whole of Central and South America, the Philippines and even India. Because of her deep attatchment to her parents' garden and also because her name itself recalls a flower, Rose is unofficially recognized as the patron saint of florists and gardeners.

> **Feast-day** 23 August
> Patron saint of Peru, New World, India, florists and gardeners

Samson

c.485 South Wales — Dol c.565

Missionary to Cornwall

Thought to be the leader of the Britons who colonized Brittany, Samson is a central figure in the Christian history of the south-west.

Born to Amwn of Dyfed and Anna of Gwent, Samson was dedicated to God as a baby and went on to be educated by St Illtud at the school of Llantwit monastery in South Glamorgan. He grew up to be ordained there as deacon and priest, but he incurred the jealous anger of two nephews of Illtud's who made an attempt to assassinate him, so he withdrew to live for some time on Caldey island (Ynys Byr), under the eremitical rule of Piro. He was joined there by his uncle Umbrafel and his father Amwn, who had suffered from a near-fatal illness, and became cellarer and then, on the death of Piro, abbot of the small community.

Mission to Cornwall

At this point Samson visited Ireland, where he may have reformed a monastery, and on his return he resigned his abbacy and lived once more as a hermit, this time on the banks of the Severn, together with his father and two companions. His solitude did not last long; he was soon consecrated bishop and appointed abbot of the nearby monastery. He continued his missionary journeys travelling through Cornwall where he lived for some time, making foundations at Southill and Golant. It is possible that he journeyed as far as the Scilly Isles, one of which is named after him.

Brittany

From Cornwall Samson moved on to Brittany, where he founded a monastery at Dol, and then to Pental in Normandy. Samson finally settled at Dol, becoming abbot there and apparently exercising some form of episcopal power of jurisdiction. According to legend he was consecrated as bishop of Dol by King Childebert, but it is unlikely that any regular see was established until several centuries later. In the political sphere, Samson supported the successful Judual against Conmor for rulership of Brittany in 555, and it was probably he who signed the acts of the 557 Council of Paris.

Death and cult

He died at Dol, having achieved a lasting reputation as a pioneer in the evangelism of Cornwall, the Channel Islands and Brittany, and was the object of several ancient church dedications throughout these areas. The spread of his cult in England was increased when Athelstan, king of Wessex from 924 to 939, secured an arm and other relics for his monastery at Milton Abbas in Dorset. In art he is usually shown with a cross or staff and often with a dove and book.

Feast-day 28 July

Sebastian

Narbonne — Rome c.288

The soldier-martyr

Although the trusted soldier of Emperor Diocletian, Sebastian's allegiance to God before duty led to his martyrdom at his master's hands.

Although the details of Sebastian's life are almost wholly derived from an untrustworthy fifth-century document (sometimes wrongly attributed to Ambrose), Sebastian's romantic legend has gained much popular credence and was a popular subject for artists especially in the Renaissance. According to his fictitious *Acts*, Sebastian was born in Gaul and enlisted in the Roman army in about 283. As a Christian in Rome he encouraged persecuted believers such as Mark and Marcellian who were in prison before their martyrdom, and as his faith was unknown to Diocletian he was appointed captain of the praetorian guard. The appointment was confirmed by Maximian in Diocletian's absence in the East, who was likewise unaware of Sebastian's faith.

Sebastian continued to support and encourage the Christians under persecution, making many converts among the prison staff and converting also the prefect of Rome, Chromatius, after curing his gout, who then went on to free his prisoners and slaves before he resigned his post. Chromatius's son Tiburtius was also converted to the forbidden faith and baptized with his father.

Martyrdom

When, as was inevitable, Diocletian finally discovered Sebastian's faith he was furious, accusing him of disloyalty and ingratitude, and he ordered him to be shot to death with arrows. The sentence was carried out and Sebastian was left for dead, but he had not been killed outright; his wounds were tended and healed by Irene, widow of the martyred Castulus. On his recovery he refused to flee the city to safety; instead, he deliberately confronted Diocletian, reproaching his cruelty. The emperor was naturally taken aback at the unexpected apparition, but he rallied to condemn Sebastian to brutal death by beating with cudgels. His body was thought to have been secretly buried by believers in a grave now marked by the Basilica of St Sebastian.

Cult

The popularity of Sebastian in artistic representation of the 15th century, usually as a young man pierced by arrows, has been explained by the rare opportunity it afforded artists to portray a male nude in an acceptable context. He became popular as the patron saint of archers and soldiers (along with Saints George and Maurice) and gained a reputation for his efficacy against the plague, maybe because of his courage in facing the arrows. It may also be because invocation to him at some point was famously followed by the end of a plague attack, and the plague of 680 in Rome has been suggested as a possibility. He was listed as one of the Fourteen Holy Helpers.

Feast-day 20 January
Patron saint of archers, athletes, soldiers and police, invoked against plague and by the dying

See illustrations on following page and p73.

St Sebastian by *Matteo di Giovanni. National Gallery.*

Simeon Stylites

c.387 Cilicia — Telanissus 459

First of the 'pillar saints'

His attempts to escape the attention of the world made him one of the most famous figures of his time.

Born the son of a Cilician shepherd, Simeon too tended flocks until the age of 13 when he experienced a vision in which he was commanded to dig ever deeper to sink the foundations of a house. Interpreting this as a call to a holy life, Simeon spent the next two years as a servant in a nearby monastery, but finding the regime here too lax, moved on to become a monk at the stricter monastery in Eusebona, near Antioch. Here he subjected himself to ever more severe self-mortification, until he nearly died after a rope of knotted palm leaves, worn next to his skin, had eaten so far in to the flesh that it took three days of careful softening and incisions to remove. As a warning against such extreme and individual austerities, as soon as he had recovered the abbot dismissed him.

From cave to pillar

Simeon lived as a hermit at the foot of the mountain of Telanissus for three years. It is said that he spent Lent there without any food or water; a kindly priest named Bassus had left him both but the bread and water were found untouched beside Simeon's unconscious body at Easter. He was brought round with the Eucharist and a few lettuce leaves. Subsequently living in a cell at the top of the mountain, Simeon was visited by hordes of visitors, drawn by the reputation of this remarkable holy man. Eventually, in 423, he decided to escape the intrusive crowds by building a pillar 10 feet high, upon which he lived for the next four years. The rest of his life was spent on a successively higher series of pillars, the last of which measured 60 feet, built for him by the people of the surrounding area, and where he spent the last 20 years of his life.

His pillar was constantly surrounded by sightseers, many of whom were converted by his kindly preaching. Despite his extreme way of life, his message was free from all taint of fanaticism; he urged his listeners to refrain from swearing and gambling, and to turn their attention instead to justice, prayer and charity. His fame had by now spread far beyond Syria and those who could not make the journey sought the prayer and advice of the holy man by letter. He was even visited by emperors.

Death and cult

Simeon died on 1 September, bowed as in prayer, and was buried in Antioch. His dramatic and extreme kind of piety has usually been regarded by the established Church as one to be admired rather than emulated, being an example more in the tradition of the Eastern fakirs than of the Church Fathers, but his effectiveness in an age of decadence cannot be denied. Most famous among his imitators are Saints Simeon the Younger and Daniel the Stylite.

Feast-day 5 January

Stephen

d. Jerusalem c.35

The first Christian martyr

Described as a man 'full of faith and the Holy Spirit', Stephen's fearless example as a martyr has inspired all who have since suffered for their faith.

Chapters six and seven of the book of Acts contain all that we know of this deacon of the early church in Jerusalem, one of the seven chosen by the apostles to supervise the administration of alms and help in the work of evangelism. Since one of his main functions was to aid the Hellenic widows of the community, it seems more than likely that he was himself a Greek-speaking Jew, and some scholars have speculated that he was born abroad and may have been educated in Alexandria.

Acts records that Stephen performed wonderful miracles after his ordination and that he was an outstanding preacher, whose wisdom was irrefutable. Inevitably he ran into opposition from the Jewish religious leaders. The elders of the synagogue attempted first to defeat him in debate, and when this proved impossible, to accuse him slanderously of blasphemy, and it was on this charge that Stephen was brought before the Sanhedrin, the Jewish council.

Trial and death

Faced with his accusers and the hostile High Priest, Stephen preached a sermon which, judging by the version recorded in Acts (which may have been elaborated on later), was one of astonishing power and authority. He appears to have been well-versed in Jewish history and in an understanding of Jesus's role as the promised Messiah, denouncing those present for their resistance to God's Holy Spirit. He ended his speech with a declaration of a vision of Jesus standing at the right hand of God in Heaven, which so inflamed the hostile court that the semblance of a trial was forgotten; they rushed upon Stephen, drove him out of the city and stoned him to death. Acts records how Stephen called out to Christ as he died, asking forgiveness for his executors in a way reminiscent of Christ on the cross. We are also told that a young man was present who looked after the cloaks of those involved in the stoning and who approved of the act; he was Saul, later to become the great apostle Paul.

Cult

Since the fourth century or earlier, Stephen's cult has enjoyed tremendous popularity. His supposed grave was discovered in 415 at Kafr Gamala and his relics were translated to Constantinople and then to Rome, along with some stones allegedly used in his murder. Numerous churches and many cathedrals have been dedicated to him; he has traditionally been regarded as the patron saint of deacons and has been invoked against headaches since late medieval times. He is usually represented in art as a deacon with a stone as his emblem, often holding a book or the palm of martyrdom. In Greek he is known as *proto-martyr*, the first of the martyrs.

> **Feast-day** 26 December
> Patron saint of deacons, invoked against headaches

Stephen of Hungary

c.975 Asztergom — Buda 1038

The first king of Hungary

Revered as both national folk-hero and saint, Stephen's work in establishing the Hungarian nation and Christianizing it are fundamental in the history of Hungary.

Son of Geza, the duke of the Magyar community recently settled in Hungary and at least partly Christianized, Stephen was baptized along with his father by St Adalbert of Prague in 985. Ten years later he married Gisela, sister to Duke Henry III of Bavaria (later an emperor and saint), and in 997 succeeded Geza as ruler of the Magyars. He faced some opposition and rivalry, but succeeded in consolidating his position and implementing his policies, one of which was the Christianization of his subjects. As a means to both ends he had himself crowned the first king of Hungary in 1001, a title sanctioned by Pope Sylvester II, who sent a crown for the coronation. This was famously captured by the United States army during World War II and was only returned in 1978.

The Christian king

As king, Stephen set about organizing his realm under a system of episcopal sees and encouraged unity among his people by reducing the power of nobles, appointing govenors responsible to himself to rule over the different counties and breaking down tribalism by means of a new legal code and by introducing an element of feudalism. He succeeded in establishing a newly-independent Hungary under his throne. He was energetic also in establishing the Hungarian church: he appointed St Astrik as ecclesiastical head and founded many new churches and monasteries, discouraging paganism by imposing heavy punishments on offenders. He made it illegal to blaspheme or to marry a pagan, and he insisted that all his subjects (except the clergy) should marry in an attempt to promote Christian morality. Although many of his measures now seem somewhat tyrannical, it must also be acknowledged that in general he governed with justice, wisdom and generosity (he was known to risk his life by going among his subjects in disguise to give alms to the poor).

Death and cult

In 1031 tragedy struck when Stephen's son and heir Emeric died in a hunting accident. His last years were marred by ill health and by the succession squabbles which broke out well before his death. His successors were to undo much of Stephen's extraordinary achievement, and this no doubt contributed to his reputation as a national hero along with the miracles reported at his tomb. His relics were enshrined at the Church of Our Lady in Buda in 1083, and he was canonized by Pope Gregory VII in that year. In art Stephen is usually represented holding a sword with a banner of the cross, and he is sometimes shown with his son St Emeric, whose relics were enshrined at the same time as those of his father.

Feast-day 16 August
Patron saint of Hungary

Swithin

c.800 Wessex — Winchester 862

Bishop of Winchester

Swithin's feast of translation has entered popular weather-lore as the day on which rainfall signals unceasing rain for 40 days.

Despite the popularity of his cult, little is actually known of Swithin's life. As a child in Wessex he was educated at the Old Minster in Winchester, and in the early ninth century he was appointed personal chaplain to Egbert, the king of Wessex. A trusted and respected advisor, he was also placed in charge of the education of the young prince Ethelwulf, who succeeded to the throne in 839.

Bishop in Wessex

In 852 Ethelwulf appointed Swithin bishop of Winchester, the capital of Wessex, one of the most significant posts in the Anglo-Saxon church. In the course of the next 10 years Wessex became recognized as the most powerful English kingdom, although it was subject to the first of the Viking attacks which were to feature so prominently in English history of the next century. Swithin was energetic in founding new churches throughout his diocese and was renowned for his compassion and charity

Feast-day 2 July

towards the needy. Before his death on 2 July he had asked to be buried in the cemetery of the Old Minster, and his grave was placed by the west door of the cathedral and marked by a tomb.

Cult

When Ethelwold succeeded to the episcopate of Winchester in 964, it was planned that Swithin's relics should be translated to a shrine inside the cathedral. The translation was scheduled to take place on 15 July 971, but it was delayed by an exceptionally heavy rainfall, which was perceived as further manifestation of the saint's power. When finally accomplished, it was accompanied by a number of miraculous cures. This is probably the origin of the famous superstition which states that rain on St Swithin's translation feast on 15 July means rain for the following 40 days. A further translation took place in 974, which probably required the separation of the head from the body to accommodate two shrines. It is thought that the shrine in the sacristy which contained Swithin's head was taken by St Alphege to Canterbury when he left Winchester to take up his new post as archbishop.

When the Norman cathedral was built at Winchester Swithin's relics were translated into a new shrine there in 1093, and this was a popular centre for pilgrimage in the Middle Ages. The shrine was destroyed in the Reformation and rebuilt in 1962. Several ancient churches were dedicated to Swithin in England, and occasional dedications also exist in Scandinavia.

Teresa of Ávila

1515 Ávila — Alba de Tormes 1582

'The eagle and the dove'

The first female Doctor of the Church, whose mysticism and charisma have made her one of the most popular of saints.

The daughter of aristocratic Castilian parents, Teresa exhibited a lively and pious disposition from an early age. On the death of her mother in c.1529 she was sent to be educated by Augustinian nuns in Ávila but was obliged to quit the convent after three years because of her poor health. It was while she was convalescing that Teresa first read the *Letter* of Jerome, which inspired her to take the veil herself, and despite initial opposition from her father she entered the Carmelite house in Ávila, the convent of the Incarnation, in 1533. After only a year her health failed again and she was forced to retire temporarily, but after recuperating with her family she returned to the convent in 1540.

The Carmelite convent of Ávila was not known for its asceticism; its many members were able to socialize freely with the townsfolk and they were allowed to retain personal possessions. Troubled by this easygoing atmosphere Teresa began the discipline of mental prayer, becoming gradually more spiritually-minded until in 1555 she began to experience ecstasies and visions and to hear voices. Much worried by these mystical experiences at first, and facing widespread misunderstanding and suspicion from the less ascetic members of her community, Teresa was greatly supported by St Peter of Alcantara who convinced her of the value and authenticity of her visions.

Calced reform

During middle-age, Teresa resolved to found a religious house which would adhere more strictly to the original Carmelite rule, distressed by the laxity of life within her unreformed convent. Encouraged by Peter and others she secured papal approval for her new foundation in 1562. The first community of Discalced (barefoot) Carmelite nuns was St Joseph's at Ávila, distinguished from the unreformed movement by the personal poverty of the nuns, the enclosed and disciplined spiritual life, and a regime of simple manual work that made the convent practically self-sufficient. With characteristic good sense and briskness Teresa insisted on recruiting only intelligent novices, believing them to be the most likely to achieve true humility and holiness. She was to found another 16 such convents in the course of her life, and in 1568 she helped St John of the Cross to found the first community of reformed Carmelite friars at Duruelo.

The Discalced Carmelites, both male and female houses, faced much opposition from their unreformed counterparts. The squabbling was ended only in 1579, when Pope Gregory XIII named the Discalced Reform as a separate and distinct association. It was during these troubled years that Teresa wrote her famous letters and books, most notably her own *Life* in 1565, *The Way of Perfection* written for nuns in 1573 and the *Interior Castle* (1577), a classic work on contemplative prayer. She also travelled widely throughout Spain founding new convents and encouraging her communities. She was beloved by her nuns, immensely cheerful and practical yet capable of a mystical spirituality, at once active and contemplative, and her vivid vernacular writing remains popular today as teaching and as an insight into one of the most likeable of all saints.

Death and cult

It was on 4 October, on her way back to Ávila after founding a new house at Burgos in 1582, that Teresa died and was buried at Alba de Tormes there. Her feast-day however is on 15 October because of the inauguration of the Gregorian calendar the day after her death in 1582, which meant the effective loss of 10 days in October of that year. She was canonized in 1622 by Pope Gregory XV and in 1970 became the first woman ever to be honoured with the title of Doctor of the Church, by Pope Paul VI.

In art she is usually represented with a dove above her head or a fiery arrow which pierces her heart, a reference to one of her most famous mystical experiences. Her legacy survives today, both in her widely-read works and in the many small communities of Carmelite nuns who still preserve her ideals and her contemplative way of life today.

Feast-day 15 October
Patron saint of lace-makers, invoked by those in need of grace

St Teresa by Bernini. Church of S. Maria della Vittoria, Rome.

Theodore of Tarsus
(Theodore of Canterbury)
c.602 Tarsus — 690 Canterbury

The organizer of the English Church

His initiatives gave structure and unity to the disorganized Anglo-Saxon church.

A native of Tarsus, Theodore was educated in Athens and took his monastic vows as a Basilian monk in Rome. In 668, at the age of 66, Theodore was appointed archbishop of Canterbury by Pope Vitalian. The post was unexpectedly vacant following the death of Wighard, archbishop-elect, in Rome, and when Vitalian had asked the African monk Adrian to accept the appointment he had declined, suggesting instead his Greek friend Theodore. When Theodore sailed for his new see, he was accompanied by Adrian as an adviser; Bede indicates that this may have been due to doubts about Theodore's orthodoxy, but his reservations appear to be unfounded. With them also was Benedict Biscop, later founder of the monasteries at Wearmouth and Jarrow.

Work in the English Church

On reaching England, Theodore made a visitation of the country: he appointed clerics to fill vacant sees, opened monastic schools (including St Augustine's at Canterbury of which Adrian was abbot), improving discipline among the clergy and introducing liturgical chants in many churches. In Northumbria he arbitrated in the disputed bishopric of York between the rival claimants Saints Wilfrid and Chad, deciding in favour of Wilfrid. At Hereford in 672 he convened and presided over the first synod of the Anglo-Saxon church, where he proposed 10 new canons, including one which calculated the date of Easter in accordance with the Roman tradition, and at which he established the diocesan system in England. He decreed that the church should hold synods annually to decide upon doctrinal, ecclesiastical and administrative issues.

Theodore ran into confrontation with Wilfrid over the division of his see, and in the subsequent appeal to Rome, Pope Agatho ordered that the division be retained but that Wilfrid himself should choose the bishops. It appears that Theodore's policy had been sound, but his manner of executing it insensitive. Egfrith refused to accept the ruling and banished Wilfrid; Theodore seems to have made no attempt to intervene. However Theodore later sought reconciliation with Wilfrid, whose biographer claims that Theodore named him successor to the see of Canterbury, an appointment which was never fulfilled.

The curriculum at Theodore's Canterbury school was exceptionally wide for the time, and it formed many future leaders of the church. Of Theodore's own writings nothing has survived: the Penitential said to be his is probably a later work incorporating some of his teaching.

Death and cult

Theodore died on 19 September; he was buried in the monastery of St Peter and St Paul in Canterbury, close to the bones of St Augustine, and his incorrupt body was translated into a shrine in 1091. Despite his enormous contribution to the organization and administration of the English church, his cult remained relatively little known and no *Life* was written until the late 11th century. The framework of the system he inaugurated has been retained up to the present day in the Church of England.

Feast-day 19 September

Thérèse of Lisieux

1873 Alençon — Lisieux 1897

The little flower

Her life-long example was one of childlike simplicity and obedience.

Marie Françoise Martin was the youngest daughter of the watchmaker Louis Martin and his wife Zélie Guérin who died when Thérèse was only four or five years old. She was brought up in a pious middle-class milieu, and when the family moved to Lisieux in 1877 was cared for by her aunt and her older sisters and educated by Benedictine nuns. Five of the sisters were eventually to join the Carmelite convent at Lisieux. Although the youngest, Thérèse was the third to enrol, at the age of only 15, taking the name Thérèse of the Child Jesus.

Life and death

For the next nine years Thérèse lived quietly at the convent, serving for a time as assistant to the mistress of novices, and living commendably under the Carmelite regime but without great distinction. Her aim was a simple, unselfconscious obedience, her 'little way' as she called it. Her tranquillity was disturbed when her father suffered two paralytic strokes and was subsequently confined to an asylum, where he lived for three years. Thérèse referred to this time as his 'martyrdom'.

In 1895 (a year after the death of her father) Thérèse suffered a haemorrhage; it was the first symptom of tuberculosis. Her condition swiftly worsened and she died at the age of 24, after silently and patiently suffering enormous pain. It is probable that nothing more would have been known of this self-effacing nun had she not written, under obedience to Mother Agnes (her sister Pauline), a short spiritual biography.

'Story of a soul'

After her death this biography was edited by her sisters and published as *Histoire d'une âme*, the story of a soul. The sweetness and simplicity of this small book charmed readers in every language into which it was translated, and suddenly the young unknown nun was accredited with interceding in innumerable miracles, attracting almost universal veneration. A great part of her popularity was her very simplicity; Thérèse had demonstrated that one need not accomplish great deeds or possess enormous talent to attain sanctity.

Cult

In 1925 she was canonized by Pius XI and a large church was built in Lisieux for the hordes of pilgrims visiting her shrine there. She was named patron of missions (along with Francis Xavier) in 1927, and in 1944 was declared joint patron of France with Joan of Arc. Thérèse said that after her death she would let fall 'a shower of roses', meaning the favours she would work by intercession. The remark has been seen as so apt to Thérèse's personality and life (she is frequently known herself as the 'little flower') that her patronage has been claimed by those who work with flowers.

Feast-day 1 October
Patron saint of France, mission and florists

Thomas

First century

The apostle of India

Told of the miracle of the Resurrection, Thomas refused to believe it until he had physical proof.

Thomas was surnamed Didymus, the twin. He was probably born in Galilee where he lived until he became a disciple of Jesus, although his calling and trade are not recorded. He was genuinely committed to Jesus, impetuously declaring himself ready to go and die with him at the raising of Lazarus (John 11: 16) but posterity remembers him best for his scepticism: when told by the other disciples that Jesus had appeared to them while he was absent, he asserted that 'unless I put my hands in his side... I will not believe'. When however he saw Christ, and was invited to touch his wounds, Thomas fell before him and cried 'My Lord and my God!', the first confession of Christ's divinity after his resurrection (John 20: 24–9). His slowness to believe has earned him reproach from some scholars but the empathy and love of the common Christian, and his confession of Christ's divinity rings powerfully throughout the ages of the Church.

Later life

Eusebius records that Thomas went on to found the Christian church in Parthia and another ancient and more prevalent tradition holds that he preached in India. The Syrian Christians of Malabar claimed to have been converted by Thomas, and it is said that he was martyred near Madras, killed by a spear, where his grave is now marked by a stone cross. The relics were supposedly translated to Edessa in Mesopotamia in 394, although some claim that they still rest in San Tome in India. From Edessa his relics are supposed to have taken a convoluted route through Chios in the Aegean Sea to Ortona.

The apocryphal *Acts* of Thomas, which occur frequently between the second and fourth centuries, are unreliable. Although the mission to India which they chronicle is not historically proven, the tradition is so strong that he was named apostle of India by Pope Paul VI in 1972.

Cult

In art he is usually shown either doubting the word of the apostles or before the wounded Christ. Sometimes he carries the spear of his martyrdom (occasionally portrayed as a sword or dagger) and often a builder's rule, from a legend that he built a heavenly palace for an Indian king. The story tells that Thomas promised to build King Gundafor a beautiful palace, but spent all the money he had been given for the work upon the poor. When challenged by the irate king, Thomas answered that he would see his new palace in the next world. Gundafor's brother died just then and appeared to him in a vision, full of admiration for his magnificent heavenly palace, and Thomas was restored to favour. This is the source of his patronage of builders and architects, and he is invoked against blindness because of his own lack of spiritual sight.

Feast-day 3 July
Patron saint of builders, architects and theologians, invoked against blindness

Thomas Aquinas

1225 Roccasecca — Fossanuova 1274

Doctor Angelicus

His greatest service to the Church was the fusing together of Greek wisdom and methods of scholarship with Christian truth.

he left his great *Summa Theologica* incomplete, saying that all his writings were like so much straw compared to the glory which had been shown to him. He died on 7 March travelling to the Council of Lyons, a corpulent man whose health had been broken by overwork.

Works

His legacy of theological, philosophical and doctrinal works, most of them dictated to secretaries, is an awesome achievement. The most important work was the *Summa Theologica*, begun in about 1266 during his years in Italy but never completed because of the vision before his death. This five-volume document earned Aquinas the title of 'universal teacher'; it is a systematic exposition which forms the basis of Catholic doctrine even today, and its authority and comprehensive scope have never been surpassed. Similarly influential was his *Summa contra Gentiles*, a treatise on God and the creation. He also wrote several hymns still used by the church and a variety of treatises and commentaries. His true place as the central intellect of the Middle Ages was only fully revealed in subsequent generations.

Born near Aquino in his family's castle in Lombardy, Thomas was educated by the Benedictine monks at Monte-Cassino. In about 1239 he went on to the University of Naples, where he was greatly impressed by the Dominican friars. He enrolled in the order in 1244 but his family were aghast, not least because the Dominicans were a mendicant (begging) order, and they imprisoned him at Roccasecca for over a year to save the family honour. Thomas however rejoined the order in 1245 and left for further studies in Paris for three years.

In 1248 he accompanied his master Albertus Magnus to Cologne and was ordained there two years later before returning to Paris to teach. From here he wrote a defence of the mendicant order in answer to William of Saint-Amour, commentaries on Aristotle and Peter Lombard's *Sentences* and some biblical works. After gaining his doctorate and teaching in several Italian cities he returned to Paris for three years in 1269, recalled by king and university alike. But in 1272 Naples demanded him back, appointing him regent of studies. It was at Naples on 6 December 1273 that he experienced a divine revelation so wonderful that

Cult

Thomas Aquinas was canonized in 1323 and his body was translated to Saint-Sernin in Toulouse in 1368 and subsequently to the Jacobins' church there in 1974. He was declared a Doctor of the Church by Pope Pius V in 1567 and in 1880 was named patron of all colleges and schools by Leo VIII, who also commanded that his teaching be studied by all students of theology. In art his emblem is a sun, and he is often represented teaching with pagan philosophers under his feet.

> **Feast-day** 28 January
> Patron saint of philosophers, theologians, booksellers, universities, colleges, students and scholars, invoked for chastity and learning

Thomas Becket (Thomas à Becket)

1118 London — Canterbury 1170

'This turbulent priest'

Probably the most famous English churchman, whose inflexible insistence on the pre-eminence of the Church brought him into tragic conflict with his sovereign.

The child of a wealthy Norman family, whose father Gilbert was a prosperous merchant and sheriff of London, Thomas was educated at Merton Abbey in Surrey and studied law in London before going on to the University of Paris. The unexpected death of his father however meant that his financial situation took a turn for the worse, and he spent some time working as a clerk before attaching himself to the household of Archbishop Theobald of Canterbury in 1141. The archbishop sent him to Rome on several occasions, and then in 1144 to Bologna and Auxerre to study canon law. Ten years later, having been ordained deacon, he was appointed archdeacon of Canterbury. In this capacity he proved a diplomatic and effective servant for the archbishop in his dealings with the court, and he endeared himself to Henry d'Anjou (later Henry II of England) by persuading Pope Eugenius III not to accept the rival claim of Eustace, son of King Stephen of Blois. In gratitude, and with the support of Theobald, Henry elected Thomas chancellor in 1155, the first native Englishman since the Norman conquest to hold such a lofty position. He became the second most powerful man in the country, with a luxurious and lavish lifestyle, and was the perfect courtier, who acted in the king's best interests on all occasions, even personally leading troops into battle at Toulouse in 1159.

Archbishop of Canterbury

This cordial relationship changed suddenly and completely in 1162 when Henry appointed Thomas archbishop of Canterbury, despite the latter's objections, following the death of Theobald. Thomas immediately resigned his chancellorship and the day before his consecration was ordained as a priest. He consciously and deliberately changed to an austere regime, adopting a hair shirt and living under strict discipline, determined to carry out properly the job he had not wanted. In addition to his new ascetic regime, he began to give away vast amounts of money to the poor. All this was immensely irritating to Henry, and the split between the two men worsened when Thomas began to support the interests of the Church over those of the Crown and took upon himself the task of ministering to and improving the spiritual welfare of the king. He even excommunicated some influential members of Henry's court for their mishandling of church estates.

In 1164 the two were in direct confrontation over Henry's 'Constitutions of Clarendon', opposed by Thomas since they denied clerics the right to be tried in an ecclesiastical court or to appeal to Rome. Neither of the strong-willed men would retreat; finally Becket was forced to flee into France where he lived as an exile for six years. Both parties appealed to Pope Alexander III who, unwilling to offend the king, did not intervene but suggested that Becket enter the Cistercian monastery at Pontigny. As Henry's strictures against him increased and his property and assets were seized by the Crown, he moved to Sens where he received protection from Louis VII of France, all the while loudly proclaiming the superior authority of the Church over the State.

Martyrdom

Finally, in 1170, Louis's efforts and the intervention of the Pope succeeded in establishing a fragile peace between the king and his priest, and Thomas returned to Canterbury. The people of his diocese, who regarded him as a defender against the exploitation of the nobles and the crown, welcomed him back jubilantly. He found however that Henry's son had been crowned Prince in his absence, a slight which was a breach of his rights as archbishop of Canterbury, and he promptly excommunicated the bishops who had presided at the ceremony. Henry was furious: 'Who will rid me of this turbulent priest!' he stormed to his courtiers, although it seems unlikely that he was in earnest. Four of his nobles however saw a chance of rendering pleasing service to their sovereign: they visited Becket in the cathedral at Canterbury and murdered him there. Whatever his way of life had been, Becket seems to have died like a saint, commending his spirit into the hands of God and the saints.

Feast-day 29 December

Cult

The whole of Europe reeled at the news of his death. He was declared a martyr and became a symbol of the freedom and authority of the Church, his personal faults forgotten in the blaze of veneration and countless reports of miracles that surrounded his name. Henry performed public penance for the death in 1174, but he actually retained most of the privileges which had been at the heart of his contention with Becket, conceding only the right to appeal to Rome. Becket was canonized in 1173 by Alexander, and his relics were translated in 1220 into a shrine in Trinity chapel which became one of the most popular centres for pilgrimage in Europe. One of the most famous English routes is the Pilgrim's Way from London or Winchester to Canterbury, along which Chaucer's pilgrims tell their *Canterbury Tales* on the way to visit Becket's shrine.

Many depictions of Becket survive, most of them showing his death at the hand of the knights before the altar, and this dramatic scene has been immortalised in TS Eliot's play *Murder in the Cathedral.* Eighty ancient churches were dedicated to him in England before Henry VIII had the shrine destroyed and removed his name from all liturgical books.

Murder of St Thomas Becket, from a manuscript in the British Museum.

Thomas More

1478 London — Tower Hill 1535

'The King's good servant, but God's first'

With simple integrity and an immovable morality, Thomas refused to countenance the political manoeuvres of Henry VIII.

Son of the lawyer and judge Sir John More, at the age of 13 Thomas joined the household of the archbishop of Canterbury, John Morton, and was sent for two years to Canterbury College, Oxford, where he studied under the famous humanist scholar Thomas Linacre. He continued his education studying law at Lincoln's Inn, and in 1501 was called to the bar like his father before him. Three years later he became a member of parliament. During these years he debated various courses for his life, whether to became a Carthusian monk (he lived at the London Charterhouse for four years), a diocesan priest or to join the Friars Minor. But in 1505 he married Jane Colt, continuing with his legal career. Even now however he would wear a hair shirt, and practise monastic discipline; it was not lack of commitment or rejection of asceticism that kept Thomas More from the cloister. It is said that More had originally fallen in love with Jane's younger sister, but married the elder to spare her the humiliation of seeing her younger sister married before her. Whatever the case, their marriage appears to have been a particularly happy one, and their home became known as a centre of Renaissance learning and humanism. Sadly, Jane died young in 1511 having borne Thomas three daughters and a son.

Already Thomas's public and political career had begun. He was recognized and applauded for his rare qualities of loyalty, integrity, intellectual brilliance and strict morality, and Henry VIII, crowned in 1509, made him a favourite. He was appointed to a series of public posts, and his reputation grew with the publication of many of his writings, most notably *Utopia* in 1516. This classic vision of an enlightened, tolerant society founded on reason rather than political expediency was quickly translated from the Latin into most major European languages. In his other writings he condemned Protestantism, arguing against the Bible translator Tyndale and ably defending Henry VIII's book on the seven sacraments (which had led the Pope to grant Henry the title 'Defender of the Faith') in his *Vindication of Henry against Luther* in 1523.

The split with Henry

Thomas was married again soon after Jane's death to a widow named Alice Middleton and they moved to Chelsea in 1524. By this time Henry had served on several diplomatic missions for Henry, speaking for him in France before Francis I and Charles V, and had been knighted two years earlier. After holding several other high positions he was appointed Lord Chancellor after the disgrace of Wolsey in 1529, despite his sustained objections. Already he was disturbed by Henry's divorce of Catherine of Aragon, which had been performed against the wishes of the Pope.

He refused to sign a petition addressed to the Pope seeking his permission for the divorce and the hostility between Henry and himself developed. Finally, in 1532, More resigned the Chancellorship in protest over Henry's measures to secure ecclesiastical power for himself. He had at first accepted Henry's title 'Protector and Supreme Head of the Church of England' along with John Fisher's provision, 'so far as the law of Christ allows', but as Henry's split with Rome became increasingly obvious he felt unable to continue in his service. He retired to Chelsea, refusing to attend the coronation of Anne Boleyn or to sign the oath in the Act of Succession which recognized the children of Henry and Anne as heirs to the throne, nullified Henry's first marriage and repudiated the authority of the Pope.

Execution

Such defiance could not be tolerated: Thomas was arrested in 1534 and imprisoned in the Tower of London for over a year, forfeiting his lands by his continued refusal to conform despite many attempts to persuade him to back down. During his imprisonment he wrote many influential spiritual works, such as the *Dialogue of Comfort versus Tribulation* and the *Treatise on the Passion of Christ*, and many letters. Finally, despite his refusal to comment on the Act of Supremacy in 1535, his silence was interpreted as treason and he was condemned. He died for refusing to compromise the dictates of his conscience, which insisted that no temporal authority could presume to usurp the spiritual power invested in the papacy by the first Bishop of Rome, St Peter. He was not alone in choosing this course; Henry was forced to execute several others, including John Fisher, John Houghton and many of the Carthusian monks in London. The execution took place on 6 July, with More memorably proclaiming himself on the scaffold 'the King's good servant, but God's first', and courteously expressing the desire to meet with his executioners in heaven. He was then publicly beheaded.

Cult

More's body was buried in the Tower of London, in the church of St Peter ad Vincula, and his head was displayed on Tower Bridge before being buried at St Dunstan's, Canterbury. He was beatified along with his friend and adviser Fisher in 1886, and canonized in 1935. They share a feast-day, and rank among the small number of English saints to be universally revered by the Catholic church. More's son-in-law William Roper wrote his biography.

Many modern schools and churches are dedicated to Thomas More, often in company with Fisher. His central importance to the literature of his age does not end with the classic *Utopia*; it has been said of his *History of King Richard III* that it was the first great work of the English humanist historical tradition. A modern play on More's life by Robert Bolt, *A Man for All Seasons*, has been very successful. He is usually represented in his chancellor's robes, often wearing a scholar's cap, together with the Chalice, Host and papal insignia.

Feast-day 22 June
Patron saint of lawyers

Sir Thomas More. Engraving by R Woodman, from an enamel by Holbein.

Thomas of Hereford
(Thomas de Cantelupe)
c.1218 Hambleden — Montefiascone 1282

The only excommunicated saint

Thomas died much as he had lived, embroiled in controversy but asserting his right.

Baron William de Cantelupe, chief steward in the household of King Henry III, was a member of a noble Norman family with connections to the earldoms of Pembroke, Hereford and Abergavenny, and married to the dowager countess of Gloucester. Their son Thomas was born in Buckinghamshire, and his education was entrusted to an uncle, Bishop Walter of Worcester. He was sent first to Oxford and then to Paris (since the atmosphere at Oxford was troubled by internal conflicts), along with his brother Hugh.

In 1245 Thomas attended the Council of Lyons with his father and probably received ordination then; he also succeeded in obtaining a papal dispensation to hold a plurality of benefices simultaneously, a privilege which he was to use freely during his life. He continued his legal studies in Orléans and Paris, where he gained his licence in canon law, and returned to Oxford as a lecturer. In c.1262 he was appointed Chancellor of the University.

In the conflict of the barons against King Henry III Thomas championed their case in Amiens before Louis IX in 1264, and after the defeat of Henry at Leves he was named Chancellor of England by Simon de Montfort. When Simon was defeated and killed in 1265 Thomas was dismissed from his post and retired to France.

After several years of lecturing in Paris, Thomas returned to England to be appointed Doctor of Divinity and Chancellor of Oxford for the second time in 1273. He also continued to rule several dioceses, all of which he visited (often without warning) to maintain a high standard of clerical and pastoral ministry. He was elected Bishop of Hereford in 1275 and set about defending the rights of his see against encroaching ecclesiastical and secular neighbours. His energetic and combative approach made him unpopular with many of the lay lords he confronted, but the common people of his parish generally loved this large-hearted holy man.

Death and cult

His most serious conflict was that with Archbishop John Peckham of Canterbury. The two men clashed over the issue of how far the metropolitan should exercise jurisdiction over his bishops; the controversy was taken up at the Council of Reading in 1279, at which Thomas acted as spokesman for a number of bishops in opposition to Peckham, and in 1282 Peckham excommunicated him. Thomas went to Rome to appeal to Pope Martin IV, but the journey exhausted him and he died near Orvieto before he could put his case. Rome eventually vindicated his cause; his heart and some bones were returned to Hereford and many miracles were reported at his shrine. Edward I, whose advisor Thomas had been, was among those who pressed the case for sainthood. He was canonized by Pope John XXII in 1320, the only canonized saint to have been excommunicated from the church at the time of his death.

Feast-day 3 October

Timothy

Lystra — 97

The young disciple of Paul

Timothy served as Paul's ambassador to many of the young Christian communities and his youth belied his abilities as a leader of the Church.

Timothy's father was a Greek and his mother Eunice a converted Jewess, and he himself studied the Jewish scriptures as a child. He was converted by Paul and became his disciple when the apostle preached at Lystra and travelled with him as a close friend and co-worker (Acts 16: 1–5). Under Paul's guidance Timothy received circumcision in order to make himself, a child of a Gentile father, more acceptable to the Jewish Christians. He accompanied Paul on his second missionary journey, although when Paul was obliged to flee Berea because of the hostility he encountered there, Timothy remained in the town for a while. Then he was sent to Thessalonica as Paul's representative to encourage the Christians under persecution there and to report on their progress. When Paul joined Timothy in Corinth, it was this information which prompted him to write the first epistle to the Thessalonians.

First bishop of Ephesus

In 58 Timothy went with Erastus to Macedonia and visited Corinth to ensure that the church there remembered and practised the apostolic teaching; from there he accompanied Paul on a preaching tour of Macedonia and Achaia. He was probably still with Paul at his first imprisonment in Caesarea and then in Rome, and although briefly imprisoned himself, was then freed. A strong legend, supported by Eusebius, claims that he then became first bishop of Ephesus, in which position he received two pastoral letters from Paul encouraging him to preserve sound doctrine and to administer his church confidently despite his youth. It is thought that the first was written from Macedonia in c.65 and the second while Paul was awaiting execution in Rome.

Death and cult

The apocryphal fourth-century *Acts* of Timothy record his martyrdom in Ephesus at the hands of pagans, who were enraged because he opposed their festival of Katagogian in honour of Diana (or more probably Dionysius). He was stoned and clubbed to death by the mob and buried in Ephesus, from where his relics were supposedly translated in 365 to a shrine in Constantinople. Many miracles of healing were reported here, and are mentioned by both Jerome and John Chrysostom. From Paul's admonition that he should 'take a little wine' with his food for the sake of his stomach, Timothy has been traditionally invoked in cases of stomach complaint. He is usually represented in art with his emblem of a club and a stone recalling his death; another common depiction has him receiving his epistle from Paul.

Feast-day 26 January
Invoked against weakness of the stomach

Turibius of Mogroveio

1538 Mayorga — Santa 1606

The reluctant, reforming archbishop

One of the first known saints of the New World, whose zeal and compassion were legendary.

Toribio Alfonso de Mogroveio was born in Spain and displayed his religious leanings even as a child. But rather than train for the priesthood, he studied to become a lawyer and took a post as professor of Law in the University of Salamanca; he was so well respected in his field that Philip I chose him as chief judge of his Inquisition court at Granada. This was a particular honour for a layman, but even more surprising was his subsequent selection as archbishop of Lima in Peru. Turibius himself was dubious about the advisability of his appointment, which technically controverted canon law, but he pleaded his unsuitability in vain. He was ordained, consecrated, and arrived in Lima in 1581.

Life in the New World

Turibius immediately ran into problems: his diocese was vast and the terrain difficult and varied (he managed a visitation but it took seven years). Discipline in the church was lax since distance and poor communication made the discovery and punishment of abuse almost impossible, and Turibius found that the Spanish authorities all too frequently tyrannized and oppressed the native Indians whom they were nominally Christianizing. He began his programme of confrontation and reform energetically, disciplining offenders within the church, representing the rights of the poor in the see, founding many new churches and hospitals and, in 1591 in Lima, the first seminary to be built in the New World.

He took it upon himself to learn as many Indian dialects as he could to enable him to communicate directly with his flock and journeyed throughout the whole of his see despite enormous personal privation and discomfort. His charity even extended to impoverished members of the ruling class; sensitive to their feelings he would give his assistance anonymously.

Death and Cult

Turibius carried on with his punishing workload right up to his death on 27 March while he was returning from a visitation of Pacasmayo. In his will he bequeathed all his personal belongings to his servants, and his property for the benefit of the poor. Canonized in 1726 he has long been popularly venerated in the Americas, but his qualities as a pioneering and reforming bishop have recently been acknowledged and his cult is now universal; even now he stands as a champion and symbol to the many Christians of South America. In art he is shown in his bishop's robes kneeling at an altar, surrounded by angels.

Feast-day 23 March
Patron saint of Peru and the bishops of Latin America

Ursula

Date unknown

Leader of 11 000 companions

Although almost wholly fictitious, her romantic legend set ablaze the medieval imagination.

The most fanciful and unsubstantiated variations upon the legend have sprung up from a bare Latin inscription of c.400 discovered in Cologne, telling of the rebuilding of a memorial church by one Clematius in honour of a number of virgin martyrs. The inscription gave no details of names, numbers or date, but the enigma caught the popular imagination and a strong local cult grew up. By the ninth century the tradition declared that the women were numerous, originated from Britain and had suffered under Maximian. Martyrologies of the late ninth century name Ursula as the leader of a group of up to 11 virgins. But by the 11th century the number had become fixed at 11 000. It seems unlikely that this exorbitant inflation can be explained by the normal processes of exaggeration; it is probably due to a misreading of a manuscript in which the M denoting 'martyres' was interpreted as the Roman numeral M, and the figure was multiplied by a thousand.

A romantic heroine

From then on the legend gained popularity and after several elaborations reached its final form, which appears in Voragine's *Golden Legend*. According to this version, Ursula was the daughter of a Christian king in Britain who was betrothed against her will to a pagan prince and managed to secure a delay of three years in which to enjoy her virginity. She spent the reprise sailing the oceans with 10 companions; each had a ship and 1000 virgin companions. They were believed to have sailed up the Rhine to Switzerland and then on to Rome for pilgrimage. On their return to Cologne they were massacred by the pagan Huns, enraged because Ursula refused to marry their chief.

The development of the cult

When a burial ground was uncovered at Cologne in the 12th century the bones were immediately declared relics of Ursula and her companions and were venerated in many churches: the fact that these relics included remains of men and children did not deter the pious but merely added fuel for the development of the legend. Many well-meaning people claimed to have spoken in visions with Ursula and her fellow sufferers, most famously Elizabeth of Schönau, and countless inscriptions were forged detailing the sufferings of the companions. Despite her alleged British origin, Ursula's popularity has been mainly concentrated around the Rhine, in northern France and in the Low Countries. Representations of her life are common, with particularly notable examples in Cologne and Bruges, and even in York and Venice. She is usually shown with a crown and sceptre, sheltering a group of companions beneath her cloak. The feast was removed from the universal calendar in 1969, and is now only permitted in certain localities. Ursula has gained popularity as a patroness of educational establishments, notably the School of St Ursula in Venice, and a teaching community was named the Order of Ursulines after her.

Feast-day 21 October

St Ursula in glory by Carpaccio. Academy, Venice.

Valentine

d. c.269

The patron saint of lovers

*The popularity of his feast owes
more to the mating habits of
birds than to the facts of
his martyrdom.*

There are in fact two Valentines, whose feasts are both celebrated on 14 February in the Roman martyrology, and neither of whom has any obvious connection with courting couples. One was a Roman priest and doctor who is believed to have been martyred under Claudius II on the Flaminian Way where a basilica was erected in his honour in 350. The other was a bishop of Turni (about 60 miles distant from Rome) who was brought to Rome and tortured and executed there in c.273 at the command of Placidus, the ruling prefect. Some believe that the two Valentines are in fact one person, that the Roman priest became bishop of Turni, was condemned there and brought to Rome for execution of his sentence. Since the *Acts* of both are equally unreliable, the final verdict may never be more than conjecture.

Development of the feast

The present popularity of Valentine's day has little to do with the historical saint or saints. It was a commonly held belief, attested from the time of Chaucer, that birds began to choose their mates on Valentine's feast-day, the very beginning of Spring, and

this is thought by many to be the origin of the tradition of choosing one's object of love as a 'Valentine'. Some scholars believe that Chaucer was actually referring to the feast-day of the bishop Valentine of Genoa, celebrated on 2 May, and that he may have had in mind the betrothal of Richard II to Anne of Bohemia on 3 May 1381. If this is the case, the conflation of the various Valentines on to a single feast-day probably occured some time after the death of Chaucer.

It is argued too that there may also be surviving elements of the pagan Lupercalia festival from Roman times which was celebrated mid-February. The subsequent commercialism of his feast and its removal both from historical fact and the observance of piety has been distrusted by the Catholic church, and his cult has recently been reduced.

Cult

No British churches are thought to have been dedicated to him, but he is often represented in art with a cripped or epileptic child at his feet whom he is believed to have cured. For this reason too he is often invoked against epilepsy. Other depictions show his beheading, or his refusal to worship idols, which led to his martyrdom.

Feast-day 14 February
Paton saint of beekeepers, affianced couples, travellers, and the young, invoked against epilepsy, fainting and plague and for a happy marriage

Veronica

First century

Woman of pity

Despite the dubiousness of her legend, Veronica's compassion and the story of her veil have awakened a response of compassion and devotion in generations.

The legend of Veronica tells how this pious woman stopped to wipe the anguished face of Christ as he stumbled beneath his Cross on the way to Calvary; the very features of his face were left imprinted on the cloth which she used for her act of simple charity. Despite the lack of evidence or collaboration the legend has understandably appealed to popular devotion for centuries, especially as interest in the human and physical aspects of Christ developed. A cloth known as 'St Veronica's veil' has been kept at St Peter's in Rome from the eighth century. Although devotion to the relic peaked in the late medieval period, it was exhibited as recently as 1933.

The debate about Veronica

In an attempt to flesh out the story, various attempts have been made to identify the enigmatic figure Veronica with other historical and legendary women. The most common of these is the woman whom Jesus healed of her bleeding. Others include the sister of Lazarus and Mary, Martha, or the wife of a Roman officer or of Zacchaeus, the tax-collector who hid in a tree to watch Jesus pass. Much debate has arisen over the derivation of her name, which many believe to be derived from 'vera icon', true image. According to this theory, the name arose as a means of explaining the relic itself, in much the same way as the word 'vernicle' in Middle English is derived, and was then attached to a fictional character to create a charming legend. It is worth noting however that the woman who suffered from internal bleeding was known in the East as Berenike long before she was associated with the image on the cloth.

Cult

Veronica is not listed in the Roman martyrology but her enduring place in popular devotion was secured by the inclusion of her story in *Stations of the Cross*, a devotional meditative work much propagated by the Franciscans in the late 18th century.

Several legends purport to record the acts of Veronica after her encounter with Christ; some claim she used the cloth to cure the emperor Tiberius in Rome, others that she accompanied her ex-tax-collector husband Zacchaeus in his evangelism of France. She is frequently represented in art, either wiping Christ's face or holding the imprinted veil.

Feast-day 12 July
Patron saint of washerwomen

Vincent de Paul

c.1581 Pouy — Paris 1660

Philanthropist and founder

His compassion and commitment were legendary even in his own lifetime.

Vincent de Paul was born into a Gascon peasant family on 24 April. He was educated at the Franciscan college in Dax and went on to study at the university of Toulouse, becoming an ordained priest at the unusually early age of 19. Some sources claim that he was captured by pirates while voyaging from Marseilles in 1605 and sold into slavery in Tunis, where he lived for the next two years before escaping to Avignon. He then studied further in Rome and on returning to France became court chaplain to Queen Margaret of Valois in Paris.

At this stage Vincent was quite contented with the prestige and comfort of his lot, but meetings with Francis of Sales and Pierre de Bérulle, working with the poor and oppressed, gradually wrought in him a conversion to a clerical life of absolute commitment and fierce devotion. During his time as chaplain to the noble Gondi family he succeeded in improving conditions for galley prisoners and evangelized the convicts of Bordeaux, and in 1625 he founded the Congregation of the Mission (the Vincentians or Lazarists), a community devoted to missionary work among peasants in small towns and villages, which quickly gained popularity right across France.

The work of the Vicentians

The order gained the approval of Pope Urban VIII in 1632, and in 1633 they were granted the church of Saint-Lazare in Paris (hence Lazarists). In the same year he founded the Sisters of Charity with Louise de Marillac, an unenclosed congregation of women ministering to the poor and sick, the first of its kind and extremely successful. He founded countless hospitals and orphanages, gave aid to victims of the war in Lorraine, sent missionaries as far as the Hebrides, ransomed enslaved Christians in North Africa, established new, high quality seminaries, and wrote many spiritual works. His deepest concern was the practical relief of human suffering and his charismatic selflessness inspired many, from all walks of life, to join his work. He was concerned also with sound doctrine, strongly opposing the heresy of Jansenism. Queen Anne of Austria recognized his value as an advisor, attracted by the same direct, good-hearted generosity that was beloved in him by so many peasants. His compassion extended to Protestants too; he instructed his missionaries to treat them with courtesy and brotherly love rather than as enemies.

Death and cult

He died on 27 September, and was canonized by Pope Clement XII in 1737. In 1833 a lay confraternity named the Society of St Vincent de Paul was founded by one Frederick Ozanam, the widespread dissemination of which did much to further his cult, and he was named patron of all charitable groups by Pope Leo XIII in 1885. In art he is usually shown with children, or sometimes with galley slaves, in remembrance of his compassion and founding activities.

Feast-day 27 September
Patron saint of all charitable societies, hospitals and prisoners, invoked to find lost articles and for spiritual help

Vitus

d. Luciana c.300

Patron saint of nervous disorders

A martyr under Diocletian, whose cult and patronage have extended in unexpected ways.

Although his cult is ancient, the historical facts about St Vitus are difficult to retrieve. He is believed to have been the son of a pagan Sicilian senator, and to have been converted to Christianity at the age of 12 by his nurse Crescentia and her husband (Vitus's tutor) Modestus. Once his proclamation of faith and the miracles which he performed came to the attention of the governor of Sicily, Valerian, Vitus was brought before him to recant. The young Christian refused, and succeeded in fleeing the country together with Modestus and Crescentia, escaping to Luciana and then on to Rome. There Vitus cast an evil spirit out of the son of Emperor Diocletian, but his compassionate gesture was to be his ruin.

Awed by the miracle, the Roman authorities demanded that Vitus offer sacrifices to pagan gods. When he refused to do so his miracle was construed as sorcery and the three were subjected to torture and executed. Some more fanciful legends record that they emerged unharmed from their tortures, and were freed from captivity amidst a violent storm, under cover of which an angel guided them back to Luciana.

Vitus's relics have been claimed by Saint-Denis and by Corvey in Saxony, where they were believed to have been translated in 836. It seems possible that two different groups of saints have been collapsed together in popular veneration: there is some evidence to suggest that there was an ancient cult of Vitus alone in Luciana, pre-dating that of Vitus, Modestus and Crescentia in Sicily.

Cult

Because he was reputed to have cured the emperor's child of demonic possession, Vitus came to be regarded as patron of those suffering from epilepsy and nervous disorders (hence the popular name for Sydenham's chorea, St Vitus's Dance). Similarly, he was invoked against the effects of bites from snakes or rabid dogs. It is interesting that his patronage was later extended to include dancers, actors and comedians. His cult was especially strong in Germany after the supposed translation of 836, and he was named one of the Fourteen Holy Helpers. In art Vitus's emblem is a cock, and he is frequently associated with the palm of martyrdom, a sword, a book or a dog.

The confusion over the exact relationship between Vitus, Modestus and Crescentia has resulted in a similarly confused iconography and cult: Vitus is often invoked alone, several monasteries omitted Crescentia from their devotions while others listed her with Vitus and Modestus on a shared feast-day.

Feast-day 15 June
Patron saint of dogs, dancers, actors and comedians, invoked against epilepsy, St Vitus's dance and snakebites

---

Wenceslas

c.907 Bohemia — Stara Boleslav 929

'Good King Wenceslas'

A young duke who had anti-pagan policies.

The education of young Wenceslas, son of Duke Wratislaw of Bohemia, was left largely in the hands of his Christian grandmother, St Ludmilla. In c.920 Wratislaw died in battle against the Magyars and Wenceslas's mother Drahomira, who had pagan sympathies despite her nominal Christianity, took the opportunity to seize power. She had Ludmilla murdered and set herself up as regent, establishing anti-Christian government and policies in her son's minority. Her rule ended with popular revolt in c.922 and Wenceslas succeeded to the duchy.

The reign of Wenceslas

The young duke proved a fair if strict ruler, who wasted no time in suppressing rebellion among his discontented nobles and in redressing the pagan policies of his mother. Drahomira had been banished from the court; she was now recalled and there is no record of any further trouble between them. Wenceslas took advice from church leaders and took steps to promote the spread of Christianity in the country by inviting German missionaries to enter on evangelistic missions. He also acknowledged the overlordship of Henry the Fowler, king of Germany, whom he recognized as successor to Charlemagne. These political and religious policies provoked a strong reaction among some of the more hardline pagan Bohemians, and especially the dissatisfied nobles. Among those opposed to the new ruler was his own brother Boleslav, whose resentment was increased at the birth of Wenceslas's son and heir, at which point he decided to join the rebels.

A treacherous assassination

Wenceslas was murdered at the hands of Boleslav and his followers on 20 September, traditionally believed to have been attacked and overcome on his way to Mass during a visit to his brother's estate. He was immediately venerated as a martyr, and Boleslav had his relics translated to the church of St Vitus in Prague, an astute political move given the immense popularity of Wenceslas's memory, whether spurred by personal remorse or not.

The cult and the carol

The church quickly became established as a popular destination for pilgrims and Wenceslas himself was soon regarded as the patron saint of Bohemia, with his image stamped on the country's coins. The crown of Wenceslas came to be regarded as a potent symbol of nationalism for the Czechs. Because of the region's reputation for producing fine beer, its patron naturally became associated with the brewing industry, although in life he was in fact more closely associated with the wine trade; he used to produce the wine for Mass from his own vineyards. In Britain, the familiarity of his name is due mainly to the famous carol by J M Neale, 'Good King Wenceslas', a reworking of the medieval carol 'Tempus adest floridum'. The story which it tells however has little to do with historical fact and everything to do with Victorian ideals of charity and social responsibility.

> **Feast-day** 28 September
> Patron saint of Czechoslovakia and brewers

Wilfrid

c.634 Northumbria — Dundee 709

The deposed bishop

Although disillusioned by the opposition he faced from both temporal and ecclesiastical potentates, Wilfrid's achievements and vision are among the greatest in the English church.

Wilfrid's father was a nobleman whose close connections with the court of Northumbria secured his child a place in the household of King Oswiu at the age of 13. Here he became a particular favourite of Queen Enfleda, and to secure the best education for him she arranged his departure for Lindisfarne, the great centre of Celtic Christianity in the north of Britain.

Although he learned much at the monastery, Wilfrid seems to have been unhappy with the inward-looking ethos of Irish Christianity. He left for Canterbury and studied briefly under St Honorius, developing a taste for Roman practices of the church, before going on to visit Rome itself with Benedict Biscop in 654. On the way they stopped off for a year at Lyons, where Wilfrid received and refused an offer of marriage to the niece of Bishop Annemund. In Rome Wilfrid studied under Boniface, the secretary of Pope Martin, receiving instruction particularly in canon law and Scripture. He once again broke his journey at Lyons on the way home, this time for three years, and it was then (if he had not already done so on his first visit) that he received the Roman rather than the Celtic tonsure. His stay was abruptly terminated after the death of Annemund in nationalistic riots; Wilfrid prudently returned to England.

The Celtic-Roman controversy

He arrived back in his native country in about 660, a staunch and persuasive campaigner for the introduction of Roman liturgical practices in preference to the Celtic traditions of the north. He was asked by Alcfrith, king of the Northumbrian province of Deira, to take on the abbacy of Ripon, where he introduced the Benedictine Rule and the Roman method of calculating Easter. Missionaries from southern England such as Paulinus had attempted to convert the northern Church to these observances, and like them Wilfrid found himself facing great and entrenched opposition, not least from Aidan of Lindisfarne and his successor, Colman.

At the Synod of Whitby in 664, Wilfrid was the chief spokesman for the pro-Roman party, and it was his articulacy and conviction which helped sway the vote of the assembly in favour of the case for Rome.

Bishop of York

After the synod, Alcfrith appointed Wilfrid bishop of York; since many northern bishops had rejected the resolutions of Whitby Wilfrid insisted on being consecrated in Compiègne, France, in the presence of 12 Frankish bishops. Unfortunately, he delayed his return to England just too long, and arrived home to find Alcfrith dead. King Oswiu had appointed Chad to fill Wilfrid's place at York, although his consecration was dubious. To avoid confrontation Wilfrid returned to Ripon, but was restored to the bishopric in 669 when the newly-appointed archbishop of Canterbury, St Theodore, decreed Chad's consecration void and removed him.

Fall from favour

Wilfrid now set about visiting and organizing his see. He promoted reform along

Roman lines throughout the diocese, improved the great Minster at York, built a magnificent church at Hexham and gained large areas of land for his monasteries. His diocese extended to the limits of the Northumbrian kingdom, a truly vast area in this time of expansion.

His life of prestige and comfort was threatened however when he aroused the anger of King Egfrith, with whom he had previously been on cordial terms, by encouraging his queen Etheldreda to leave him and enter a convent in 672. Meanwhile, his opulent lifestyle had become something of an embarrassment, attracting criticism from his enemies, and in 678 Theodore (working closely with Egfrith) set about dividing Northumbria into four dioceses without consulting Wilfrid. The move was of itself reasonable, but in going over Wilfrid's head so blatantly he effectively deposed him against the spirit of canon law. Smarting from this insensitive treatment, Wilfrid took his case to Rome, the first English bishop ever known to do so. On his journey to the continent he was caught in a storm and driven off course to the coast of Friesland. He spent a year preaching there, the first of many Anglo-Saxon missionaries.

Imprisonment and restitution

His case for restoration was vindicated by Pope Agatho, but on his return to England Egfrith had him imprisoned for nine months, in defiance of the papal command. He was freed into exile; settling in Sussex Wilfrid evangelized the pagans there, almost the last in England, and founded a monastery at Selsey. Not until 686 was he finally reinstated in Northumbria by Theodore, and even then his powers were reduced. Five years later he quarrelled with Egfrith's successor Aldfrith and was exiled again. He retired this time to Mercia, becoming bishop of Lichfield and founding several monasteries.

The final compromise

In 703 Theodore was succeeded by St Bertwald who, in collaboration with Aldfrith, convened a council at Austerfield in West Yorkshire at which Wilfrid was ordered to resign his episcopal seat. Once again Wilfrid had recourse to Rome and once again his case was upheld by the Pope. John VI commanded Bertwald to call a synod to clear Wilfrid's name, but it was not until Aldfrith's death in 705 that an acceptable compromise was reached at the Synod of the River Nidd. Its terms were that Wilfrid should agree to the continued rule of St John of Beverley as bishop of York, but that he should enjoy complete control of the diocese of Hexham, living at his monastery in Ripon, and of his various monasteries.

Death and cult

It was while visiting his monasteries in Mercia that Wilfrid died, and according to his wishes his substantial personal wealth was divided between the poor, the Roman Church, his loyal followers, and his abbots, to enable them to 'purchase the favour of kings'. Given the circumstances of his life, the cynical tone revealed here is perhaps understandable. From his own experience he probably regarded this as much the best way to secure the continuation of his foundations.

He was buried at Ripon, the centre of his cult, and was succeeded at Hexham by his follower Acca. When both Canterbury and Worcester claimed his relics by 10th-century translations his cult increased to national proportions. In art he is usually represented as a bishop, either baptizing or preaching, holding his pastoral staff.

Feast-day 12 October

Glossary

The following glossary provides brief explanations of some of the unfamiliar or specifically religious words found in *Saints*.

antipope One who proclaims himself pontiff in opposition to the one canonically appointed.

apostasize To abandon one's religious vocation or obedience.

apostle One who spreads the gospel message, especially one of Christ's 12; the first to bring Christianity to a country.

apostolate The state of being an apostle.

Arianism Pertaining to Arius of Alexandria (c.250–336), whose doctrine denied the equality of the three persons of the Trinity.

ascetic (adj) Very strict in terms of mortifying the flesh for the sake of holiness.

Austin Pertaining to the writings of St Augustine.

canon An ecclesiastical law or rule; a clergyman living under a rule and serving a cathedral or church.

Canon Regular A member of an order which is based on the teachings of St Augustine, or else intermediate between monks and secular clergy.

canonry A canon's benefice, or living.

catechism A question-and-answer system of Christian teaching.

catechumen One who is being taught the basics of Christianity.

chapter An assembly of members of a religious order or of eg canons of a cathedral or collegiate church (so-named because a chapter of the Rule or of the Bible was customarily read).

chapter-house A meeting place for a chapter.

Charterhouse A Carthusian monastery (a strict order founded by St Bruno in 1086).

collect A short prayer for a specific purpose or day.

conventual Belonging to a convent; a monk or nun; a member of one division of the Franciscans (friar Conventual).

crozier The pastoral staff of an abbot or bishop.

discalced Bare-footed, as are some of the Carmelite order.

Doctor of the Church A saint whose doctrinal writings have special authority; the early Christian Church has four Latin or Western doctors: SS Ambrose, Augustine, Gregory the Great and Jerome, and three Greek or Eastern doctors: SS John Chrysostom, Basil the Great and Gregory of Nazianzus. Western Christianity adds St Athanasius the Great to those Eastern doctors. The Roman Catholic church has proclaimed others doctor since the 16th century.

episcopate The office of a bishop.

eremitical Reclusive, like a hermit.

exarch A metropolitan; a legate; a Byzantine provincial governor.

father-general A monk in charge of an order that has many houses.

Forty Martyrs English and Welsh Roman Catholics who died between 1535 and 1680. They were canonized in 1970.

Fourteen Holy Helpers A group of saints venerated for the supposed efficacy of their prayers for human necessities.

heterodoxy Heresy; opinion opposed to conventional belief.

Holy See The Pope's bishopric of Rome.

incorrupt Unaffected by decay.

investiture The often ceremonial giving of an office or benefice.

legate An ambassador of the Pope; governor of a papal province.

martyrology A history of those who have died or suffered for their belief.

metropolitan The bishop of a cathedral city or chief see of a province.

monstrance In Roman Catholic churches, the venerated receptacle containing the consecrated host.

novice One in a religious house who has not yet taken the vows.

novitiate The state of being a novice.

Observant (eg friars Observant) Of the stricter division of the Franciscans.

office An act of worship or order of service.

pallium (pl. **pallia**) The Pope's double Y-shaped white woollen vestment, also given by him to archbishops.

penance A voluntary or imposed act to show repentance for sins; the sacrament which conveys absolution.

penitential A rule book pertaining to penance.

pontificate A pope's office or reign.

Poor Clare A Franciscan order of nuns founded by St Clare.

protonotary A chief secretary of the chancery at Rome.

recusant A dissenter; usually a Roman Catholic who refused the compulsory Church of England attendance.

relic Any part of the body or previous possessions of a saint which is revered to inspire faith and piety.

sacramentary A book of all the Roman Catholic prayers and ceremonies used at eg Baptism, Confirmation, Penance etc.

Sacred Heart Christ's physical heart, adored by Roman Catholics since the 18th century.

schism A breach in the unity of the Church; the Great Western Schism (1378–1417) occurred when there were antipopes under French influence at Avignon.

see The office of bishop.

shrine A hallowed receptacle for a saint's relics; a place built especially to house them, or simply hallowed for its historical significance.

stigmata Marks resembling the wounds on Christ's body.

superior The head of a religious house or order.

take the habit/veil To become a monk/nun.

tertiary A lay member of a third order of a monastic order, who may live an ordinary life.

translate To transfer a saint's body or relics to a different place from where they originally came to rest.

viaticum Money or provisions for a journey; the eucharist given to those in danger of death.

Index

Note: Saints are listed under their names, as they appear in the book, eg Andrew, St. Places named after saints are listed in true alphabetical order, eg St Andrews, St Michael's Mount. Popes, kings etc are also listed under their names. Councils and synods are listed in groups under C and S respectively. Entries in **bold type** refer to specific articles in the text. Entries in *italic* refer to illustrations.

A

Abbo of Fleury 187
Abbo of Maine 184
Abelard 51
Abingdon 98, 107, 198
Abraham 178
Acacius 86
Acca 230
Acre 160
Adalbert of Prague, St **3**, 207
Adalbert the Elder 3
Adalric, Lord 182
Addai 156
Adela 64
Adelaide, St **4**
Adeonatus 35
Adomnan, St **5**, 56, 76
Adrian II, Pope 84
Adrian VI, Pope 28
Adrian of Canterbury, St **6**, 14, 211
Aegidius, St — see Giles, St
Ælfheah — see Alphege, St
Ælfmar 17
Aelfric, Archbishop of Canterbury 17
Aelred, Æthelred, St — see Ailrid
Aesidius 167
Æthelfrith, King of Northumbria 186
Æthelred the Unready, King of England 17, 57, 93, 99
Aetius 159
Afra, St 7, 135
Agatha (German princess) 169
Agatha, St **8**, 9
Agatho, Pope 48, 211, 230
Aghowle 112
Agiloff, King 77
Agincourt, Battle of 79, 124
Agnes (sister of St Clare) 74
Agnes, St **9**
Agricolaus 53
Aidan of Dalriada 76
Aidan, St **10**, 71, 81, 132, 136, 186, 229
Aigulf of Maguelone 49
Ailred, St **11**, 88, 181
Akar 23
Alacoque, Claude 166

Alba de Tormes 209
Alban, St **12**, 04
Albano 54
Alberic of Rome 184
Albertus Magnus (Albert the Great), St **13**, 214
Albezzeschi, Bernardino degli
  — see Bernardino, St
Albinus 159
Alcala 151
Alcantam 196
Alcfrith, King of Deira 48, 71, 81, 229
Aldfrith, King of Northumberland 5, 230
Aldhelm, St **14**, 132
Alençon 212
Alexander III, Pope 27, 215, 216
Alexander IV, Pope 54, 74
Alexander VI, Pope 115
Alexander VII, Pope 120
Alexander, Bishop of Alexandria 33
Alexander, King of Scotland 88, 169
Alexander Severus, Emperor 70
Alexandria 29, 31, 32, 33, 66, 85, 108, 134, 159, 170, 193, 206
Alexis, St 3
Alfonso IV, King of Portugal 102
Alfonso XI of Castile 102
Alfonso Maria de Liguori, St **15**
Alfred, King of England 14, 132
Alipius 35
Almachius 70
Alnwick 169
Aloysius Gonzaga, St **16**
Alphege, St **17**, 93, 107, 208
Alpheus 176
Alphonsus Rodriguez, St 195
Alvarez, Juan de Yepes y —
  see John of the Cross, St
Alvastra 58
Amalfi 22
Amand, St **18**, 126

Ambrose, St 9, **19**, 21, 35, 132, 133, 135, 203
Amiens 163
Amphibalus 12
Amwn of Dyfed 202
Anatolius 87
Andrew, St **22**, 194, 197
Andrew II, King of Hungary 101
Anlaf 17
Anna, King of the Angles 106
Anna of Gwent 202
Annaghdown 56
Anne, St **23**, *24*, 174
Anne of Austria 109, 226
Anne of Bohemia 23, 224
Annecy 120
Annegray 77, 122
Annemund, Bishop of Lyons 43, 229
Annesi 42
Anselm, St **25**
Anskar, St **26**
Anthelm, St **27**
Antioch 40, 87, 108, 124, 146, 149, 159, 161, 167, 190, 191, 194, 205
Antoninus of Florence, St **28**
Antony, St *xii*, **29**, 134
Antony of Padua, St **30**
Antony Zaccaria 40
Antwerp 94
Aosta 25
Aphrodisia 8
Apollonia, St **31**
Apostles' Council 40
Aquila 52, 191
Aquileia 20, 146
Aquinas 200
Arbogastes 20
Arbon 122
Arcadius, Emperor 32, 149
Arcella 30
Arculf, Bishop 5
Ardfert 56
Arenas 196
Ariconium 92
Aristotle 13, 54, 214
Arius 33
Arles 127
Armagh 164, 189
Armentius 57

Arnold, Matthew 56
Arona 65
Arrowsmith, Brian — see
    Edmund Arrowsmith, St
Ars-en-Dombes 145
Arsenius, St **32**
Arsenius, Bishop 33
Arthur, King 92
Arundel 106
Ashton-in-Makerfield 97
Assisi 30, 74, 116, 119
Astrik, St 205
Astyages, King of Armenia 41
Asztergom 205
Athanasius, St 29, **33**, 34, 108,
    135
Athelm 93
Athelstan, Anglo-Saxon king
    4, 93, 107, 202
Athens 42, 90, 127, 128, 191,
    211
Attila the Hun 123, 159
Aubert, St 178
Audrey, St — see Etheldreda,
    St
Augsburg 7
Augustine, St 11, 20, 25, 31,
    35, *37*, 105, 108, 125, 131,
    132, 147, 188
Augustine of Canterbury, St
    38
Augustus 25
Aurelius Augustinus — see
    Augustine, St
Aust 38
Austerfield 230
Austregisilus, Bishop of
    Bourges 18
Auvergne 183
Auxentius, Bishop of Milan
    19, 108, 135, 172
Auxerre 189, 215
Avalon 140
Avignon 58, 68
Avila 151, 155, 196, 209

B
Badajoz 196
Baeza 151
Bagnoregio 54
Baius 200
Baldwin, Emperor 160
Bailey, Abbé 145
Baltonsborough 93
Bamburgh 10, 186
Banmgor (Ireland) 77, 122,
    164
Bannockburn, Battle of, 110
Barat, Jacques 163
Barbara, St **39**
Barberi, Dominic 193

Barcelona 195
Bardney Abbey 71
Bardsey Islad 92
Bari 180
Barking 14
Barnabas, St **40**, 170, 190
Barr, St — see Finbar, St
Barra 111
Barrow (Lincolnshire) 71
Bartholomew, St **41**, 197
Barton, Elizabeth 150
Basil the Great, St **42**, 45, 128
Basilia 42
Basilicus 87
Bassus 205
Bastia 74
Bath 17
Bathild, St **43**, 103
Baudricot — see de Baudricot
Baume-les-Dames 182
Baume-les-Messieurs 184
Beaumont, Lady Margaret
    150
Beauvais — see de Beauvais
Bec 25
Becket — see Thomas Becket,
    St
Beddington 107
Bede, the Venerable, St 5, 10,
    43, **44**, 48, 61, 71, 81, 106,
    131, 132, 143, 181, 186,
    188, 211
Bedricsworth 95
Begga, St 126
Bellarmine, Roberto — see
    Robert Bellarmine, St
Belley, 27
Benedict, St 42, **45**, *47*, 84,
    132, 187
Benedict I, Pope 131
Benedict XIII, Pope 193
Benedict XIV, Pope 15, 143,
    148, 159
Benedict XV, Pope 166
Benedict Biscop, St 6, 44, **48**,
    211, 229
Benedict of Aniane, St **49**
Beneventum 41
Benincasa, Giacomo 68
Berea 220
Berengarius 4
Bereswindis 182
Bernadette, St **50**
Bernadone — see di
    Bernadone
Bernard of Clairvaux, St 11,
    27, **51**, 125, 164, 183
Bernardino of Siena, St **52**
Bernini 210
Bertwald, St 230
Bérulle — see de Bérulle

Bethlehem 146, 155, 174
Bethsaida 22, 197
Bevegnati Giunta 168
Beverley 150
Birha 26
Birmingham 71
Bjorn, King of Sweden 26
Blaise, St **53**
Blanche of Castile 160
Blanche of Namur 58
Boleslaus, Duke of Poland 3
Boleslav, Duke of Bohemia
    228
Bollstädt, Count of 13
Boleyn, Anne 218
Bologna 52, 91, 198, 215
Bolt, Robert 218
Bonaventure, St **54**, 117
Bonelli, Cardinal 115
Boniface, St 3, **55**, 77, 198, 229
Bordeaux 226
Borromeo, Count Gilbert 65
Boswell, St 81
Boulogne 189
Bourges 18
Brabant 138
Bradford-on-Avon 14
Bregenz 77, 122
Bremen 26
Brendan the Navigator, St **56**,
    112
Breuil 109
Brevnov 3
Brice (or Britius), St **57**
Bride, St — see Brigid, St
Bridget, St **58**, 155
Brig 56
Brigid, St **59**
Brude, King 76
Brueghel the Elder 192
Bruges 222
Brunhilda, Queen 43, 77
Bruno, St **60**
Budapest 207
Burgas 210
Bury St Edmunds 95
Byzantium 22, 42

C
Cadoc, St 112
Cadwallon, King of Gwynedd
    186
Caedmon, St **61**, 136
Caen 25
Caerleon-on-Usk 92
Caesarea 42, 128, 191, 220
Caesarius of Arles, St 127
Cajetan, St **62**
Calaruega 91
Caldey Island 202

Callistus I, St (and Pope) **63** 137
Callistus II, Pope 89
Callistus III, Pope 139, 148
Calpurnius 189
Calvin, John 36, 142
Cambridge 38, 150
Campion, Edmund 142
Cana 41, 174
Canapus 32
Canassa 139
Canice 112
Canisuius, Peter 142
Cantalupe — see de Cantalupe
Canterbury 6, 17, 23, 25, 38, 41, 55, 89, 93, 98, 100, 105, 184, 188, 198, 208, 211, 215, 216, 218, 229, 230
Canute, St (King of Denmark) **64**
Capernaum 22
Cappadocia 108, 124, 128
Capua 200
Caravaggio 192
Carlisle 36, 88
Carlo Borromeo, St 64, **65**
Carlyle, Thomas 95
Carpaccio 223
Carpophorus 62
Cartagena 195
Carthage 35, 83
Casa degli Esercizi Pii 113
Cascia 199
Cashel 164
Casseneuil 91
Cassian 45
Castellazzo 1193
Castiglione 16
Castiglione, Friar John da — see da Castiglione
Castra — see de Castra
Catania 8
Catherine of Alexandria, St **66**, *67*, 148
Catherine of Aragon 150, 217
Catherine of Siena, St **68**, *69*, 201
Catherine of Vadstena, St 58
Catherine wheel 66
Caxton, William 124
Ceadda, St — see Chad, St
Ceawlin, King of Wessex 105
Cecilia, St **70**
Cedd, St 71
Celestine I, Pope 85, 159, 189
Celian Hill, Rome 131
Cellach of Armagh 164
Celsus, St 164
Cemetery of Callistus 63, 70
Ceolfrid 5

Ceolfrith, St 44
Chad, St **71**, 211, 229
Chamoisy — see de Chamoisy
Chantal — see de Chantal
Chaptel 103
Charlemagne, Emperor 26, 49, 127, 143, 228
Charles V, King of France 62, 217
Charles VII, King of France 148
Charles VIII, King of France 119
Charolles 166
Chartres 157
Chartreuse, La Grande 27, 140
Châtillon-sur-Seine 51
Chaucer, Geoffrey 70, 103, 216, 224
Cheddar Gorge 93
Chelles 43, 103, 136
Chester 97
Chicago 114
Chichester 198
Childebert, King of Brittany 202
Childeric II, King of the Franks 43, 123
Christopher, St **72**, *73*, 157
Chromatius 202
Cicero 11, 35
Cîteaux 11, 51, 60, 140
Civita Vecchia 78
Clairvaux 51, 164
Clare, St **74**, 116, 117
Claudius II, Emperor 224
Clematius 222
Clement, St (Pope Clement I) **75**, 84, 90, 191
Clement IV, Pope 54
Clement VI, Pope 58
Clement VII, Pope 68
Clement VIII, Pope 200
Clement X, Pope 201
Clement XIII, Pope 166, 226
Clement of Alexandria 170
Clerkenwell 97
Clermont 120
Cletus, Bishop of Rome 75
Clitherow, John 165
Clonard 76, 112
Clonfert 56
Clotaire II, King of the Franks 103
Clotaire III, King of the Franks 43
Clotaire II, King of Neustria 77
Clovis, King of the Franks 43, 123

Cloyne 111
Cluain Inis 77
Cluny 4, 46, 107, 139, 140, 183, 184
Cnut, King of England 17, 64, 95, 99, 185
Codogno 114
Coimbra 30, 102
Coldingham 106
Colette, St 74
Colman, Abbot of Lindisfarne 10, 81, 229
Cologne 7, 13, 60, 126, 214, 222
Colombaio 52
Colt, Jane 217
Columba, St (Colmcille) 5, 56, **76**, 112, 158, 169
Columban, St **77**, 122, 136
Columbia 195
Columbus, Christopher 114
Comgall, St 77, 122
Comgan 110
Commodius, Emperor 63
Compiègne 148, 229
Compostela 58, 102, 144
Confraternity of Divine love 62
Confraternity of Our Lady of Mercy 168
Congregation of the Mission 226
Conmor, King of Brittany 202
Conrad, King of Mercia 100
Conrad of Marburg 101
Constantina 9
Constantine, Emperor 9, 33, 133, 180
Constantinople 22, 23, 29, 32, 42, 54, 84, 87, 128, 132, 133, 149, 159, 161, 206, 220
Constantius, Emperor 33, 86, 108, 135, 172
Constantius Chlorus 133
Corbie 26
Corinth 40, 75, 191, 220
Cork 111
Cornelimunster 49
Cornelius, St **78**, 83
Coroticus 189
Corrigan, Archbishop 114
Cortona 28, 168
Council of Aachen 44, 49
Council of Antioch 86
Council of Bari 25
Council of Chalcedon 159
Council of Chaldon 103
Council of Clermont 139
Council of Constantinople 86, 128
Council of Ephesus 85

Council of Florence 28
Council of Lyons 13, 54, 214, 219
Council of Nicaea 33, 128, 180
Council of Paris 202
Council of Reading 219
Council of Seleucia 86, 135
Council of Sens 51
Council of Seville 143
Council of Toledo 143
Council of Trent 62, 65
Coventry 178
Crediton 55
Crispin, St **79**, *80*
Crispinian, St **79**, *80*
Culross 158
Curubis 83
Cuthbert, St 10, 44, 76, **81**, *82*, 186
Cyneburga 186
Cynegils, King of Wessex 186
Cynewulf 133
Cyprian of Antioch 83
Cyprian of Carthage, St 78, **83**
Cyril, St 75, **84**
Cyril of Alexandria, St **85**, 159
Cyril of Jerusalem, St **86**

D
da Castiglione, Friar John 168
Dagobert I, King of the Franks 18, 103, 126
Dalfinus 44
Dalmatius, Count of Demur 139
Damascus 190
Damasus I, Pope 32, 146, 147
Damietta 116, 160
Danei, Paul Francis — see Paul of the Cross, St
Daniel 137, 178
Daniel the Stylite, St **87**, 205
Dante 13, 44, 143
d'Arc, Jacques 148
Dardilly 145
David, King (biblical) 155
David, St (King of Scotland) 11, **88**, 138, 169
David of Wales, St **89**, 92, 111, 158
Dax 226
de Baudricot, Robert 148
de Beauvais, Vincent 157
de Bérulle, Pierre 226
de Cantalupe, Baron William 219
de Castra, Eleanor 115
de Chamoisy, Mme 120
de Chantal, Jane Frances 120
de Flores, Isabel — see Rose of Lima, St

de Loyola, Iñigo de Recalde — see Ignatius Loyola, St
de Marillac, Louise 226
de Massa, Don Gonzalo 201
de Medici, Cosimo 28
de Medici, Francesco 16
de Montfort, Simon 219
de Paul, Vincent — see Vincent de Paul, St
de Sales, Francis — see Francis of Sales, St
de Sandovel, Father Alfonso 195
de Saumaise, Mother 166
de Voragine, Jacobus 1, 39, 46, 124, 157
Decius, Emperor 3, 12, 72, 78, 83, 130
Deerhurst Monastery 17
degli Albezzeschi, Bernardino — see Bernardino, St
Deinol St 92
Della Tome 60
Demetrius, St 124
Denis, St **90**, 123
Denis, King of Portugal 102
Derbend 41
Derry 76
Devereux, St — see Dubricius, St
Devie 145
di Bernadone, Pietro 116
di Fidanza, Giovanni — see Bonaventure, St
di Giovanni, Matteo 204
Diana (goddess) 153, 191, 220
Diarmaid, King of Ireland 76
Diego de Avezedo, Bishop 91
Diocletian Emperor 7, 53, 104, 124, 167, 180, 188, 203, 227
Diodorus of Tarsus 149
Dionysius (god) 220
Dionysius of Alexandria, St 31
Dionysius the Areopagite 90
Dioscorus 39
Discalced Reform 151, 209
Dol 202
Dominic, St **91**, 117
Domitian 153, 197
Domrémy 148
Donatus 146
Doncaster 88
Douai 97, 169
Doulting 14
d'Outremer, Prince Edward 169
Dover 198
Downpatrick 59
Drahomira (mother of Wenceslas) 228

Drepanum 133
Droitwich 198
Dryden, John 70
Dubricius, St **92**
Duchesne, Sister Philippine 163
Dumbarton 189
Dumfries 158
Dundee 229
Dunfermline 88, 169
Dunkeld 76
Dunstan, St 17, **93**, 103, 107, 187
Dürer, Albrecht 23
Durham 11, 82, 186
Duruelo 209
Dyfrig — see Dubricius, St
Dympna, St **94**

E
Eadmor of Canterbury 25
Eata, Abbot 81
Ebbe, St 106
Eddius 43, 71
Edessa 213
Edgar, King of England 93, 107, 187
Edinburgh 127, 138, 169
Edith (Queen of Edward the Confessor) 99
Edith (Queen of Otto the Great) 4
Edmund, King 93, 136
Edmund, St **95**, *96*, 99, 198
Edmund Arrowsmith, St **97**
Edmund Ironside 169
Edmund of Abingdon, St **98**
Edred, King 93
Edward I, King of England 88, 219
Edward III, King of England 124
Edward the Confessor, St (King of England) 11, **95**, *96*, **99**, 124, 169
Edwin, King of Northumbria 136, 186
Edwy, King 93
Egbert, King of Wessex 208
Egbert, St 71
Egfrith, King of Northumbria 48, 81, 106, 211, 230
Egwin, St **100**
Eilaf 11
Elias of Cortona 117
Eleutherius 90
Eligius, St — see Eloi, St
Eliot, T S 216
Elizabeth (mother of John the Baptist) 152, 174
Elizabeth of Hungary, St **101**

Elizabeth of Portugal, St **102**
Elizabeth of Schönau, 222
Elmo, St — see Erasmus, St
Elnone 18
Eloi, St 79, **103**
Ely 12, 99, 106, 107
Emeric, St 207
Emma, Queen 41
Enfide 45
Enfleda, Queen 229
Ephesus 153, 173, 174, 191, 220
Epidaurus 134
Epiphanius 134
Erasmus, St **104**
Erasmus, Desiderius 72, 150
Erasmus of Antioch 104
Erastus 220
Erc, St 56
Erchinoald 43
Erconwald, St 106
Erhard,St 182
Eric III, King of Denmark 64
Erik, King of Jutland 26
Estremoz 102
Estrithson, Swein 64
Etargabail 111
Ethelbert, St (King of Kent) 38, **105**, 131
Ethelburga, St 106
Etheldreda, St **106**, 230
Ethelred, St — see Ailred, St
Ethelred, King of Mercia 100
Ethelred II, King of England 185
Ethelwold, St 17, 93, **107**, 187, 208
Ethelwulf, King of Wessex 208
Eudoxia, Empress 149
Eugenius III, Pope 51, 215
Eugenius IV, Pope 28, 113
Eulogius of Alexandria 105
Eunan, St 5
Eunice (mother of St Timothy) 220
Euphemius 87
Eusebius of Nicodemia 33, 41, 42
Eusebius of Vercelli, St **108**, 146, 161, 170, 213, 220
Eustace, St 138
Eustathius, St 108
Eustochium 146
Eustratius, St 53
Evesham 64, 100
Exeter 55
Exning 106

F
Fabian, St 78
Fabian, Pope 137

Fabius, Bishop of Antioch 31
Faro, St 109
Fatima 175
Faustus, Bishop 35
Faversham 79
Felix, Bishop of Messana 38
Felix (Roman governor) 191
Ferdinand V, King of Aragon 115
Ferdinand the Catholic, King of Spain 141
Feriach 110
Ferrante, Marquis of Castiglione 16
Ferrara 53
Fiacre (or Fiachrach), St **109**
Fidanza, Giovanni di — see Bonaventure, St
Fiesole 28, 52
Fillan, St **110**
Fillan the Leper, St 110
Finbar, St **111**
Finbar of Moville 111
Findlugh of Tralee 56
Finistère 176
Finnian St 77, **112**
Fisher, John — see John Fisher, St
Flaubert, Gustave 157
Flavian, Bishop of Antioch 149
Fleurs 46
Fleury 107, 184, 187
Florence 28, 74, 200
Florentian, St 143
Florentius 45
Flores, Isabel de — see Rose of Lima, St
Foillan, St 126
Fontaines 51, 77
Fontiveros 151
Formiae 104
Fossanuova 214
Fourteen Holy Helpers 39, 53, 104, 124, 167, 203, 227
Fra Angelico 28, 68
Frances of Rome, St **113**
Frances Xavier Cabrini, St **114**, 141, 211
Francis Borgia, St **115**
Francis of Assisi, St 30, 54, 74, **116**, *118*, 119, 196
Francis of Paola, St **119**
Francis of Sales, St **120**, 226
Francis Xavier, St **121**
Francis I, King of France 218
Frederick II, Emperor 74
Friars Minor 116
Frome 14
Fulda 55
Fulgentius, St 143

Fulk II, Count of Anjou 184

G
Gabriel (Archangel) 174, 178
Gaeta 104
Galileo 200
Gall, St **122**
Gallus, Emperor 78
Gamaliel 190
Gandia 115
Garavito, Peter — see Peter of Alcantara, St
Gaza 134
Geismar 55
Gelasius, Pope 167
Genoa 193
Geneva 120
Geneviève, St **123**
Genseric 36, 159
Geoffrey of Monmouth 12, 92, 133
George, St 99, **124**, 203
Geraint, King of Dumnonia 14
Gerald of Aurillac, St 184
Gerebernus, St 94
Germanus of Auxerre, St 123, 189
Gerona 7
Gertrude of Hackeborn 125
Gertrude of Helfta, St **125**
Gertrude of Nivelles, St **126**
Gethsemane 144, 153, 194
Geza, Duke of Magyars 207
Gheel 94
Ghent 18, 93, 200
Gilbert of Limerick 164
Gildas, St 89, 112
Giles, St **127**
Gilla, Abbot of Derry 164
Giovanni — see di Giovanni
Glasgow 158
Glasnevin 76
Glastonbury 89, 93, 107, 136
Glendochart 110
Gnostic Priscillianists 172
Goa 121
Godwin, Earl 99
Golant 202
Gordianus 131
Gospel of St John 41
Gougane Barra 111
Granada 151, 221
Gratian, Emperor 19, 20
Grecchia 117
Greenwich 17
Gregory the Great, St (Pope Gregory I) 20, 38, 46, 77, 105, 125, **131**, *132*, 173, 188
Gregory II, Pope 55
Gregory IV, Pope 26

Gregory V, Pope 3
Gregory VII, Pope 139, 207
Gregory IX, Pope 30, 74, 98, 101, 117
Gregory X, Pope 54
Gregory XI, Pope 58, 68
Gregory XIII, Pope 209
Gregory XV, Pope 210
Gregory of Nazianzus, St 42, **128**, *129*, 146
Gregory of Nyssa, St 46, 86, 130
Gregory of Tours 57, 90
Gregory Thaumaturgus, St **130**
Grenoble 60
Griezno 3
Grimkell, Bishop 185
Gudmarsson, Ulf 58
Guiscard, Robert 60, 176
Guiscard, Roger 60
Gundafor, King 213

H
Hambleden 219
Hamburg 26
Hannah 23
Harold, King of Denmark 26, 64
Harold, King of England 99
Harold Grenske, Lord 185
Harthacnut 99
Hartlepool 136
Heiu 136
Helena, St **133**
Helfta 125
Heliopolis 39
Hellesdon 95
Helvetic College, Milan 65
Henllan 92
Henry I, King of England 25, 88, 169
Henry II, King of England 27, 140, 215, 216
Henry III, Duke of Bavaria 207
Henry III, King of England 98, 160, 219
Henry V, King of England 124
Henry VIII, King of England 150, 216, 217, 218
Henry the Fowler, King of Germany 228
Hereford 211
Herewitha 136
Herman I, Landgrave of Thuringia 101
Herod, King 155, 174
Herod Agrippa I 144, 194
Herod Antipas 152

Herodias 152
Herrings, Battle of 148
Hertford 71
Hesychius 134
Hexham 11, 81, 186, 230
Hierapolis 170, 197
Hilaria 7
Hilarion, St **134**
Hilary of Poitiers, St 108, **135**, 172
Hilda, St 61, **136**
Hilduin 90
Hippo 35, 36
Hippolytus, St 63, **137**
Hippolytus (son of Theseus) 137
Holmhurst Hill 12
Honorius, St 32, 229
Honorius III, Pope 91, 117
Houghton, John 218
Hubert, St **138**
Hugh of Avalon, St — see Hugh of Lincoln
Hugh of Cluny, St **139**, 184
Hugh of Grenoble, St 60
Hugh of Lincoln, St 27, **140**
Hugh of Provence 4, 184
Humbert III, Count of Maurienne 27
Huntingdon 88
Hypatia 85

I
Ibor, Bishop 59
Ignatius Loyola, St 62, 121, **141**, 155
Illtud, St 202
Illyricum 104
Imar, Abbot 164
Inde 49
Ine, King of Wessex 14, 55
Ingwar 95
Inishadroum 56
Innocent II, Pope 51, 164
Innocent III, Pope 74, 91, 116
Innocent IV, Pope 198
Iona 5, 10, 76, 112, 169
Irenaeus, St 137
Isabel, St — see Elizabeth of Portugal
Isaiah 146
Isidore of Seville, St **143**
Islip 99
Ita (nun) 56

J
James (the Great), St 23, **144**, 153, 155, 173, 190, 197
James the Younger, St 144, 156

James I, King of England 97, 200
Jarrow 6, 44, 211
Jean-Baptiste Vianney, St **145**
Jerome, St 7, 8, 9, 20, 76, 124, 132, 134, 135, 137, **146**, *147*, 161, 209, 220
Jerusalem 5, 23, 40, 58, 86, 141, 144, 152, 155, 161, 170, 174, 190, 191, 194, 206
Jesus Christ 22, 23, 39, 41, 144, 152, 153, 155, 161, 170, 173, 174, 176, 190, 193, 194, 197, 206, 213, 225
Jette 163
Joachim (husband of St Anne) 23, 174
Joan of Arc, St **148**, 167, 212
Joanna 173
Joanna I of Naples 58
Job 132
Jocelin of Brakelond 95
Jocelin of Furness 158
John (Abbot of St Martin's Rome) 48
John, King of England 140
John III, King of Portugal 196
John VI, Pope 230
John VIII, Pope 84
John XI, Pope 184
John XII, Pope 4
John XV, Pope 3
John XVIII, Pope 17
John XXII, Pope 219
John Cassian 159
John Chrysostom, St 85, **149**, 220
John Dominici 28
John Eudes, St 166
John Fisher, St **150**, 217, 218
John Mark 40
John of Antioch, Archbishop 85
John of Beverley, St 44, 136, 230
John of Joinville 160
John of the Cross, St **151**, 209
John the Baptist, St 11, 22, 144, **152**, 173, 174, 194, 197
John the Dwarf, St 32
John the Evangelist, St **153**, *154*, 174, *177*
John the Spaniard 27
Joigny 163
Jona (father of St Andrew) 22
Jordan, River 22, 152

Joseph, St **155**, 174
Jovian 33
Jovinian 147
Judas Iscariot 156
Jude, St **156**, 178, 194, 199
Judual, King of Brittany 202
Julian I, Pope 33
Julian the Apostate 31, 33, 42, 85, 86, 108, 128, 152
Julian the Hospitaller, St **157**
Julien, Bishop of St David's, Wales 89
Julius II, Pope 62
Julius III, Pope 196
Justinian, Emperor 23, 66

K

Kafr Gamula 206
Katagogian, festival of 220
Kentigern, St **158**
Kentigerna, St 110
Kerry 56
Kildare 59, 112
Kilfiachra 109
Kimacahil 111
Kilpatrick 189
Kirkcudbright 81
Knights Hospitallers 152
Koman 29
Köningsberg 3

L

la Colombière, Claude 166
La Motte 29
La Peñuela 151
La Salette 175
Ladislas of Naples 113
Lake Genasareth 22, 144, 153, 194
Lambert, St 138
Lammermuir Hills 10
Lancaster 97
Landen 126
Landuin, Prior 60
Lanfranc 25,100
Langres 51
Laoghaire, King of Ireland 189
Lastingham 71
Lateran Palace, Rome 9
Laud, Archbishop 88
Lauingen 13
Laviano 168
Lawrence, St 137
Lazarus 173, 213
Leander, St 143
Leantius 19
Leinster 76, 77
Leo VII, Pope 184
Leo VIII, Pope 214
Leo IX, Pope 139

Leo X, Pope 60, 102
Leo XII, Pope 163
Leo XIII, Pope 44, 84, 85, 155, 195, 226
Leo the Great, St **159**
Lérins 189
Lewes 139
L'Hautecour 166
Liberius, Pope 33, 108, 146
Lichfield 71, 230
Licinius, Emperor 53, 133
Ligugé 172
Lima 201, 221
Limoges 103
Linacre, Thomas 217
Lincoln 95, 140
Lindisfarne 10, 71, 82, 186, 229
Linus, Bishop of Rome 75
Lipara 41
Lisbon 30, 196
Lisieux 212
Lismore 164
Lisnacaheragh 111
Liudhard 105
Llandaff 92
Llanelwy 158
Llantwit 202
Lombard, Peter 54, 214
London 38, 93, 127, 138, 140, 150, 215, 217, 218
Lothair, Prince of Italy 4
Louis, King of Westphalia 26
Louis IV of Thuringia 101
Louis VI, King of France 119
Louis VII, King of France 215
Louis IX, St (King of France) **160**, 219
Louis XII, King of France 119
Louis XIII, King of France 109
Louis the Pious 49
Lourdes 50, 175
Louvain 200
Loyola, Iñigo de Recalde de — see Ignatius Loyola, St
Luciana 227
Ludmilla St 228
Luke, St 155, 156, **161**, *162*, 170, 174, 176, *177*, 191
Lupercalia festival 224
Luther, Martin 23, 142, 150
Luxeuil 77, 122
Lycia 72
Lydda 124
Lyons 54, 120, 145, 229
Lystra 220

M

Maastricht 138

Macarius 29
Madeleine Sophie Barat, St **163**
Maderna 70
Madras 213
Madrid 169
Mael Maedoc, St — see Malachy, St
Maeldubh 14
Magdala 173
Magdeburg 3
Magnus, King of Norway 185
Magnus II, King of Sweden 58
Mainz 55
Majolus of Cluny, Abbot 4
Majuma 134
Malachy, St **164**
Malchus of Lismore, St 164
Malcolm III (Malcolm Canmore), King of Scotland 88, 169
Malek al-Kamil, Sultan 116
Malmesbury 14
Manesses, Archbishop 60
Manjarates 196
Manresa 141
Mantua, Duke of 16
Maratha 87
Marburg 101
Marcellina St 20
Marcia (mistress of Commodius) 63
Margaret Clitherow, St **165**
Margaret Mary Alacoque, St **166**
Margaret of Antioch, St 148, **167**
Margaret of Cortona, St **168**
Margaret of Provence 160
Margaret of Scotland, St 88, **169**
Margaret of Valois, Queen 226
Marianelli 15
Marilloc — see de Marillac
Marina, St — see Margaret of Antioch, St
Mark, St 155, 156, **170**, *171*, *177*, 194
Marmoutier 57,172
Marseilles 226
Marta Tana Santena 16
Martel, Charles 55
Martin, Marie Françoise — see Thérèse of Lisieux, St
Martin IV, Pope 219
Martin V, Pope 52
Martin of Tours, St (Pope Martin I) 28, 57, **172**, 181, 184, 229

Mary, St (mother of Jesus) 23, 24, 155, 161, 173, **174**, *175*, 183
Mary Celesta of Scala 15
Mary Magdalene, St **173**
Massa — see de Massa
Massa di Carrara 52
Matilda, Empress 144
Matilda (Queen of Henry I) 169
Matthew, St 144, 146, 155, 156, 161, 170, 174, **176**, *177*
Matthias, St 105
Maurice, St 203
Maxentius, Emperor 66
Maximian, Emperor 79, 133, 203, 222
Maximinus, Emperor (Gaius Galerius Valerius), 29, 39, 124
Maximinus, Emperor (Gaius Julius Verus) 137
Maximus, Emperor 19
Maximus, St 86
Mayeul, Abbot 183
Mayorga 221
Meaux 110
Mechtilde 125
Medici — see de Medici
Medina 151
Medjugorje 175
Mel of Armagh, St 59
Meletius, Bishop 108
Melin, Mother 166
Mellifont 164
Melrose 81
Memphis 32
Mendelssohn 192
Menevia (later St David's, Wales) 89
Messina 30
Methodius, St 75, **84**
Metras 3 1
Metz 77
Michael, St 126, 148, **178**, *179*
Michael III, Emperor 84
Michaelangelo 91, 175, 192
Middleton, Alice 217
Middleton, Thomas 165
Milan 16, 19, 20, 35, 40, 65, 108
Milchu 199
Milton Abbas 202
Minim Friars 119
Missionary Sisters of the Sacred Heart 114
Moccas 92
Molville 76
Monica, St 35

Monserrat 141
Mont St Michel 178
Monte Argentaro 193
Monte Cassino 45, 46, 214
Monte Gargano 178
Montefiascone 167, 219
Montepulciano 168, 200
Monterepido 52
Montfort — see de Montfort
Montmartre 90, 121
More, Sir John 217
More, Thomas — see Thomas More, St
Morton, John 217
Mount Athos 137
Mount Brandon 56
Mount Calvary 133
Mount Etna 8
Mount Kolzim 29
Mount La Verna 117
Mount Lebanon 104
Mount of Olives 144
Mount Oliveto 113
Mount Sinai 66
Muirchertach 164
Munga Sulcain 112
Mungo, St — see Kentigern, St
Myra 180

N
Nanna, St 128
Nanterre 123
Naples 15, 23, 28, 62, 200, 214
Napoleon 1, Emperor 145
Narbonne 203
Narcissus, Bishop of Gerona 7
Nathanael 41, 197
Navarre 121
Nazareth 23, 155, 174
Nazianzus 128
Neale, J M 228
Neocaesarea 130
Nerida 6
Nero, Emperor 194
Nestorius 85
Nevers 50
Neville, Ralph 198
New Corbie 26, 227
New York 114, 189
Newman, Cardinal 193
Niall, Archbishop of Armagh 164
Nicholas, St **180**
Nicholas I, Pope 26, 43
Nicholas V, Pope 28, 52
Nicomedia 39, 124, 133
Niedermünster 182
Nîmes 127

Ninian, St 11, **181**
Nivelles 18, 126
Nocera 15
Non, St 89
Novatus 83
Novitian 78, 83
Noyon 103
Nynia, St — see Ninian, St

O
Oak of Thor 55
Obernheim 182
Oblates of Mary 113
Oblates of Tor de Specchi 113
Odense 64
Odilia, St **182**
Odilienberg 182
Odilo, St 4, 139, **183**, 184
Odo of Cluny, St **184**
Odo the Good, St 184, 187
Offa, King of the East Saxons 100
Offa, King of Mercia 12, 95
Ohrdruf 55
Olaf (brother of St Canute) 64
Olaf, St 58, **185**
Opsikion 84
Oratory of St Jerome 62
Order of Barnabites 40
Order of Hospitallers of St Antony 29
Order of Ursulines 222
Order of the Garter 124
Order of the Visitations 120
Orestes 85
Origen 130
Orléans 148, 198
Ortona 213
Osgar 107
Oskitall, Archbishop of York 187
Osma 91
Oswald of Northumbria, St 10, 82, **186**
Oswald of Worcester, St 187
Oswestry 186
Oswin, King of Deira 10
Oswiu, King of Northumbria 5, 10, 48, 71, 81, 188, 229
Ottilia, St — see Odilia, St
Otto, Cardinal 98
Otto II, King 4
Otto III, King 4
Otto the Great, King 4
Ouen, St 43
Ovada 193
Oxford 98, 127, 198, 217, 219
Ozanam, Frederick 226

P

Padua 13, 30, 62, 120, 161, 200
Palencia 91
Palermo 15
Palladius 189
Palma 95
Pancras, St **188**
Pantaenus, St 41
Paola 119
Paphos 134
Papias, Bishop 170, 176
Paray-le-Monial 166
Paris 13, 43, 54, 90, 103, 109, 120, 123, 141, 148, 163, 198, 214, 215, 219, 226
Paschal I, Pope 70
Paschal II, Pope 25, 64, 139
Pasicrates 124
Patara 180
Patmos 153
Patras 22
Patricius 35
Patrick, St 59, **189**
Patrophilus, Bishop 108
Paul, St 40, 90, 121, 147, 161, 170, **190**, *192*, 194, 220
Paul, Vincent de — see Vincent de Paul, St
Paul II, Pope 84
Paul III, Pope 141, 142, 150
Paul IV, Pope 62, 96
Paul V, Pope 113, 200
Paul VI, Pope 46, 68, 165, 210, 213
Paul of the Cross, St **193**
Paul of Thebes 146
Paul the Hermit, St 29
Paula 146
Paulinus (scribe) 89
Paulinus (bishop) 136, 146, 229
Pavia 4, 36
Peckham, Archbishop John 219
Pedrosa 196
Penda, King of Mercia 186
Pelagius II, Pope 131
Pental 202
Pepin 49, 126, 138
Perga 40, 170
Persson, Berger 58
Perugia 52, 74
Peter, St 8, 22, 75, 153, 156, 159, 170, 190, **194**, 218
Peter III, King of Aragon 102
Peter Claver, St **195**
Peter of Alcantara, St **196**, 209
Peter of Castlenau 91
Peter of Cattaneo 116

Peter of Tarentasia 13
Peterborough 105
Philempora 87
Philiberte 166
Philip, St 41, **197**
Philip, Emperor 31
Philip I, King of Spain 221
Philip II, King of Spain 16
Philip of Hesse 101
Philippi 40, 161, 191
Photius 84
Pierozzi Nicolo 28
Piro, Abbot 202
Pisano, Giovanni 168
Pisano, Nicolas 91
Pispir 29
Pittenweem 110
Pius II, Pope 28, 68
Pius IV, Pope 65
Pius V, Pope 65, 214
Pius VIII, Pope 51
Pius IX, Pope 15, 155, 175
Pius XI, Pope 13, 16, 50, 97, 113, 121, 142, 145, 166, 212
Pius XII, Pope 30, 114, 174, 175, 176
Placidus 224
Plato 35
Plessis 119
Poissy 160
Poitiers 135
Poitou 18
Pontian,Pope 137
Pontigny 198, 215
Pontius 83
Pontius Pilate 194
Pontus 128, 130, 149
Ponziani, Lorenzo 113
Poor Clares 74, 102, 116, 166
Pope, Alexander (poet) 70
Porphyrius 66
Portes 27
Portiuncula 74
Portus 63
Poussin, Nicolas 175
Pouy 226
Prague 3, 228
Priscilla 191
Prudentius 9

Q

Quinta 31
Quintian 8
Quintinus, St 79

R

Ramsey 187
Raphael (archangel) 178

Raphael (painter) 70
Rathmelsigi 71
Ravenna 131
Raymond of Capua 68
Raymond VII of Toulouse 160
Reading 144
Redemptorists 15
Rederech Hael, King 168
Redwold of East Anglia 186
Reggio 60
Remaclus, St 18
Rheims 60, 148, 156
Rhygyvarch 89
Rich, Edmund 198
Rich, Reginald 98
Richard I, King of England 140
Richard II, King of England 23, 95, *96*, 224
Richard of Chichester, St 98, **198**
Rictiovarus 79
Rievaulx 11
Ringan, St — see Ninian, St
Ripon 71, 81, 229
Rita of Cascia, St **199**
Robert Bellarmine, St 16, **200**
Robert of Molesmes, St 60
Robert the Bruce, King of Scotland 110
Roccaporena 199
Roccasecca 214
Rochester 38, 105, 150
Rodriguez, Fr Simon 121
Romanos (a monk) 45
Rome 3, 4, 6, 9, 16, 23, 25, 28, 32, 35, 38, 39, 41, 45, 48, 55, 57, 58, 60, 63, 65, 68, 75, 79, 84, 85, 90, 91, 100, 108, 113, 115, 119, 121, 127, 128, 131, 133, 137, 141, 142, 146, 147, 153, 159, 161, 164, 178, 181, 190, 191, 193, 194, 197, 203, 206, 211, 215, 220, 222, 224, 225, 226, 229, 230
Romera, Francesca — see Frances of Rome, St
Roper, Weillism 218
Rose of Lima, St **201**
Roskilde 64
Rostislav, Duke of Moravia 84
Rouen 148,157
Rudolf II, King of Upper Burgundy 4
Ruffin 71
Rufinus 147
Rule, St 22
Rusticus 90

S

Sabelius 63
Sabert, King of the East Saxons 105
Sacred Congregation of Rites 176
St Andrews 22
St Antony's bread 30
St Agnes Church, Rome 9
St Albans 12
St Bartholomew's Church, Rome 41
St Bride's Bay 59
St Davids (Wales) 89
St Devereux 92
St Elmo's fire 104
St Helena Island 133
St Honorat, Lérins 48
St Martin's summer 172
St Michael's Mount 178
St Pauls Cathedral, London 17
St Peter's, Rome 128, 156, 159
St Vitus's Dance 227
Saint-Denis 227
Saint-Fiacre-en-Brie 109
Saint-Gilles 127
Saint Maximin 173
Saint-Seine 49
Sainte-Chapelle, Paris 160
Salamanca 151, 196, 221
Salamis 40
Sales — see Francis of Sales, St
Salome 152, 173
Samosata 130
Samson (biblical) 92
Samson, St **202**
Samuel 23
San Andrea, Rome 16
San Marco, Florence 28
San Paolo, Forli 30
San Pietro della Valle 167
San Tome 213
Sandovel — see de Sandovel
Sanhedrin (Jewish council) 206
Sant (father of St David) 89
Sant' Agata de Goti 15
Sant' Angelo Lodigiono 114
Santa 221
Santa Claus 180
Santa Maria Novella, Florence 28
Santa Maria sopra Minerva, Rome 68
Saros 101
Saul of Tarsus — see Paul, St
Saumaise — see de Saumaise
Sauvigny 183

Saumaise — see de Saumaise
Scholastica, St 45
Sea of Galilee 173
Sebastea 53, 152
Sebastian St **203**, *204*
Seghine, Abbot 5
Segovia 151
Seigneur de Nouvelles 120
Selsey 230
Seltz 4
Semur 139
Sens 215
Septimus Severns, Emperor 12
Serf, St 158
Severin, Tim 56
Seville 143
Sexburga, St 106
Shakespeare, William 79, 89
Siegebert, St 18
Siena 52, 68
Sigebert, King 122
Sigfrid, St 26
Silas 191
Simeon Stylites, St 87, **205**
Simeon the Younger, St 205
Simon, St 22, 156, 173
Simon IV, Count of Montfort 91
Sinell 77
Sisters of Charity 50, 226
Sixtus II, Pope 119
Sixtus III, Pope 159
Sixtus IV, Pope 54
Sixtus V, Pope 147, 200
Skete 32
Society of Jesus (Jesuits) 141, 142
Society of St Vincent de Paul 226
Society of the Sacred Heart 163
Soissons 79
Solignac 103
Sophronius, Eusebius Hieronymus — see Jerome, St
Soubrious, Marie Bernarde — see Bernadette, St
Southill 202
Southwell, Robert 142
Stachys, Bishop 22
Stephen St (martyr) 190, **206**
Stephen I, Pope 83
Stephen, King of England 88
Stephen of Hungary, St 169, **207**
Stiklestad 185
Strathfillan 110
Strido 146

Subiaco 45
Swein 17, 57, 185
Swein, Earl 185
Swithin, St **208**
Sylene 124
Sylvester II, Pope 207
Synod of Antioch 130
Synod of Béziers 135
Synod of Brefi 89, 92
Synod of Chalons 77
Synod of Druim Cetta 76
Synod of Innishpatrick 164
Synod of Tara 5
Synod of the Oak 149
Synod of the River Nidd 230
Synod of Troyes 51
Synod of Twyford 81
Synod of Whitby 10, 81, 136, 229

T

Tagaste 35
Tara 189
Tarragona 195
Tarsus 40, 86, 190, 211
Telanissus 87, 205
Tennyson, Alfred 92
Teresa of Avila, St 151, 155, 196, **209**, *210*
Tertullian 63
Thaddeus (St Jude) 156
Thenew, Princess 158
Theobald Archbishop 215
Theodebert, King 77
Theoderic II of Burgundy 77
Theodore of Canterbury, St (also called Theodore of Tarsus) 6, 14, 48, 71, **211**, 229, 230
Theodore the Studite, St 32
Theodosius I, Emperor 19, 20, 32, 128
Theodosius II, Emperor 85
Theophano, Queen 4
Theophilus of Alexandria 85, 149
Theotimus 167
Thérèse of Lisieux, St **212**
Theseus 137
Thessalonica 20, 84
Thierry III, King of the Franks 43
Thomas (the Doubter), St 176, **213**
Thomas Aquinas, St 13, 25, 54, 175, **214**
Thomas Becket, St 17, 25, 27, 140, **215**, *216*
Thomas More, St 150, **217**, *218*

Thomas of Hereford (Thomas de Cantelupe), St **219**
Thor (Norse god) 180
Thorney 48, 107
Three Holy Hierarchs 42
Tiberius, Emperor 203, 225
Tiburtius 70
Timothy, St **220**
Toledo 151
Tonbert Prince 106
Tondini, Antonio 114
Toribie, St 201
Toulouse 95, 156, 214, 215
Tournai, 103
Tourraine 57
Tours 18, 57, 172, 181, 184, 189
Trier 19, 33
Trinity House 75
Troë 32
Trondheim 58, 185
Troyes 148
Tunis 160, 226
Turibius of Mogroveio, St **221**
Turni 224
Tyndale, William 217
Tyre 33

U
Ubeda 151
Urban I, Pope 137
Urban II, Pope 60, 139
Urban IV, Pope 74
Urban V, Pope 58
Urban VI, Pope 23, 68
Urban VIII, Pope 102, 226
Urbanists 74
Urbino 52
Urien, Prince 158
Ursula St **222**, *223*

V
Valens, Emperor 19, 33, 42, 86, 128

Valentine, St **224**
Valentine of Genoa, Bishop 224
Valentinian II, Emperor 19, 135
Valerian (husband of St Cecilia) 70
Valerian, Emperor 83, 90
Valcrian, Bishop 146
Valerian, governor of Sicily 227
Valerius, Bishop 35
Varin, Abbé 163
Venerea of Antioch 7
Venice 121, 141, 167, 170, 222
Vercelli 108
Verdu 195
Veronica, St **225**
Verulamium 12
Vicenza 62
Vicovaro 45
Victor IV (Antipope) 27
Villardbenoit 140
Vincent de Paul, St **226**
Visitandines 120,166
Vitalian, Pope 6, 188, 211
Vitus, St **227**
Voragine — see de Voragine
Voytech — see Adalbert, St

W
Waldef, St 88
Wallace Collection, London 138
Walter Daniel 11
Walter of Worcester, Bishop 219
Wartburg 101
Wearmouth 5, 6, 44, 48, 211
Wenceslas, St **228**
Westbury-on-Trym 187
Westminster Abbey 99
Whitby 61
Whithorn 181
Wighard, Archbishop 6, 211

Wilfred 55
Wilfred, St 43, 48, 71, 81, 100, 106, 136, 211, **229**
William, Duke of Aquitaine 184
William of Avalon 140
William of Malmesbury 43
William of Saint-Amour 214
William of York 11
William the Conqueror, King of England 64, 99
William II, King of England 25
Willibrord 55
Wilton Diptych 95
Winchester 55, 107, 208, 216
Witham 140
Withburga, St 106
Wolsey, Cardinal 217
Womba, King 127
Worcester 93, 100, 187, 230
Wratislov, Duke of Bohemia 228
Wulfhad 71
Wulfhere, King of the Marcians 71
Wynfrith — see Boniface, St

Y
Yelverton, Sir Henry 97
Yeu 18
York 54,64, 71, 81, 82, 133, 165, 187, 211, 222, 229, 230

Z
Zacchaeus 225
Zebedee 144,153,156
Zechariah 152, 161
Zeno, Emperor 87
Zephyrinus, Pope 63, 137